CONTENTS

KU-502-874

FOREWORD
David Coulthard MBE

It is a great pleasure to have been asked to write the foreword to Mark's book *The Business of Winning*. It seems incredible to me when I think about it, but Mark and I go back over 20 years, right back to when we worked together at the Pacific Racing Formula 3000 team in 1993.

I was a young, wet-behind-the-ears driver in those days, although I would grow up quickly enough. Ayrton Senna's tragic death at Imola in 1994 handed me the chance to drive for Williams and I never looked back.

Mark, meanwhile, was back then a journalist turned media consultant who would go on to become head of marketing for Eddie Jordan's nascent F1 team. The fact that he survived nearly 10 years working for EJ without losing his job or his marbles, before going on to a number of senior roles at Jaguar, Red Bull Racing and Cosworth, tells you everything you need to know about Mark's qualities as a survivor. I also know that he learned a great deal from his experience of working with EJ, experiencing the ups and downs of building a winning team from the inside.

There is a serious point here, which is that longevity in Formula One is a valuable commodity, one to be respected. Not for nothing is Formula One known as the Piranha Club.

The paddock is one of the most thrilling, cut-throat environments on Earth, drawing hugely successful characters from all walks of life: people who are used to winning, to getting their own way; people chasing their dreams with the resources and the skill sets to back up their ambitions.

The combination of these hugely competitive characters being thrown together in such a supercharged environment is both intoxicating and explosive.

Formula One is positively Darwinian in the way that it chews up and spits out those who are not up to the task.

Mark has not only survived; he thrived in a number of demanding roles, including leading Cosworth's return to Formula One in 2009 and building his own championship-winning team, Status Grand Prix.

Naturally, the lessons that can be applied to businesses from working in such an environment are many and varied. Everywhere you look are examples of winning and losing behaviour, and wonderful anecdotes with which to illustrate the points you are making, because, let's face it, Formula One is a marvellous soap opera as well as a sport.

Take leadership, for example. With all those alpha males strutting around thinking they know best, it takes a strong person to get everyone working together.

Formula One has produced some outstanding, inspirational leaders. I have been fortunate enough to work with some of the best, from Frank Williams and Ron Dennis to Christian Horner and Dietrich Mateschitz.

Each had his own qualities, but what they had in common was an ability to bring out the best in their employees, whether that was by using the stick or the carrot, sometimes a combination of the two. In the case of Red Bull Racing the right leadership, talent and technical structure enabled it to go from strength to strength.

In this book, Mark covers all of the key areas of good business practice, using experience gained in over 30 years in the sport. Whether it is performance management, another area in which Formula One excels, or risk management, I cannot imagine another walk of life where the rate of development is so relentless and everyone is so driven to succeed. Factories hum away 24/7, running CFD programs, test benches, dynos.

This is a people sport above all, though. Data is the lifeblood of Formula One, but it does not collect itself. It needs to be harnessed, interpreted, applied.

When you are at a smaller team, as Mark was with Jordan Grand Prix, you necessarily have to be more creative, more selective in the way you go about things. That can make you more efficient, but compromising on quality is never an option.

Formula One pushes the boundaries of what is achievable. Its record in areas such as safety and innovation is being felt across our societies, driving up standards, effecting change.

Since my retirement as a driver I have been fortunate enough to speak alongside Mark at a number of talks and conferences, and my respect for him has grown immeasurably. It is easy to underestimate Mark, as he is self-effacing, not one of the sport's loudest characters, but he knows what he is talking about. As I said before, you do not survive for 30 years in our sport without knowing your way around. Mark has seen the sport from the outside, as a journalist, and from the inside, at the heart of a team. That rounded insight is invaluable.

What is more, he has that gift of storytelling so common among the Irish. When he speaks, when he tells an anecdote, it is always interesting, always stimulating.

It has been a good 20 years, Mark. Here's to the next 20.

David Coulthard MBE
Monaco

PREFACE

The origins of this book can be traced to a strange convergence: the 20th wedding anniversary of Formula One team boss Eddie Jordan in 1999, a decision by telecommunications giant BT to hold a leadership conference in Vienna, and a long speech by former Soviet president Mikhail Gorbachev.

It was when Eddie's wife Marie surprised him with tickets on Concorde for a romantic weekend in New York that he withdrew from BT's event in Vienna, leaving me to take his place and present a keynote address on the use of technology and innovation in Formula One. I was not unduly nervous, as one way or another I have been speaking about Formula One throughout my career. I was, however, concerned that a speech by Mikhail Gorbachev to the delegates earlier in the day might prove a hard act to follow. I need not have worried. His speech was long, and in Russian, and when I stood up to give my 45-minute address on Formula One the audience seemed delighted.

So began a 15-year professional public speaking career on the business lessons to be learned from Formula One motor racing, and the background to why I have written this book.

I have been fortunate indeed to turn my favourite sport into a career, starting in 1983 when I landed a job working for *Autosport* magazine in south-west London. Eight years in the media as a journalist, broadcaster and then PR consultant gave me an opportunity to get to know the sport as a close observer. However, it was only when I jumped the fence into working with a team that I really began to understand how the business of Formula One works.

My 10 years in management at Jordan Grand Prix enabled me to work closely with immensely talented people, and learn what it takes to win in a sport of high technology and high finance. I also came to appreciate the complexity of a sport where each team has to be able to design, manufacture, develop and operate products that integrate technologies from the automotive, aerospace and IT sectors – and do so against a backdrop of immovable deadlines and strict regulation.

In speaking to hundreds of multinational companies about the lessons to be learned from Formula One, I have been struck by how similar the problems and challenges are facing businesses the world over. This book aims to bring together my observations, insights and conclusions from working in a sports business that I know has lessons relevant to business leaders.

Great leadership and team work are a prerequisite for success in F1, but so too are the need to develop an innovation culture, embrace constant change and focus on performance whilst placing safety and risk management at the centre of everything we do. We also work with, and build, global brands and communicate with our audiences using multiple digital platforms and outlets.

It has taken two and a half years to complete this book, which I started when I left Cosworth after two happy years leading one of Formula One's most famous engine suppliers. After leaving Jordan my time with Jaguar and Red Bull Racing taught me new lessons, while co-founding and leading Status Grand Prix to success in the A1GP World Cup of Motorsport in 2009 added a new dimension to my experience.

I have written this as a book that readers can either tackle cover to cover or pick up and put down whenever they wish to delve into a particular theme or topic. For the reader who relishes all aspects of Formula One I have also included a variety of stories and anecdotes that may not necessarily contribute to any great business learning but will perhaps explain why the sacrifices inherent in committing myself to this career have been worthwhile.

It would be unfair to credit any particular list of people for helping me in the writing of this book, mainly because I have realized that each and every person whom I have met, worked with, observed or competed against has contributed in some way. I have been privileged to meet some of my heroes, develop lifelong friendships and witness this extraordinary sport from the inside. I hope that some of my conclusions will resonate with the reader.

I will, however, thank my agent Brendan O'Connor for his support in bringing this book to market, and Helen Kogan and Melody Dawes at Kogan Page for their advice, guidance and commitment. Finally, it would be remiss of me not to thank my wife Natalie, who has nudged me along since 2011 with timely quips about 'How's that book going?', and our children Frank and Laura.

Mark Gallagher
Aynho, Oxfordshire

For Harry and Eithne

CHAPTER ONE
FORMULA ONE
A global business

At the wheel of his ornately decorated Proton, bounding its way along one of Kuala Lumpur's wide, smooth but undulating motorways, the Malaysian taxi driver worried me a little because of the amount of time he spent looking in his rear-view mirror as opposed to the road ahead. For several minutes we'd been engaging in conversation, covering a range of topics, starting with the form shown by Manchester United. We'd since moved on to discussing the weather in England, the flying time to KL and the prospects for this weekend's Malaysian Grand Prix.

This was all very interesting, because not only was it making the journey into central KL pass more quickly but the fact that neither I spoke Malay nor he English was having no discernible effect on our ability to communicate.

His car was a shrine to Manchester United. Everything was red. A United scarf bedecked the dashboard, causing the team's name and crest to reflect alarmingly in the windscreen, while every surface appeared to have team and player stickers, photos of tackles and goal celebrations applied to them. A figurine of goalkeeper Peter Schmeichel hung, gallows style, from the mirror.

I had been initially very impressed with the collection, not least since we were six and a half thousand miles from Old Trafford, while among the things I least expected to learn about on my first trip to Malaysia for their inaugural Formula One race in 1999 was the skill and prowess of Messrs Sheringham, Yorke, Cole, Cantona and Giggs.

I had opened the conversation with the question, 'You like Manchester United?', rather stating the obvious. Had it been England I am sure I'd have had a deadpan 'How did you guess?' response, but my driver was very happy to have this pointed out. After responding in Malay, interspersed with the odd 'Giggsy' and 'Mr Teddy', he went on to give a no-doubt authoritative and insightful critique of the team's Premiership winning season, one that perhaps Alex Ferguson might have found useful.

It was when we progressed to discussing the weather in England, summoned by frantic hand gestures simulating wind and rain, that we got as far as him apparently asking why I was in Malaysia.

'Formula One,' I replied, simply.

'Eff one?' he shouted, looking at me intently again in the rear-view mirror, and then weaving the taxi from side to side to show me that he knew exactly how to keep the tyres warm whilst running behind the safety car.

'Schumacher!' he shouted, more loudly, and then 'Hakkinen!' More weaving, now more violent than before.

'Go, go, go!' he added, delighted with his knowledge of the latest sport to descend upon his country.

I'd already been impressed by his knowledge of an English Premiership football team, his awareness of two of Formula One's key protagonists and his ability to keep his remoulded tyres up to temperature whilst in traffic. It was as nothing compared to my shock on realizing that his only English was one word, repeated three times, in the style of a certain Murray Walker, BBC F1 commentator and icon of the sport.

If ever I needed an education in the power and reach of television, and the fact that by 1999 Formula One really was beginning to 'go global', this was it. Malaysia's addition to the F1 calendar had surprised many, not least because the sport did not hold particular interest for the indigenous population, but also the fact that ticket prices were likely to make attendance well beyond the means of your average Malaysian household income of £500 per month for city dwellers and half that for those in rural areas.

Any confusion about the addition of this event to the calendar was quickly dispelled as we began to see how much Formula One was changing. It was reflecting the needs of its customers, team owners and the opportunities afforded by the rapidly shrinking world in which we live. Here was a new development within the business model of the sport –

one where a country's sovereign government, the strategists behind its nationhood, had taken a hard look at Formula One and decided that it represented an unrivalled opportunity to promote Malaysia's international interests. Here was a worldwide televised sport that demonstrated the country's confidence in itself as a global player, attracted international media attention for a full week to 10 days each year, and ensured that 'Malaysia' as a brand reached hundreds of millions of households and billions of eyeballs.

If globalization has been with us for centuries, the modern definition with which we are all familiar combines the notion of global trade with the breaking down of physical and commercial barriers, the speed and ease of communication across continents and the ability to build truly global brands with a commonality of look, feel and purpose – a commercialization that reaches and appeals to people wherever they may live on the planet.

The giant US brands such as Coca-Cola, Kellogg's and Campbell's Soup have been with us internationally since the latter part of the 19th century, but the sporting world did not embrace the commercial, professional model on an international basis until much later. While sponsorship was nothing new in itself, it could be argued that it wasn't until the 1960s that it really took off when a Cleveland-based Yale law graduate by the name of Mark McCormack decided to suspend his own golfing ambitions in favour of managing a young Arnold Palmer, soon after adding Gary Player and Jack Nicklaus. When he negotiated his first deal, a US$5,000 endorsement by Palmer of Wilson sporting goods, I doubt even Mark McCormack and his fledgling International Management Group could have imagined the transformation that would overtake the world of sport in the five decades ahead.

The US lawyer was 10 years ahead of the man who would buy a Formula One team, realize the old adage that in F1 the easiest way to make a small fortune is to start off with a large one, and set about building the global enterprise that this unique business has become.

Unique?

Over the last 40 years Bernie Ecclestone has been the key player in creating the Formula One business we know today, and, whilst there are countless other highly professional, commercialized sports, none possesses the combination of ingredients of Grand Prix motor racing. The cries of derision will no doubt go up, but I include the downsides as well as the upsides in viewing F1 as a sports business without parallel. Yes, of course the races can be tedious to watch at times, though those times are far fewer than its critics will have you believe. And, of course, 'it's not really a sport', they will add, considering that the car is the star and the role of the driver is merely to guide the missile around a closed circuit for 300 kilometres.

The uniqueness of the sport of Formula One is the range of challenges it creates for the competing teams and drivers, and the compression of those challenges into immovable timescales and deadlines that have to be met at venues around the world and at all times under the scrutiny of a global media and viewing public every week or fortnight from March through to November. While public companies concern themselves with meeting quarterly targets, Formula One teams see their results published every other Sunday in front of a highly critical audience that includes their own customers, staff and suppliers. There is no room to hide.

Other sports offer the same results-based scrutiny of teams and competitors, of course, but I would argue that none involve the multifaceted challenges faced by Formula One teams, and in this regard they are unique in sport and offer a very specific opportunity to study a broad range of business issues set against a sporting background.

To be a successful Formula One team requires the ability to establish, develop and sustain a profitable engineering business operating in the low-volume prototype-manufacturing sector, producing a high-end product using a range of technologies from within specialisms including automotive, aerospace, electronics, software and advanced materials. This product, the result of a collaboration between people and companies spanning many months, must be produced against a backdrop of legislation and regulation – compliance, in the modern parlance – and produced with the very specific task of accommodating continuous improvement as it competes against its opposition day to day, event to event.

This high-technology product, designed to meet new regulations each season, will incorporate developments that in some cases have been in gestation for years. It then competes directly against the opposition in a truly hostile environment where the heat, vibration, noise and speed of operation offer a most alien experience. The F1 product is a piece of technology of which the end user demands high performance, innovation and competitive edge, uneasy bedfellows for technology that must also be strong, safe and utterly reliable. Finishing first may be the goal, but first you have to finish.

The F1 engineering business therefore faces the numerous challenges of any business operating in the manufacturing sector, but with the time frames compressed to meet immovable deadlines. To design, manufacture, develop and bring to market this high-end product requires not only the collaboration of those employed in the relevant disciplines within the business, but seamless operation with key suppliers such that procurement and effective supply chain management become a fundamental aspect of the foundation for any team.

In the last 20 years F1 teams have been through both extremes of the supply model, from running very small teams utterly reliant on suppliers for the vast majority of the goods and services needed to operate in this field, through to very large organizations that bring most operations in-house. At the turn of the century a team such as Jordan Grand Prix employed little more than 250 full-time staff yet had almost 400 suppliers, whilst Toyota's F1 operation employed over 1,000 staff at its peak and did as much as possible in-house. That Jordan, a small, bespoke, profitable F1 engineering concern, became a winner whilst Toyota, the world's largest car manufacturer, failed to do so is a story to which we shall return. But, in manufacturing culture and supply chain management alone, these were two very different businesses.

Since the advent of carbon fibre and associated composite materials in F1 in the early 1980s, teams have developed sophisticated manufacturing facilities producing aerospace-quality components designed for lightness, strength and high performance. An F1 car is, in effect, an inverted aircraft. We fly them into the ground, with the wings, upper body and critical floor design generating tonnes of aerodynamic downforce such that these machines can corner at velocities far beyond the capabilities of any other road vehicle. The speed with which F1 technicians are obsessed is not of the straight-line, top-speed variety – indeed there are road cars that can match or exceed the straight-line speed of an F1 car – but the cornering speed. Creating the ability for the car to maintain its velocity through turns, and over undulations in the road, is the holy grail for F1 designers, and it is for that reason that it tends to be aerodynamicists and vehicles dynamicists who hold the keys to success.

While these engineers focus on optimizing cornering speeds, the team must ensure that this inverted aircraft protects the human being tasked with piloting it, sustaining up to 5G in corners, and many times that in the event of an accident. Thus the manufacturing process is about ensuring the integrity of the product in terms of safety, before anything else. Once again, the trade-offs and potential compromises come to light. But in F1, as within the wider business world, product safety, operational safety and risk management at every level are critical topics. Reputational damage is one thing but, when your product can kill its operator or those watching it perform, the focus becomes even sharper.

When I started working in Formula One in the mid-1980s the championship consisted of 14 races, of which 10 were staged in Europe and four at 'long-haul' destinations. Its 'world' status was bestowed upon it by virtue of having races in Australia, Japan, Brazil and Canada. The United States figured at times, but until recently the US love affair with F1 has involved a series of desperate flings rather than anything enduring. Only now, with a purpose-built facility in Austin, Texas, does Formula One have a permanent presence in the United States.

As a Euro-centric business, therefore, Formula One's nod towards the rest of the world meant that for 48 weeks of the year the sport, and the business, was almost entirely focused on a single continent. The teams were all European based in Italy, France and the UK, while the predominance of the European press corps underlined the almost parochial nature of the sport.

In 2012 Formula One's calendar featured 20 events, with more than half outside Europe. As a business it has gone where the money is and shunned where the money isn't. In a little over two decades F1 has become a truly global sports business. The combined demands of its shareholders and customers have seen to that.

Having changed hands several times, whilst always under the leadership of F1's CEO Bernie Ecclestone, F1 has ended up owned by debt-funded private equity, with all the demands on growth, profitability and cash generation that has bought. While the revenues generated from television, the hosting of races, trackside advertising and corporate hospitality have been pushed ever higher, ultimately the demand for more events worked in parallel. Fourteen races became 16, 18 and then 20. Although placing an enormous human and logistical burden on the teams, this exponential growth has seen the sport move into new markets, attract new audiences, and accelerate the presence of F1 around the world as never before.

The internal customers of the sport, the sponsors, the brands that require a return on investment as never before, have also demanded more events, new markets and fresh audiences. It all goes hand in hand. As the principally European marketing dollars gave way to worldwide marketing spends, and the globalization of brands became ever more striking, so Formula One had to go where the clients demanded. Asia was a natural place to start, for Japan had been on the calendar since 1973, while the presence of the Australian Grand Prix since 1985 meant that logistically Formula One was already geared towards visiting the eastern hemisphere up to twice a season. Malaysia in 1999 was followed by China in 2004, the Grand Prix in Shanghai confirming that, when it came to investing in Formula One and building world-class facilities, the new markets would be teaching the old world a thing or two. The palatial facilities in Sepang and Shanghai made the traditional venues of Silverstone, Monza, Spa, Monaco and even the new and unloved Nurburgring appear very mid-20th-century.

The recognition that sovereign funds and governments could see the benefit of one week of global advertising led inexorably to the Gulf, the creation of the Bahrain Grand Prix in 2006 and the addition of Abu Dhabi in 2008. Not to be outdone, Singapore joined the fray with a downtown street circuit, a race held at night, and a glittering Asian spectacle that instantly put the city state among the elite events and gained a profile worth every one of the estimated $400 million that the circuit construction and initial five-year deal cost.

By 2010 the championship featured a further race, Korea, and a calendar with 19 Grands Prix, while in 2011 India came on board, completing F1's invasion of the two most highly populated countries in the world. Consider that China in 2004 and India in 2011 exposed a potential 2.63 billion people to this very Western, aspirational, high-technology sports business, which not many years before had struggled to extend its reach beyond Europe. With Russia scheduled to host its first Grand Prix at Sochi in 2014, and the United States enjoying another reconciliation with its race in Austin, it is no wonder that the growth is leaving even industry veterans breathless.

The old world was always the foundation and mainstay of F1, right from that first race at Silverstone in May 1950, but the new worlds of the Americas and Australia have now been joined by the BRIC economies, the economic powerhouses that Malaysia and Korea represent, and the financial capability of the oil- and gas-rich Gulf states. Others keen to join include former venues South Africa and Mexico, raising the prospect of a World Championship that may in the future extend to half the weekends in the year. More events will mean increased revenues for F1, and ultimately for the teams able to stiffen their sponsorship rate card as the championship visits additional key markets. Inevitably this will further increase pressure on the sport to re-evaluate whether Friday practice sessions, poorly attended and of limited media interest, serve any valuable purpose. A larger series with two-day events would appear an obvious development for the future.

Each new territory brings with it multiple benefits: new audiences, more media, potential new sponsors from among the domestic, regional and global brands, and the increased prestige that comes with the cumulative effect of racing in the largest economies combined with the most important developing ones. Consider that China and India rank first and second in the world in terms of mobile phone usage, with 740 million and 630 million mobile users respectively in 2012, and you start to understand why Formula One technology sponsors will struggle to ignore a sport that can only grow in popularity as the populace becomes ever more aspirational, car usage increases and the affluent middle and upper classes proliferate.

The role of sponsors in helping to drive demand for Formula One should not be underestimated, for, whilst Bernie Ecclestone and the team at Formula One Management have grown the television revenues and negotiated the addition of new venues, the changing face of sponsorship and the power of the sponsors' marketing spend have pushed the popularity of F1. With over 200 sponsors across the sport, the benefit to the F1 business of having customers trumpeting its appeal to a broad demographic is clear. In 2011 UK television audiences were exposed to multiple advertising campaigns featuring McLaren driver Lewis Hamilton and Jenson Button, with brands including Vodafone, Santander, TAG Heuer and Head & Shoulders exploiting the success, profile and appeal of Britain's World Champions.

It's generally acknowledged that the first commercial sponsorship in Formula One was undertaken by Imperial Tobacco in 1968 when Gold Leaf commenced support for Team Lotus with drivers Jim Clark and Graham Hill, a full 18 years after the inaugural World Championship. This is not to say that major companies had not utilized Formula One for marketing reasons previously, but the support provided by oil giant Castrol, tyre suppliers Dunlop or automotive brands including Ferrari, Honda and Ford could be categorized as essentially industry or trade sponsors. Gold Leaf marked a pivotal change as non-automotive brands recognized the appeal and reach of the sport.

Whilst the F1 teams with their manufacturing, operational, logistics and team management challenges provide a broad insight into a range of business challenges familiar to companies around the world, it is perhaps the commercial lessons from acquiring, retaining and developing sponsor-customers that have helped the sport to become an international business barometer. The ability of F1's major teams to adapt their commercial model to the fast-moving economic realities of the modern world, mitigating commercial risk and sustaining and growing revenues in the face of multiple recessions in the 1980s, 1990s and 2000s, has been impressive.

The types of customer and their requirements, geographical markets and industry sectors have changed remarkably over time. If, in the 1950s and 1960s, F1 teams were less businesses and more the philanthropic efforts of private individuals sometimes supported by the automotive trade and its suppliers, the 1970s saw the creation of profit-focused businesses and the arrival of serial racing entrepreneurs such as Bernie Ecclestone, Ron Dennis and Frank Williams. They, along with Enzo Ferrari's legendary team, would be at the heart of the commercial development of the sport.

It was appropriate that the Gold Leaf deal became viewed as the trigger point of commercial sponsorship in the manner we know today. As the 1970s progressed, the values that F1 promoted to a growing audience attracted the first wave of sponsor-customers eager to take advantage of its appeal. Young men, fast cars, exotic destinations, beautiful women and innate danger made for a heady combination, a sex appeal that proved as attractive for brands as it was to the general public.

Tobacco's affair with the sport well and truly began, with Gold Leaf soon replaced at Team Lotus with the stunning black and gold livery of John Player Special, and in an instant one of the most iconic and widely referenced sponsorships in sport was created. Even 40 years after it began, market research was showing that 'JPS Lotus' was a recognized composite brand in Western markets, long after its disappearance from the sport following successful forays in both the 1970s and 1980s. Lotus F1 even uses the colour scheme today, such is its appeal. The ability of sports sponsorship, and particularly F1 at that time, to create a sustained association between the brand and the activity was given its foundation.

JPS was joined by Marlboro, Philip Morris's brand marketing prowess initiating a sponsorship relationship with Formula One that, against the odds including anti-tobacco advertising legislation, continues to this day. Marlboro started with the Iso Marlboro team in 1972, migrated to McLaren in 1978 and developed the Marlboro World Championship Team programme that supported multiple teams and drivers throughout the two decades that followed. The red and white chevron became synonymous with the sport, the Marlboro brand managers developing a highly sophisticated programme that ensured they not only achieved global recognition for the brand, but developed a template that to this day is followed by FMCG brand sponsors throughout the sport.

Aside from using Formula One cars as a high-speed billboard, Marlboro added Grand Prix race sponsorships, developed more effective circuit signage, bought up the tobacco sampling rights so that promotions staff could hand out free cigarettes to race goers, created huge promotional stands, and ran consumer competitions. They operated a media information service that was years ahead of its rivals or other sponsors, and helped their teams to invest in the facilities, equipment and presentation such that anything Marlboro-related was inevitably best in class.

Such was the power of Marlboro's Formula One sponsorship that, when one of their senior executives made a speech at the time of the Monaco Grand Prix in the late 1980s, he stated that the reason Marlboro had achieved its status as the world's number one consumer brand was down to two things: Formula One sponsorship and the iconic 'Marlboro Man' advertising campaigns.

As an example of tobacco sponsorship, Marlboro was the benchmark. Directly involved in bringing Ron Dennis in to take over and run the

McLaren team in 1982, Marlboro invested the dollars necessary to make the Woking-based team one of the heavyweights after years of underperformance.

Philip Morris's sponsorship through Marlboro was to be followed by a raft of other tobacco brands in the 1980s and 1990s; Camel, JPS for a second time, Barclay, Gauloises, Gitanes, Mild Seven, West, Rothmans, Winfield, Benson & Hedges, Sobranie, 555 and Lucky Strike would follow. By 2000 the sport had become addicted to tobacco funding in a manner that caused anyone concerned with long-term planning to wonder where the sponsorship revenues would be found at a time of increasing anti-tobacco advertising legislation around the world.

If tobacco had become a mainstay of Formula One sponsorship over the first three decades of the sport's commercialization, it was perhaps unsurprising that the alcohol industry followed, for, in spite of the drink-driving and social responsibility concerns that may come to mind these days, the 1970s and 1980s saw brands such as Martini, Molson's, Labatt's and Guinness appear. The same attributes that attracted the tobacco brands applied to drinks, and if the sexiness of the sport needed to be under-lined many further brands including Durex contraceptives and *Penthouse* magazine followed. Tobacco, alcohol and sex: Formula One was associated with all three, and happily reciprocated.

No one industry compared with the power of the tobacco spend within F1. For those of us who wondered just where the sport would go to replace its revenues, the last 15 years have proven to be an education in the ability of the industry to diversify its customer base, adjust its offering and demonstrate an impressive flexibility.

As the tobacco spend began to wane, the teams began to mine for dollars in other rich seams: automotive, oil and gas, soft drinks, financial services, IT, telecommunications. During the initial dot-com boom we saw Yahoo briefly, and then the telecommunications giants Nortel, Lucent and MCI WorldCom. F1 seemed to have swallowed the NASDAQ whole.

In a few short years they were gone, however, but mobile communications followed with sponsorships from Orange and then Vodafone, growing international brands with strong cash flow and the dollars to spend. IT was there, too, HP having joined the sport once the information technology revolution started to hit F1 in the early 1990s, and that grew further with Compaq, Acer, Dell, Toshiba, Intel, EMC, Sun Micro-systems and others besides. Tobacco was giving way to tech.

One of the drawbacks of tobacco sponsorship was that it had a limited B2B activity; thus all the activity and promotion within Formula One were centred on reaching consumers, the general public. So too with automotive, and to some degree oil, tyres and other automotive 'trade' sponsorships. With IT, telecommunications infrastructure and mobile the corporate audience grew; B2B was important. The same applied with financial services, as banking groups such as HSBC joined the fray, and brands such as the UK's Pearl Assurance and MasterCard tapped into the F1 show.

If tobacco wanted to make the act of smoking appear sexy, it was no less true of those peddling technology, communications and finance. One of MasterCard's corporate guests at F1 races in the late 1990s was Fred Goodwin, NatWest bank having fallen to RBS and the NatWest/MasterCard branding on the Jordan F1 cars at the British Grand Prix being one of the results. Goodwin, later to preside over the UK's largest banking collapses, loved the sport and would bring RBS into F1 in 2005 with a multi-year sponsorship of the Williams team. Credit Suisse, ING, Santander and UBS were to be found there too.

The ability of F1 and its teams to redirect their efforts into creating not only a compelling advertising medium but an unrivalled corporate experience drove the B2B business perhaps even more strongly than B2C. The Formula One Paddock Club hospitality business, operated from Geneva by Allsport Management under Paddy McNally, was able to charge thousands of dollars for a five-star experience, where technologists, bankers and dot-com boomers could rub shoulders with celebrity guests and taste the high-energy cocktail of F1.

If all this reads as a rose-tinted view of F1, it isn't meant to be. It's simply a restatement of the development of the sport commercially, and an insight into how it has adapted to meet the challenges as well as the opportunities that have developed. With each new source of revenue, so the challenges also had to be faced. Tobacco was on borrowed time from the late 1970s. The only miracle is that it lasted as long as it did and, with Marlboro, continues to this day with unbranded, red and white Ferraris. Legislation was always going to catch up with it, but for 30 years the tobacco industry used Formula One very effectively.

Similarly the dot-com and technology stock boom and bust showed that new sectors did not necessarily have the staying power. The 2000s witnessed the overindulgence of car manufacturers wooed by the prospect of F1 fame only to see their management and organizational abilities found wanting in this most demanding of arenas. This was soon followed by the bloodbath of the 2008 financial crash and its near-apocalyptic effects on the car industry. As quickly as they had arrived, they departed.

What's interesting about F1 is how, in spite of the challenges, the entrepreneurial skill of those involved and the fast-paced nature of the businesses mean that the challenges have repeatedly been faced down. In the wake of Ford's departure in 2004, Red Bull arrived, turning Jaguar Racing into Red Bull Racing and dominating the sport between 2010 and 2013. The withdrawal of BMW, Toyota and Honda, each of which owned a team, was further insight into the inability of automotive companies to easily achieve success in F1; their teams were predominantly cost centres and, as such, were unsustainable when the corporate belt had to be tightened.

When Honda withdrew, its team continued under the ownership of technical boss Ross Brawn, winning the World Championship in its first year. It was quickly snapped up by Mercedes-Benz and is today one of the sport's major players. Post-2008, however, the sport did look fragile, but the response was typically robust.

New entrants were sought, over 40 applied, and three new, entrepreneurial-style teams arrived to bolster the show; Malaysian businessman Tony Fernandes, fellow airline owner Sir Richard Branson and Spanish hopeful Jose Carabante picked up where the car companies left off and, against all the odds, two of them have survived.

Formula One is a microcosm of global businesses. To be successful in it requires strong skills: leadership, vision, communication – the ability to design, manufacture, develop and bring to market a constantly improving high-technology product, working to immovable deadlines with hundreds of suppliers and demanding customers and all in the face of a relentless 20-event schedule around the world where your results are posted every fortnight and the successes and failures are there for all to see. This international operation requires a global outlook on business and the ability to manage complex logistics, ensuring just-in-time delivery from one continent to the next, and to do so seamlessly.

Human resource management, the ability to motivate, lead, build a winning team and get a group of international employees to work together to achieve a range of goals with the ultimate focus on delivery at a pivotal moment, winning the race: these are extreme challenges, as any business knows.

I often ask businesspeople if they can imagine 20 of their colleagues having to perform a team task upon which the company's future depends, except that it has to be accomplished in 3 seconds in front of 120 million television viewers and the world's media. You get some insight into how a pit stop alone can represent just one extraordinary task for these businesses.

The final layer, perhaps the critical one for any real business, is the customer base: the ability to attract, sustain and develop customers internationally in the face of a dynamic economic environment, coping with the ebb and flow of global business. Growing the offering, diversifying and becoming customer-centric have been central to the success of entrepreneurial F1 businesses. It is for that reason that some of us find F1 just as compelling Monday to Friday as those who follow its fortunes on a Sunday afternoon.

CHAPTER TWO
INSIGHTS ON
LEADERSHIP

Good leaders and empowered managers build businesses; poor leaders with bureaucratic regimes destroy them. It may not be the accepted wisdom that successful companies should rely heavily on the ability of one individual to devise, communicate and create the framework for the delivery of his or her vision. In Formula One it is certainly the case that we witness the benefits of entrepreneurial, individual leadership over the malaise created by purely process-driven, committee-style management.

The term 'benevolent dictatorship' is often discussed in hushed tones by many people I have worked with, simply because, once you have experienced the compromise and ineptitude displayed by cosy consensus, having someone with whom the buck finally stops, and who will make a decision, is refreshing.

It is my firm belief that every business needs a single, clear leader who has the ability to define the direction that organization should take and then fully empower and support his or her management to unleash their own leadership skills and cascade that throughout the enterprise. The leader of an organization must set the tone and style he or she wishes the organization to follow. Marina Nicholas, CEO of Franco Formula Entertainment, on whose board of directors I sit, runs leadership training courses under the 'Navigator' headline, the analogy being that the leader of a company is like the captain of a ship. I relate fully to that – the leader should be determining the destination, setting the course and making sure he or she gets the best performance from the crew for the journey.

My evidence for the inadequacy of committee-led management can be seen in the dramatic inability of four of the world's major car companies to achieve significant sporting or commercial success in Formula One over the last decade. These failures resulted in their ignominious withdrawal, whilst the entrepreneurial teams flourished and now dominate the industry just as they did during its growth phase of the 1980s and 1990s. Indeed, in the cases of both Ferrari and McLaren, although they are themselves heavyweights in the luxury automotive sector, both were born out of individual entrepreneurship and retain the essence of such.

Ford, Honda, Toyota and BMW each created their own teams, ran them as divisions of their businesses, and yet failed to achieve their objectives within the sport. Harsh words, perhaps, but if the KPIs were the ability to win races and championships, or create profitable businesses, they didn't succeed. If 'brand marketing' was the raison d'être, that too rings hollow, since in F1 the inability to win leaves a brand associated with the alternative: losing.

BMW and Honda each won a race during the 2000s, but in some ways those singular successes underlined an inability to discover the formula for achieving sustained success. Four companies, spending billions of dollars, were unable to crack the code to achieve and sustain success in the F1 business.

As though to drive this hard-to-swallow message home, in two of these cases the withdrawal from Formula One was achieved by a fire sale of the businesses, only for the new owners to take the very same organizations and become World Champions – not simply win a few races, but actually achieve multiple victories and tie up the title. In the case of Ford, an ignominious foray into the sport in the guise of Jaguar Racing saw an abject lesson in poor leadership, management structure and delivery followed by a takeover by Austrian energy drinks company Red Bull. Within a few short years the approach taken by the producer of a fizzy drink produced a World Championship-winning car, which Henry Ford's successors had been unable to do in spite of the vast resources and capabilities of their global automotive empire.

If that wasn't enough, Honda's sudden withdrawal from the sport in December 2008 – ostensibly because of the recession – was followed by British engineer Ross Brawn taking over the business with a group of colleagues and promptly winning the very next year's World Championship in a Mercedes-Benz-powered Brawn. Quite what Honda's management will have made of this, one can only imagine. An estimated US$2 billion spend had failed to achieve the glory required by a company in whose DNA racing could be found. From the outset, Soichiro Honda's vision of powered bicycles had grown into a legendary success story, a post-war Japanese business that came to produce some of the best motorcycles and cars and prove their pedigree through racing.

In the white heat of contemporary Formula One, however, Honda was unable to find the winning formula, yet under Ross Brawn's leadership the same team, with technology created whilst still owned by Honda, took the World Championship by storm and would be snapped up by Mercedes at a relatively knock-down price one year later.

All too often when discussing the reasons for Ford, BMW, Toyota or Honda's difficulties, the answer from senior management would come back that the issue was 'Tokyo', 'Munich' or 'Detroit'. The point was clear: the F1 teams were answerable to head office, to an extent that meant there was a layer of management bureaucracy that does not lend itself easily to the fast-paced business of Grand Prix motor racing.

As mentioned elsewhere in this book, David Coulthard often relates that when he joined Red Bull Racing shortly after their takeover of the Jaguar Racing team, he found a culture where 'doing reports' in order to justify your existence was more important than developing strategies to ensure success for the business. It was as though the financial reporting for previous quarters or years had become in itself more important than delivering successful outcomes in the future.

Eddie Jordan was a very interesting man to work with, and he possessed leadership qualities that remain overlooked by people within the industry, including former staff, customers, suppliers and drivers. It is not likely, in response to the question 'What was Eddie Jordan best known for?', that many people will state 'leadership'. And yet I would promote Eddie's reputation in that regard, because our team undeniably achieved both sporting and business success under his leadership. None of it happened by accident, and none of the individual managers can take credit for the success the team achieved.

It's likely that some people will say Eddie was only interested in money, a frustrated rock star better known for his parties than his podiums, certainly unorthodox, sometimes foul-mouthed, with a whacky dress sense, something of a rebel whose approach often appeared contrary to the world of corporate sponsorship.

Eddie could be, to a greater or lesser extent, all of the above, but ultimately he created something out of nothing: a highly profitable business that he successfully sold a large chunk of at the peak of its value, winning races and almost a World Championship in 1999 – more, in other words, than four major car companies ever achieved. He was a businessman, and he provided a leadership that could be inspiring, sometimes frustrating, but ultimately set the tone for a team that achieved a great deal.

It was an off-hand comment by myself to none other than Dietrich Mateschitz, founder and owner of Red Bull, that prompted me to be brought up short and reflect on Eddie's achievements. I made a comment, the kind we all make from time to time, half-serious, half-light-hearted, about 'EJ's manner of doing business', to which Mateschitz responded by saying that Jordan had done more than most and was someone he admired. An accolade indeed, given that was only a few weeks after Mateschitz himself had taken over Jaguar Racing from Ford Motor Company and set Red Bull Racing on a path to F1 glory.

I first came across Eddie Jordan in the paddock of a Formula Atlantic race in Kirkistown, Northern Ireland, in 1978. I asked him for his autograph; he told me to 'f*** off'. I was 16, a teenage fan; he was 30 and driving for Marlboro Team Ireland. It wasn't exactly the response I was expecting.

The next time was in the Lisboa Hotel in Macau in 1987 when I was reporting on the Macau F3 Grand Prix and supporting my friend Martin Donnelly, who would win the main event and in doing so launch himself towards an international career leading to F1. One of my contracts meant I was providing editorial services and media support to Marlboro, through its Marlboro World Championship Team sponsorship programme. EJ realized that my race reports were influential in so far as the Marlboro management would use this information in their quest to pick and choose which teams in the lower formulae in which to place their drivers.

'Gallagher, I need to see you,' was EJ's greeting on seeing me. He was vying with rival F1 team West Surrey Racing to land a young Northern Irish driver by the name of Eddie Irvine, fully backed by Marlboro, and the deal he offered me was simple. If I put in a glowing report about

Eddie Jordan Racing and helped Marlboro's agency based in Chiswick, London, to select his team as the best option for Irvine, there'd be £5,000 in it for me. A commission, an inducement, a fee or perhaps simply a bribe: to a 25-year-old freelance journalist with a large overdraft and rent to pay, it was attractive. I am glad to say I didn't take it, since I didn't know EJ other than my previously brief encounter at Kirkistown, and I did know that my contract with Marlboro was important to me.

This unpromising start to our relationship did not hint at things to come because, by 1990, EJ was on the cusp of entering Formula One. Championship wins in Formula 3 and Formula 3000 had demonstrated the capabilities of his team, with Eddie doing the deals and team manager Trevor Foster ensuring that the money was spent wisely with immaculately maintained, well-engineered cars and talented drivers providing a winning combination. In parallel to his race team, EJ had developed with his lawyer Fred Rodgers a driver management business, Eddie Jordan Management, which had nurtured talent and brought to F1 drivers including Johnny Herbert, Martin Donnelly and Jean Alesi.

EJ always had vision and, yes, that included making money. Some might say it was his only motivation, but that's simply wrong. There are many, easier ways of making money than going motor racing; in fact it is a harsh and unforgiving industry, which has buried many a dreamer. Just as profit can be a dirty word to some, EJ's commitment to making money, whether for his team or himself, was often criticized. Yet it was difficult to understand this, since as a self-made man he knew that in the expensive world of international motor racing you have to work seriously hard to make deals work and to make money. Money is the lifeblood of an industry where everything needed to compete to win comes at a high price: cars, engines, tyres, gearboxes, transporters, top engineers and mechanics. Eddie, though, had a passion for what he did, for motor racing, and on top of that he had a passion for making money and therefore doing business. And, ultimately, he knew that the best place to make serious money would be in Formula One, if he worked hard, built a team that could deliver on the track and win customers off it.

After a failed attempt to buy Team Lotus, EJ opted to take his own team into F1 in 1991, and it was at the Italian Grand Prix in Monza, 1990, that I found myself typing out a one-page press statement announcing the arrival of Jordan Grand Prix. Compared to today's sophisticated PR wire services, distribution of the release was rather straightforward; I stood in the middle of the F1 paddock and handed releases to passers-by. Our first press conference, to launch the Jordan–Ford 911 as tested by ex-F1 star John Watson, was attended by around 20 of the media, and infamously caused the late, but celebrated, French journalist Jabby Crombac to wonder why EJ was bothering. Failure seemed inevitable.

Twenty years later, Eddie Jordan has a tattoo under the watch on his arm. It reads simply FTB. The acronym means 'F*** The Begrudgers' and gives an important insight into the complex motivations that drove him to create a highly successful, profitable Formula One team that did indeed make him serious money. If making money and going motor racing were key motivators, so too were the fear of failure and a deep desire to prove the critics wrong. Irish people are not alone in begrudging their peers their success, but EJ knew from years of experience that to achieve success often means attracting adulation and jealousy in equal measure. Not only that, but your competitors often don't simply want to beat you; they want to see you fail. FTB was a motivation, and Jabby Crombac's article would never be forgotten by Eddie. 'Why I am bothering? I'll show you.'

As a leader, Eddie could be many things: difficult, and sometimes impossible because he had very fixed ideas about what he wanted. He could be prone to fierce outbursts, and be highly litigious, but he could also be funny, charming, inspirational and stylish. Frankly, he was different, and his leadership style reflected this as he set out to differentiate Jordan Grand Prix from the morass of competitors. He succeeded.

Importantly, he liked to remind us that it was his name that hung over the door to the business and that, since the buck stopped with him, he would also have the ultimate say in key decisions.

His tiny Irish-registered team based at Silverstone entered F1 with a spectacular green livery, top-quality brand sponsors in the form of 7UP, Fujifilm and Marlboro, and a quick car designed by a tight-knit team under technical director Gary Anderson. They brought a well-conceived, competitive product to market, and in its first season Jordan would finish fifth in the Formula One World Championship for Constructors, out of 17 entrants. It would score multiple points finishes, embarrass the factory Ford-based Benetton team, have one driver sent to prison as the result of a traffic incident in London, and replace him with a relatively unknown German driver by the name of Michael Schumacher whose backers would pay for the privilege of seeing him make his F1 debut for Jordan. You cannot say that was anything other than a memorable debut season.

Add to that the infectious enthusiasm that the Jordan team brought to F1, with EJ's sometimes manic sense of fun and his ability to take the qualities of being Irish and apply them to the creation of an F1 team brand, and the stage was set for a decade and a half of highs and lows that would see Jordan among the most recognizable brands in the sport.

Although it's going too far to state that there was a carefully crafted strategy from the outset, there was certainly an approach that EJ took from the start. He was different, so the team would be different; the Jordan brand would be differentiated.

The Irish traditions of being welcoming, open, friendly and up for a bit of 'craic' or gossip became values the team espoused. Friday morning breakfasts for the media became de rigueur and ground-breaking; for a travel-weary British press corps, a proper fry-up in the Jordan hospitality unit set the weekend off, and inevitably led to some banter with EJ, a running commentary on current events, and the odd bet or two. A love of music and of storytelling would lead to languorous and sometimes riotous evenings with media, sponsors, suppliers and officials. Win, lose or draw, Jordan promised noisy parties, a sprinkling of celebrities, and a glass or three.

This was a powerful combination. We couldn't sell sponsorship on the basis of winning races and World Championships; that would take time. It was clear that the experienced opposition sold sponsorship on the premise of achieving success on the track, and perhaps some corporate hospitality or PR to support it. But that was an all-or-nothing strategy and, since there can only be one race winner on the Sunday, the majority of teams and thus their sponsors can easily feel a deep anticlimax. To finish second is to be the first of the losers.

At Jordan the sales pitch was different: the team will try hard and work to win, as it had done in Formula 3 and Formula 3000. But it would guarantee other things: a strong media profile, and an engagement that would offer rewards beyond merely the rolling of the dice to see whether we could win or not. I used to say to sponsors that the difference with Jordan was that you could call us on a wet Tuesday in February and ask to borrow our F1 car or arrange a driver appearance and we'd say 'yes'.

Did this come from Eddie? I would say yes, because his determination to win deals, make them happen and make money meant we worked hard at that and we knew that going the extra mile to win the customer over was supported from the top down. Sometimes, in later years, he'd kick back hard if he thought we were overservicing customers; he had a keen sense of the value that the team was delivering.

If his charisma, sense of fun and ability to entertain and frustrate in equal measure were qualities that come to mind, so too were a relentless work rate and energy that often left the rest of us wondering where it came from. If he seemed to disappear to his yacht or house in Spain for half the summer, it was no less true that he was working the phone and the fax, and networking with celebrities and businesspeople like crazy. He had never done a deal, he would say, sitting 'on my arse in the office waiting for the phone to ring'.

Departing Kidlington airport near Oxford early one morning, EJ's HS125 private jet took us to Amsterdam's Schiphol Airport for a sponsorship contract signing with DiverseyLever, part of the global Unilever group, and a deal I had worked on with agent Graeme Glew. Eddie, immaculately suited, was charm personified when we met the management, signed the contract, enjoyed light refreshments and celebrated the start of another million-dollar deal. From there we headed to Germany and a meeting with the owner of Liqui Moly, producer of automotive lubricants, fluids and cleaning products, a difficult meeting where the owner complained that a small sponsorship of the Jordan F1 would be a 'chickenshit' deal and he worried that he'd be treated accordingly – not an easy meeting, but we persevered. On arriving back at the airport, Eddie announced we had a third, previously undisclosed meeting, which required us to fly to a small regional airfield, touching down for less than an hour. I didn't know who he was meeting, and never did. He could be extremely discreet when needed, since sometimes deals required the utmost secrecy. The meeting was over quickly and we were gone. Ten hours and three countries later, we were on our way back to Kidlington.

Or not. Partway home EJ realized that Coventry City football club were playing away at Newcastle and so, with the pilots having been informed and spoken to air traffic control and Newcastle Airport, we diverted north and landed shortly after 7 pm. We were collected by a chauffeur-driven car and deposited outside the ground, were met by a Coventry City runner with tickets for the directors' box, grabbed a sandwich and sat down with one minute to go before the start. By 10 pm we were out of the ground, back to Newcastle Airport and bound for Kidlington to arrive by 11 pm and get home by midnight. Just another day with EJ, and an insight into his relentless work ethic.

With the passage of time we all suffer from looking back with rose-tinted glasses, but there's never been any question in my mind that the success Jordan achieved was down to Eddie's unique blend of leadership qualities that excited, motivated, cajoled and sometimes browbeat staff into looking for the next deal, the next result, the next PR triumph for a team that achieved more column inches than many who had won more on the track. If you needed to see EJ's enthusiasm for the job, his excitement, witness his dance to the podium when Jordan won its first Grand Prix in Spa-Francorchamps, Belgium, in August 1998. It became the first team in the history of the sport to achieve its maiden victory with a 1-2, and on a day when we had our fan club, our factory staff and the majority of our major sponsors present: a unique turnout to see the team's moment of glory.

Three months later Warburg Pincus concluded a deal to purchase half the equity in Jordan Grand Prix for around £50 million, making Eddie a very rich man. He and CFO Richard O'Driscoll had read the market perfectly, sold at the peak, and flipped the company onwards. It annoyed a lot of people but, FTB, it was good business for Eddie, and who can begrudge him that? In business terms, for an entrepreneur, it was a super-successful outcome after decades of hard work.

With money came many things: new friends, new projects and, perhaps, the beginning of a decline in the Jordan F1 business. Although 1999 was to be the zenith of the team's fortunes on and off the track, with two Grand Prix wins, third in the World Championship and a host of sponsorships, by 2000 it was clear there was a malaise setting in.

I have a theory about why that decline began, but in part I think the very fact of the Warburg Pincus deal having happened altered the motivations and rationale behind Eddie running a Formula One team. He was the leader of the business, but his motivations began to change. Simply put, the private equity people didn't understand the business and began to drive it in directions that were alien to the management, EJ included. By the end of 2005 the business was sold on to a Russian businessman, and Eddie was gone from F1: a loss to the sport, but with 15 years of enormous success behind him.

As leaders go, Eddie Jordan showed what can be achieved through a combination of charisma, graft, focus on the bottom line, and inspiring staff, customers and suppliers to want to work with him to achieve the goal.

Two observations about his style.

One was his list of deals and tasks, neatly written, edited, scored out or underlined, in his Filofax. Every day, when he was in the office, I'd get the call to join him, often with Ian Phillips or Richard O'Driscoll, to run through the list of deals, issues, opportunities and challenges – always with a view to managing how we were doing and where the next incremental deal could be clinched. It was very disciplined and relentless and kept us all focused on what mattered: securing customers and growing the business.

The other was his daily phone call to his mother Eileen back in Dublin. Around eight o'clock in the morning he would often be on the phone to his mother for a quick chat, staying in touch. In the midst of the high-tempo work rate demanded by Formula One, with constant travel, lots of pressures and deadlines, he always remembered to call his mother, and I felt that showed something about him as a leader. Ultimately he had very grounded human feelings, and he wasn't afraid for us as managers to see that side of him; a little bit of humanity goes a long way.

In Formula One the businesses led by an individual with vision and entrepreneurial flair, supported by a highly professional management team who can deliver, inevitably win out over those with top-heavy, committee-style structures where the vision and power are pushed out and downwards. If the failure of Ford or Toyota to build winning teams was evidence of the latter, the consistent success achieved by McLaren and Williams illustrates the former.

In both instances their leaders, Ron Dennis and Sir Frank Williams, forged their skills in the fires of disappointment brought on by their early forays into the complex, expensive and unforgiving world of running an international motor racing team. It would be too easy to describe Ron Dennis's experience with the Rondel F2 team or Frank Williams near bankruptcy caused by the collapse of Frank Williams Racing as mere failures. As we have seen many times in business, it is these trials that often shape entrepreneurs and develop their skills, lessons from the school of hard knocks.

Ron Dennis today presides over arguably the most successful business in Formula One. Success can be measured in many ways in this business: success on the track, as we have seen, and profitability off it, and in these respects McLaren has proven itself time and again. However, there have been successful, profitable F1 teams in the past, so perhaps what makes McLaren the standout organization has been its ability to attract, sustain and develop long-term customer relationships, expand its offering as a business to include electronics, advanced technologies and business processes that can be applied in other industries, and now a fast-developing automotive business that is seeing McLaren take its bitter on-track rivalry with Ferrari into the high-end sports car marketplace.

By 2015 McLaren Automotive aims to be producing 4,000 vehicles a year from its state-of-the-art production centre near Woking in Surrey, UK, while its Formula One team continues to thrive. Its new partnership with GlaxoSmithKline brings F1 decision making and business processes to bear in one of the world's largest companies, and its Applied Technologies business takes the knowledge gleaned from 50 years of race-bred technology and applies it in areas as diverse as designing world championship-winning bicycles and data analytics to aid London's Heathrow Airport.

All this stems from a Formula One team that became a business, and ultimately from the vision of Ron Dennis supported by a strong board and skilled management team.

I first met Ron Dennis in 1984 when I applied for a job as marketing executive at McLaren International and was interviewed by him in his pristine office in the team's headquarters situated, at that time, in Station Road, Woking. He was businesslike and polite, asked fairly straight-forward questions of a 22-year-old Irish economics graduate with one year's experience in the advertising department at *Autosport* magazine, and ultimately decided I wasn't the one for the job. I was disappointed not to get it, but impressed even to have been interviewed and had a glimpse behind the scenes of what was already a highly successful F1 team.

The next time I met him in person was for a one-to-one interview in the McLaren motor home in 1989. Ron was having breakfast, a bowl of something very healthy, and my hopes for the meeting were damaged as I fell up the step into the inner sanctum of the motor home and banged my head on the ceiling. Ron found that very amusing, and his staff told me after that, 'Everyone does it, and Ron quite likes it.'

Pride dented, I spoke to him at length about his team's continued high fortunes after a year in which they had won 15 of the 16 Grands Prix thanks to the combined capability of the team, the McLaren MP4/4 car, its Honda engine, and two drivers by the name of Ayrton Senna and Alain Prost. Something of an A team, that, and Ron had pulled it all together. Interestingly, he told me that he felt they should have won all 16 races in 1988 and, of course, he was right. Only a hasty mistake by Senna had caused them to lose in Italy.

Ron is known for being extremely determined in the manner he runs his business and obsessive about attention to detail. Sometimes his critics make fun of these attributes, but, as with those who said Eddie Jordan was only interested in money, this shows a lack of understanding about what's really going on. Eddie's interest in money meant he was determined to run a highly profitable business, while Ron's attention to detail is not a flaw but part of his inherent desire to ensure that everything McLaren does is very precisely planned and executed as well as possible.

If the Formula One World Championship was awarded for presentation alone, I suspect McLaren would have won it every year. Everything about its presentation – the cars, the garages, the trucks, the team's motor homes, the livery, the team clothing, its headquarters – screams attention to detail. The immaculate presentation suggests a very clinical approach to the engineering disciplines that lie at the heart of success in Formula One: a strong message.

McLaren has been the benchmark team in terms of presentation, perhaps matched only by Ferrari's upmarket Italian design. Both have undoubtedly benefited from the input of Philip Morris's Marlboro marketing managers, the brand backing McLaren between 1973 and 1994 and supporting Ferrari to the present day.

If Marlboro's brand guidelines demanded clean lines – the crisp white and red chevron with easily read black-on-white lettering, and best-in-class designs for everything from press kits to drivers' race suits and hospitality units – then they can only have contributed to Ron Dennis's belief in the importance of presentation. Prior to taking over the running of the McLaren team in 1982, Ron's Project 4 Motorsport organization had already attracted Marlboro backing for its championship-winning BMW M1 sports car racing programme, and established a reputation for building cars that were reliable, high-performing and impressively turned out, the key ingredients for any engineering business keen to attract customers and build for the future.

Attracting commercial partners was therefore an established skill when Ron Dennis secured what would become a pivotal business relationship with businessman Mansour Ojjeh, a Saudi-born French national whose company Techniques d'Avant Garde was known in the aviation sector as well as one-time owner of the elegant watch brand brought about by TAG's acquisition of the Swiss brand Heuer in 1989.

In taking over the running of McLaren at the behest of Marlboro in 1981, Ron Dennis and his new partner Ojjeh convinced none other than Porsche to design a V6 turbo engine with which McLaren would be powered for the following three years. Funded by TAG, this unit would power McLaren to success in the World Championship for Drivers in 1984 with Niki Lauda and 1985 with Alain Prost.

Marlboro had identified in Dennis a man who had the attention to detail and commitment to continuous improvement necessary to win in Formula One. These attributes were supported by another ingredient common to all success in this sector: a desire to innovate. The MP4/1 featured the first all-carbon-composite chassis, a development that in one fell swoop changed the direction of F1 car design, combining great strength with lightness. In order to produce this vehicle McLaren entered into yet another partnership, this time with the US aerospace company Hercules, and under the technical direction of John Barnard the car set new standards in terms of safety and performance, paving the way for the development of the F1 cars we see today.

Another aspect of McLaren's development was that the initially successful business partnership between Ron Dennis and John Barnard ultimately came to an end in 1989 when the pair split, Barnard leaving to join Ferrari. Whether intentionally or not, this helped Dennis to move away from a technical structure over-reliant on the skills of one man, a facet within F1 teams that has been commonplace.

It may be one thing to have someone leading the charge at the head of the company, but ultimately the need for structure, process and sustained performance means that the spread of management skills must remain evenly balanced. A contemporary example of the dangers here lies in Red Bull Racing, a team that many people feel has been dominant because of the technical leadership of one man – Adrian Newey – without whom the team would retreat from its position as industry leader.

Newey, too, was once a McLaren technical director, joining in 1998 after a successful, championship-winning, seven-year spell at the Williams team. He achieved much at McLaren, including presiding over the championship-winning cars piloted by Mika Hakkinen and David Coulthard, and when he departed many felt that Ron Dennis had made an error in not doing all in his power to retain him. As with the departure of Barnard, however, McLaren proved that it had strength in depth, subsequently winning the World Drivers title with Lewis Hamilton in 2008.

In 2004 McLaren moved into a new headquarters facility near Woking, and if ever the world needed to see an example of Ron Dennis's single-minded approach, attention to detail, belief in innovation, commitment to growth and desire to move constantly to the next level the 'Paragon' facility design by Britain's Sir Norman Foster is it. Originally spread over a 150-acre site, the futuristic design houses all the facilities required for the design, manufacture, development and operation of championship-challenging F1 cars, and spacious accommodation for all the other disciplines. The McLaren Technology Centre was born, and stands as testimony to Ron Dennis's vision for the business.

As ever at McLaren there was a keen emphasis on presentation with a view to impressing the customers, but on a level that had never previously been seen in F1. The lines of previous championship-winning cars, innovative designs and heritage models from the days of McLaren's Can-Am and Le Mans sports car racing programmes help visitors to become immersed in a long tradition of excellence. This is underlined by the ability to see today's cars being developed and manufactured behind floor-to-ceiling glass walls. In 2013 the team celebrated 50 years since founder Bruce McLaren incorporated the company. McLaren's heritage is an extremely important part of its business story.

The fact that visitors can see precisely what the workers are doing, the culture of their work environment, the cleanliness and the immaculate presentation underlines the deep conviction that Ron Dennis has in his business and his pride in his staff. While many companies would hide their operations away, McLaren gets them out in the open, free to view, as a demonstration of self-confidence.

When visiting for a luncheon with director of communications Matt Bishop I was struck by many things: yet again the cleanliness and present-ation, the fact that lunch was served by professional staff from yet another of McLaren's diverse businesses – Absolute Taste – and the provision of ample meeting space. Not for McLaren the discourtesy of 'Let's see if we can find a free room' such as you get in many businesses. However, on that day, the item that struck me most was the butter; chilled, served on a dish, and shaped in the form of the McLaren logo. Even in the presence of this transient product, soon to melt or be con-sumed, the attention to detail and pride in the brand were present.

McLaren's approach is not to everyone's taste in Formula One. I myself have often teased them for being somewhat 'bland' or 'corporate' in a sport where noise, excitement and the feverish support of fans around the world appear to lend themselves more to the passion of the racing red Ferraris. Think also of the 'extreme sports' lifestyle marketing of Red Bull or even the brash, showy, rock'n'roll approach that Jordan took. This misses the point; McLaren's customers are multinational corporations and, for a customer-focused business, that comes first.

If the positioning of the McLaren brand has been a tad boring to some, and underlined at times by media criticism of Ron Dennis's tendency to verbosity – coined 'Ron-speak' in the industry – this has rather missed the point about McLaren as a business. For McLaren, more than any team in F1, has created an identity around attracting, sustaining and developing customers, and in this respect Ron Dennis's attention to detail has worked right down to the bottom line.

Helped in no small part by the demands of Marlboro as its sponsor, McLaren under Ron Dennis has, since the 1980s, maintained an impressive array of customers. Having been involved in sponsorship throughout my career, I take the view that the majority of Formula One teams have failed to maximize their income potential from sponsorship simply because at no stage did they put in the effort required to research potential customers, woo them through presenting relevant, compelling, business-led proposi-tions, and then deliver on all their obligations to those sponsors.

I recall many in the media, and other teams, decrying McLaren for creating a McLaren Marketing entity under Ekrem Sami, one of the lynchpins of the McLaren business. But in making the effort to carve out 'marketing' this showed that Ron Dennis understood a business imperative that passed others by, namely that if you are serious about securing customers you need to get serious about resourcing the sales, marketing, client services, hospitality and communications departments necessary to deliver customers to the organization and deliver results for the customer.

Having put that structure in place McLaren went on to show its understanding of another fundamental: that the decisions to buy global commercial sponsors are not made by the media or fans hungry for a brash, racy image, but by senior executives at board level of multinational businesses where a corporate approach is more likely to be understood. When senior executives aged in their late 40s, 50s or 60s are making multimillion-dollar commitments to associate their closely guarded and valuable brands with a company that races cars, it is understandable that they will relate to a highly polished, corporate identity that wants to deliver real value rather than a team selling 'car racing' and 'publicity'.

This may be disappointing for those who would still like Formula One to be risqué, but times have changed and the approach to securing and maintaining customers has had to evolve. There are many in our sport who yearn for the 'old days' – most often the 1960s and 1970s when the race tracks of the world were graced by a cosmopolitan mix of drivers with strong personalities and a wide range of ages, drivers with the quiet brilliance of Scotland's Jim Clark, the taciturn nature of Australian 'Black Jack' Brabham or the quintessential English qualities of Graham Hill.

It is understandable, for many of us in Formula One grew up watching those drivers race, and it was an apparently more glamorous affair than the one we view today. That, however, is mainly myth, since it was also a time when sponsorship was in its infancy, the sport was at best semi-professional, and running a Formula One team required patronage because no business model worth the name existed. It was also a sport that sometimes seemed to kill as many drivers as it made famous.

The T-shirts that emerged a few years back with the legend 'The 1960s – when sex was safe and racing was dangerous' raised a few laughs and emphasized our rose-tinted view of the past. There was a similar reaction when the latest in a line of biographies of British star James Hunt was published in 2009, including a photograph of him wearing race overalls on which he had sewn a badge reading 'Sex – Breakfast of Champions'.

But if F1 back then was sexy, dangerous and glamorous, it also wasn't very corporate; it wasn't a business. As that changed, so too did the approach to wooing customers, and the progression of sponsorship through the decades has followed a fixed path. If in the 1970s and 1980s it can be said that a great many sponsorships were decided by individual executives of major companies for whom corporate governance, accountability and responsibility were unknown tenets, there is no doubt that this has changed dramatically over the last two decades.

As the sponsorship industry has grown and matured, with global companies and their brands now advised by an entire industry of sponsorship consultants, marketeers and communications specialists, so too the managements of those companies have had to adhere to stricter corporate discipline. Making a decision to sponsor a Formula One team 'because the CEO likes it' is much less common that it used to be. There are some who maintain those days are over; they are not, and never will be, because there will always be self-made entrepreneurs who enjoy a particular sport presiding over their own businesses and deciding how to spend their company money. Witness Dietrich Mateschitz at Red Bull, for one. But it is no longer the mainstay of sponsorship, and so teams have had to evolve a more sophisticated approach to wooing and retaining customers than merely appealing to the fans within the boardroom.

The ravages of the global recession following the financial crash of 2008 will unquestionably have made the quest for new business more difficult, and corporate decision makers will inevitably have to be more careful than ever to follow good corporate process and governance before signing off on major sponsorships. It will be those teams that can demonstrate and reflect their understanding of this that will stand a chance of benefiting from the upswing when it comes, and in that regard McLaren is likely to lead the field.

In 2004, whilst head of commercial affairs at Jaguar Racing, I was advised to go and meet a senior executive of the Royal Bank of Scotland on the basis that there was evidence of a potential Formula One sponsorship. The background to this was that Fred Goodwin, RBS's CEO, was known to be a great fan of Formula One and was allegedly using the good offices of close friend Sir Jackie Stewart to secure headline sponsorship of a major team.

The meeting duly took place, and I found myself in RBS's main London office seated opposite Howard Moody, the director of corporate communications, who explained to me that RBS was not considering F1 sponsorship for a variety of reasons, including the cost, the fact that Bernie Ecclestone's Formula One Management (FOM, the commercial rights holder of the Formula One World Championship) TV figures did not appear realistic, and that half of the bank's customers were women, who did not like F1.

I then got to the point and said that we were informed that Jackie Stewart was working on a sponsorship opportunity with Fred Goodwin, and Howard responded by saying that they were indeed good friends but that did not mean RBS would be sponsoring Formula One. He was emphatic on that point, and unsurprisingly the meeting was not a long one.

Fast-forward a few months and in January 2005 RBS announced title sponsorship of the Williams F1 team, with Jackie Stewart acting as brand ambassador, and none other than Howard Moody quoted in the press statement as advocating Formula One as a logical step for their brand.

There can be two ways of looking at this. One is to say that I had been quietly sold a dummy; the other is to imagine that Fred Goodwin's now infamously known dictatorial style won through and the company was instructed to sponsor Williams. This was at a time when RBS's fortunes were riding high, two years before it would begin a dramatic slide into achieving the largest loss in UK corporate history, subsequent near collapse, and rescue by the British taxpayer.

Whatever the case, the rise and fall of RBS as both global banking giant and major customer of a Formula One team provide the ultimate argument that all future sponsorships of this size, and certainly from the financial services sector, will come under greater corporate scrutiny than before. This scrutiny of executive decision making cuts across every area of business, of course, but in the world of Formula One – where potentially vast sums of money can change hands because of the scale of the sport – this is going to be increasingly the case when it comes to justifying sponsorship.

McLaren's approach to creating a corporate F1 team identity addresses some of these fundamental questions. It has set out to create an environment that its customers can relate to and in which they feel comfortable doing business. This has been one of the master strokes of Ron Dennis's leadership, developed and executed with the help of lieutenants such as Sami.

Consider the colour palette used in McLaren's corporate identity and the livery of its F1 cars. The silvers, blacks and greys with a flash of red on its logo promote a corporate image, reflecting the grey-suited executives who represent its customer base.

First to move away from the motor homes, which were converted buses used as hospitality units in the paddocks of Formula One races in Europe, McLaren created a portable building – the Communications Centre – in 1999, with a suite of offices that reflected technology, innovation, attention to detail and success.

That was replaced in 2006 by the enormous Brand Centre, a three-storey building that takes a fleet of trucks to carry it – and all for the five days of a Grand Prix, and only in Europe. The very name 'Brand Centre' shows what McLaren is all about: working with and building brands – its own brand, or the customer's brand. It's about adding value, promoting excellence, and ultimately winning the race off the track to achieve the most important goal of all: profitability.

Before finishing with McLaren, with its uber-corporate approach to Formula One and relentless desire to sustain and develop its customer relationships, there are two final points worth making.

The first is that McLaren enjoys some of the longest-standing unbroken customer relationships of any team in Formula One. Hugo Boss has been with the team since 1983, Exxon Mobil since 1982, and they have enjoyed a relationship directly or indirectly with TAG Heuer for the same 30-year period. As a metric for client-centricity, customer relationship management and customer satisfaction, there can be no simpler test than the longevity of relationships. Through decades, with the natural ebb and flow of business and the inevitable cycles that brings including changes of management and strategy reviews, these companies have repeatedly chosen to remain customers of McLaren. The team has not won every race, won every championship or dominated the sport, but it has been relentless in its pursuit of sporting success on the track and commercial success for itself and its customers off it.

The second is that this most corporate of teams knows success, celebrates success, and in a unique way. Winning in Formula One usually means that hot, sweaty, dishevelled team personnel, drivers and managers are photographed in less than photogenic circumstances in the very moment of achieving their goal. As part of its partnership with Vodafone, McLaren introduced victory shirts, not in the corporate silvers and greys, but in the mobile phone giant's 'rocket red', which every member of the team changes into when they win. Whilst the rest of the pit lane wearily sets about packing their equipment away, hot and bothered, the McLaren crew are visibly successful, trumpeting their victory, posing for the cameras in their fresh tops, faces beaming.

As if to illustrate, or even illuminate, the attention to detail, this visible sign of celebrating success, showing the world that they are winners, extends to the McLaren headquarters in Surrey. Outside the $700 million facility, on a busy roundabout adjacent to Farnborough Airport, the McLaren company sign stands proudly. When they win, the sign is lit with the same orange hue as that of the T-shirts worn by the team personnel at the track. Even the factory celebrates the success of its products.

Dietrich Mateschitz is seldom written about in the international business press, and indeed I have often wondered how, in this age of Silicon Valley celebrities such as Gates, Jobs and Zuckerberg, when billionaire businesspeople are so often feted and wooed by media celebrity, the founder and owner of Red Bull has managed to remain relatively low-key.

One reason is undoubtedly that, although a giant of the soft drinks industry, Red Bull is also a privately owned company and thus does not have its results put under the media microscope each quarter.

When Red Bull first appeared in Formula One as a personal sponsor of Austrian driver Gerhard Berger, few imagined that the sweet, fizzy drink with a taste some described as being akin to cough medicine would go on to achieve dominance in one sector of the global beverages market and embarrass giants of the car industry by achieving complete success as a team owner in Formula One.

From my perspective there are two distinct strands to the Red Bull story: the development of the brand into the success story it is today, and the manner in which this upstart Austrian drinks company was able to take over the largely failed Jaguar Racing Formula One team from Ford Motor Company and turn it into a winner. I was there the day Mateschitz addressed the workforce at Jaguar Racing in late 2004, hot on the heels of Red Bull's takeover, and he told a relieved but tense staff about his vision for the team and his ambitions for the future. If any of us doubted him, we only had to look at what he had achieved with Red Bull in the two decades since it was founded to know that this was a man who knew how to get things done.

Having worked in marketing for Unilever, Mateschitz later joined German cosmetics company Blendax, where he had an international marketing role for products including toothpaste. It was while on a business trip to Asia that he came across an invigorating tonic drink known as Krating Daeng, which a Thai company was selling widely in the region. Popular for its ability to boost energy thanks in part to its caffeine and taurine constituents, it featured a pair of fighting gaur, or Indian bison, as a logo.

I was fortunate in 2004 to meet with Peter Huls and Roland Concin, two of Mateschitz's right-hand men, and during a day-long introduction to the world of Red Bull they explained how he had taken this regional product and turned it into a global brand phenomenon. Huls was head of engineering and technology, Concin responsible for operations, and they explained how Mateschitz had taken the original drink and had it modified to appeal to a Western palate before setting about producing it. They also explained how product differentiation was key from the start, including the choice of slim, tall can with its cool blue and silver colours.

The Red Bull production lines at the Rauch factory in Rankweil illustrated the scale of Red Bull's success less than two decades after Mateschitz had the vision to create an 'energy drink' and in so doing invent an entirely new sector of the soft drinks industry. The automated production lines were busy when we walked around, each producing 90,000 cans of Red Bull an hour, or 25 a second. And there were four lines.

Later I met Jurgen and Roman Rauch, whose family business is primarily known for producing fruit drinks, and who recalled the moment when this man named Dietrich Mateschitz came to them with the idea of producing his 'new' product in their factory. His initial order quantities were so small they really didn't want to know, but when the original batch quickly sold out and he came back for more they began to realize Red Bull might be worth the effort.

From the outset Mateschitz's vision for Red Bull was to eschew traditional advertising techniques and instead to promote the product by creating events and getting cans of Red Bull into the hands of consumers. Event-based marketing was a core philosophy from the outset and, in embracing extreme sports, motor sport and aviation, Red Bull was very much reflecting the personal energy and enthusiasm Mateschitz himself had for skiing, Formula One and flying. As a lesson in leadership it illustrates that, when you combine your passions with your business, success can follow.

Many people in Europe will remember the early days of Red Bull's roll-out when Minis began appearing in our streets with a large Red Bull on the rear deck of the converted car. Guerrilla marketing was part of the Red Bull game plan, targeting everything from major events to traffic jams where promotional staff on scooters would hand out the product to frustrated motorists.

I asked Mateschitz about this when we met in 2004, and he told me that the whole point of their marketing is to motivate people to try the product. Their own research showed that some consumers simply did not like the taste at all – as many as 50 per cent – but that left half the world's population who might come to regard a can of Red Bull as a convenient way of getting the same caffeine rush as from a cup of coffee, and the more regular users will drink perhaps four to six cans a week.

From the start Red Bull was associated with high energy, youthfulness and vitality; it was edgy. Mateschitz was very clear about the brand values. Extreme sports showed cool young people performing outlandish feats on skis and snow boards, from base jumping to free climbing. Drink Red Bull and this 'is' you.

Aviation sport was by no means a mainstream activity to reach consumers, but by using base jumping and free-fall parachuting, and then extending it into the creation of the Red Bull Air Race, which visited major cities around the globe, Mateschitz was again combining high energy and underlining the slogan adopted in their advertising: 'Red Bull gives you wings.'

Other events soon followed, from the motocross-based stadium events called Red Bull X Fighters to the very popular Red Bull Soap Box derby and amusing Red Bull Flugtag, which involves members of the public trying to build homemade, human-powered aircraft. There have been more than two dozen Red Bull-created event formats, each underlining the brand's values and putting the product into the hands of consumers worldwide. Each activity was carefully crafted so that it could travel well from market to market and be scalable.

Probably the most well-known event was Red Bull Stratos, when on 14 October 2012 Austrian free-fall parachutist and wing flyer Felix Baumgartner jumped from a special capsule floating at 128,100 feet above New Mexico. He broke the sound barrier during his free fall, reaching a terminal velocity of 833.9 mph, setting new world records for the highest free fall and highest human balloon flight. More importantly it was widely broadcast, with 80 television stations in 50 countries taking the live feed and rolling news channels replaying the jump end-lessly. There were 52 million views online. It took Red Bull to new heights in terms of its message of 'energy', being on top of the world and, of course, giving you 'wings'. It also contributed directly to Red Bull's record year, selling 5.2 billion cans worldwide.

Mateschitz's prowess for creating a brand marketing phenomenon is well established, therefore, but perhaps his greatest achievement in showing how his vision and leadership can drive success whatever the industry comes in the form of Red Bull Racing.

Jaguar Racing, owned by Ford Motor Company and formed as the result of the US firm's acquisition of Stewart Grand Prix from three times World Champion Jackie Stewart in 2000, was markedly unsuccessful and something of an embarrassment to the brand it represented. Between 2000 and the end of 2004 the team scored only two podium finishes, in the hands of Eddie Irvine, but failed to win a race, score a pole position or finish higher than seventh in the Constructors Championship.

Ford, frustrated by the team's lack of success and unwilling to under-write the budget for 2005, put the team up for sale with the threat that if a buyer could not be found then the team would close with the loss of several hundred jobs.

I had just joined the team to handle commercial affairs and found myself dispatched to China to work on a rather complex deal whereby Ford would sell the team to a Chinese entity. In so doing we would create a Ford Team China team, which would take the F1 liability off Detroit's desk and at the same time build a joint venture relationship with investors in China. Somewhere in Shanghai, to this day, lies a quarter-scale Jaguar F1 car painted in Ford Team China colours, much to the confusion of anyone who might find it.

Fortunately back in Europe a more obvious deal materialized when Red Bull, which had been sponsoring the team via its driver Christian Klien, came to the table with the idea of buying Jaguar Racing outright. Tony Purnell, Jaguar Racing's diligent team principal and CEO, was thankfully able to conclude an agreement with Mateschitz and the deal was done; Red Bull Racing was the result.

Those hundreds of jobs had been saved too, but what, everyone wondered, would a Red Bull Formula One team be like? If Ford and Jaguar failed to produce a winning car, what chance would a producer of energy drinks have to compete against the likes of Ferrari, McLaren and Williams? The only thing that seemed certain was that the parties would be good, for even in Milton Keynes the staff knew that Red Bull had a legendary reputation when it came to staging events.

When Mateschitz came to the factory a few days later he addressed the staff and explained very clearly what his vision for the business would be. He explained how, in the 1960s, he had become a big fan of Formula One. He liked the technology, the purity of the racing, the challenge that was involved. He said he liked the lifestyle around Formula One, but that it had all become a little bit serious, and so Red Bull would be putting the fun back into the sport and doing things differently from the rest. He also said that he wanted to win, to find the right people and spend the money in the right areas. He was very clear that Red Bull did things properly, and that Formula One would be no different.

Christian Horner and Adrian Newey, the team principal and technical director of the Red Bull Racing that came to dominate Formula One in 2010–13, weren't even in the audience that day. They had yet to be employed. This moment was ground zero for the creation of Red Bull's F1 project.

With his vision outlined, Mateschitz began to make the changes that he felt were absolutely necessary to turn Jaguar Racing from a loss-making, unsuccessful embarrassment into a team capable of winning. One of the early changes was to replace the senior management, notably Tony Purnell and David Pitchforth, with a fairly brutal 'clear your desks' approach. New management was installed, with Horner brought in by Mateschitz's motor sport adviser Helmut Marko. A successful and ambitious team boss in lower formulae, Horner was regarded as a reliable lieutenant who could be trusted to deliver on Mateschitz's vision.

David Coulthard was recruited as one of the drivers for the 2005 season, and 'DC' brought with him some vital qualities. He knew how to win and had worked with two of the most successful teams in the sport – Williams and McLaren. Understanding the culture of a winning team was important, and Mateschitz wanted to get the right people into key roles as soon as possible.

By the end of the team's first year changes had already been made to the way things were done, but some of this 'pain' was balanced by the recruitment of Newey from McLaren. As a multiple championship-winning car designer, and someone whom DC had worked with at both Williams and McLaren, he was a key appointment. He was then empowered to put in place the people, structure and technology necessary to haul Red Bull Racing up the league table.

Newey's first full design for Red Bull came in 2007, since the 2006 car was already 'done' when he joined, but in the meantime DC had scored the team's first podium finish in Monaco 2006. Regular points-scoring results and more podiums began to come the team's way, but 2009 became the breakthrough year with an inaugural victory in the Chinese Grand Prix. By season's end the team and lead driver Sebastian Vettel were second in both the Constructors and the Drivers World Championships, but little hinted of what was to follow: complete dominance of Formula One in the four seasons that followed, with successive titles from 2010 to 2013 inclusive.

Behind all of this success is Mateschitz's vision, outlined on that day in November 2004 when he stood in front of the relieved staff in their Milton Keynes factory. He had a clear vision of what he wanted to achieve, put in place the right people for the job, empowered them, provided the resources necessary to invest in the areas that mattered, and used Red Bull's global marketing power to build the team into a giant of the sport both on and off the track. In so doing he created not only a winning racing team, but a winning business, which is now itself sponsored by major global brands including Infiniti cars, Total oil, Pepe Jeans, Geox apparel and even Rauch – the Austrian fruit juice company that gave Mateschitz the production capability he so desperately needed all those years ago.

Working with Eddie Jordan and Dietrich Mateschitz, competing against Ron Dennis's McLaren, teaches a lot about leadership. In each case they eat, sleep and breathe their businesses and are relentless in their quest for success. They are consistent and clear in their vision for the business, require their staff to buy into that and drive businesses where everyone is responsible for their role and accountable for their actions.

EJ was focused on the bottom line, in his quest for the next deal. Ron Dennis wanted nothing left to chance; everything is about attention to detail. And in Dietrich Mateschitz we had someone who combined his business with his passions, found the right people to deliver for him in each area, and in so doing showed how to be the best in the world, from drinks to Formula One.

LESSONS IN LEADERSHIP

Leadership requires a broad range of skills, and although not every leader can possess every quality it is worth reflecting on those attributes that have made successful business leaders in Formula One.

There are some common features. Although it is a much overused word these days, having a genuine 'passion' for the industry helps. Having that innate interest in the subject makes it much easier to make the commitment necessary to become the very best. It is clear that the really successful leaders work extremely hard at what they do, put in the hours and find that the returns are proportionate.

Eddie Jordan, Ron Dennis and Dietrich Mateschitz achieved success as the result of a lifetime's commitment to what they do. There was never any half-measure; each in his own way was relentless in his quest to achieve success. In each case it was a question of working harder than the competition in every area, driving towards having the best-engineered product, developing the most powerful brand and landing the most lucrative deals.

They set the tone for their businesses, and expected their employees to buy into the vision they set out. Whether it was Ron Dennis's attention to detail, EJ's focus on sales or Mateschitz's belief in the importance of the brand, each drove his business with great conviction and focus.

Great leadership requires that the leader is fully empowered. In each of the examples I have given the leaders of these top Formula One businesses were self-made entrepreneurs. As Eddie Jordan said, his name was 'over the door' of the business, and this translated into his leadership style; the business meant everything to him personally, and ultimately he knew the buck stopped with him. Leadership without authority is impossible, and it is for this reason that Formula One's most successful teams have traditionally been entrepreneurial in nature with strong, centralized leadership.

TO SUMMARIZE:

▪▪▪➡ *Centralized leadership works.* Formula One teams have seen the advantages of strong centralized leadership supported by managers empowered to run the business functions. A 'benevolent autocracy' is seen to be preferable to consensus-led management.

▪▪▪➡ *Empowered leaders can transform a business.* As we saw with Jaguar–Red Bull and Honda–Brawn, empowered leadership can deploy resources faster and more efficiently, and create a culture of innovation and continuous improvement.

➠ ***Be yourself, but look after the fundamentals.*** A leader can be unorthodox, like Eddie Jordan, but a strong work ethic and relentless sales drive were combined with a strong human touch that inspired personnel and drove success on and off the track.

➠ ***Be different.*** Both Eddie Jordan and Dietrich Mateschitz saw the importance of differentiating their brands, standing out from the competition, and deploying the 'fun factor' as an important weapon in nurturing staff loyalty and attracting customers.

➠ ***Have greater attention to detail than your rivals.*** McLaren has always been a team with a pin-sharp focus on engineering excellence combined with world-class presentation. Aiming to be the very best in every single area has been a core message.

➠ ***Understand who your customers are and focus accordingly.*** Designing the business to attract customers may seem obvious. McLaren's success in retaining clients for decades reflects their ability to match their proposition continuously to customer demands.

➠ ***Don't be afraid of failure.*** Many leaders make mistakes, or suffer failures, on their way to the top. Ron Dennis, Frank Williams and Eddie Jordan all endured tough times early on in their careers; it didn't put them off, because they had the determination to keep trying.

➠ ***Put the right people and resources in place.*** The McLaren story showed how Ron Dennis assembled the best customers, technical suppliers and investors to enable his business to create great products and place innovation at the heart of his business.

➠ ***Communicate your vision to your staff.*** As Dietrich Mateschitz showed in his address to the staff of Red Bull Racing upon its creation in November 2004, it's important to be clear about what you are doing, why you are doing it and how you plan to go about it.

➠ ***Believe in your brand.*** As leader you are 'brand ambassador in chief', and it's important to have complete belief in your brand, its values and its proposition. Jordan, McLaren and Red Bull were very clear about their core values, attributes and goals.

CHAPTER THREE
BRAND BUILDING

As one of the most successful global sports, Formula One has played an important role in building some of the world's most famous brands. I often ask delegates at conferences to give me a show of hands for those who follow Formula One; in a typical European audience there will be perhaps 30–40 per cent who raise their arms. I then ask how many people have heard of Ferrari. It's 100 per cent, every time, and not only in Europe. An interesting response considering that Ferrari has never used traditional advertising or marketing; Formula One, and its associated PR value, has been its principal avenue for brand building.

Not bad considering that in February 2013 it was announced by Brand Finance that Ferrari was the world's most powerful brand and in 2012 had enjoyed the best sales figures in its history, with total revenues of €2.4 billion.

Brands fascinate me because my career in Formula One inevitably involved working with major sponsors eager to promote their brands and create associations with the speed, technology, glamour and global appeal of the sport.

Considering that at any one time there are over 200 brands involved in Formula One, and that at Jordan Grand Prix we were adept at securing a broad portfolio of sponsors from across a wide range of industries, brand watching was always an inherent part of my job.

Along the way, to coin a phrase, we saw the good, the bad and the ugly: brands whose owners knew what they stood for, had a vision of how to develop them and did so relentlessly and successfully; others whose senior executives had a vision but were playing fast and loose, unsure of brand attributes, aspiring to develop values that remained out of reach; and some that, as things turned out, used sponsorship at the whim of CEOs, simply because they liked Formula One motor racing or wanted to have fun in glamorous, far-flung destinations. This meant that sometimes the selected sponsorship was entirely irrelevant to the brand and its business.

In over six decades, however, Formula One has produced some extraordinary successes in relation to brand building. Ferrari might hog the number one title, but in the sport's key markets in the 1970s, 1980s and 1990s brands including John Player Special, Goodyear, Honda and Benetton made the most of the opportunity and imbued their brands with strong, positive values backed up by effective marketing communications.

As the sport went truly global in the 2000s, adding the giant Asian economies and the burgeoning Middle East to its footprint, companies such as Red Bull showed what can be done when you embark on a strategy with real focus, and in doing so embarrassed the also-rans paralysed by short-termism, knee-jerk thinking and management turnover. How many times I have been told 'The new boss is reviewing everything and we are going through a period of change' – transformation for transformation's sake, and often at the expense of the brand.

It's not often that you remember a specific date, but Saturday, 10 January 1987 was a memorable one for me because of a phone call. Ian Phillips, former editor of *Autosport*, called me to say that he had been invited to run the March Formula One team and would be quitting life as a freelance journalist; and would I like to take on his media work for Marlboro?

For the next six years I would dovetail all my other work in motor racing with providing media information for Marlboro, working for one of the tobacco giant's agencies in London. The Marlboro World Championship Team (MWCT) was a global sports marketing phenomenon, for not only did the Philip Morris-owned brand sponsor top Formula One teams including McLaren and Ferrari, but they were principal sponsors of at least two teams in all the lower formulae. This included Formula 3000, Formula 3, Vauxhall/Opel Lotus and Formula Ford, while Marlboro's presence stretched across other major forms of motor sport on both two wheels and four.

This all-pervasive sponsorship of motor sport extended not only to teams but to drivers, with Marlboro also allocating budgets on a regional and national basis to support local stars, thereby guaranteeing uptake by their domestic media.

Working on the MWCT programme taught me a great deal about brands, and specifically what makes a world-class brand stand out from the crowd. It was an education in brand building and brand management because, although it may seem strange for modern eyes to read, Marlboro was the world's number one consumer brand at the time. Yes, a cigarette was top of the list.

Anti-tobacco legislation was just around the corner, with France's Loi Evin removing advertising and sponsorship in this key European market in 1991. However, the EU-wide ban and global restrictions championed by the World Health Organization were still a decade and a half away.

In the meantime, the tobacco companies were able to market and advertise their products freely in international motor sport. Budgets were good, but what really struck me was the way in which Marlboro built their brand by keeping things very simple, the message strong and always consistent.

'Keep it simple, stupid' should be engraved on every brand marketeer's desk folder because, much as I have admired the sophistication of modern marketing, the reality is that most consumers don't have the time, energy or motivation to take on board any messaging that's too complicated.

Marlboro got it right for lots of reasons, including the fact that its brand name is a simple eight-character word, its primary colour palette of red, white and black is easy to spot, and the 'roof-top' chevron of white and red is iconic.

The alliteration of 'Marlboro McLaren' also helped during the brand's 23-year association with one of Formula One's most successful teams. It's not difficult to write and it's easy to say, which made it easy for print media, broadcasters and fans alike to recall. Marlboro McLaren developed into a conjoined brand identity, each feeding off the other, a symbiotic relationship between a number one F1 team and a number one tobacco brand.

I remembered the success of that Marlboro McLaren association when I was a lowly Jordan commercial manager in the mid-1990s and found our team named 'Benson & Hedges Total Jordan Peugeot'. As brand building went in relation to sponsorship, it was appalling, for this was a team named by committee, an amalgam of brands that worked for none. Not surprisingly, I don't think I met a journalist or fan who referred to us by our official name, and 'Jordan' was all that mattered.

Brand names benefit from simple, single words or, sometimes even better, a short acronym. The John Player Special Team Lotus entries of the 1970s might have gone the same way as Benson & Hedges Total Jordan Peugeot had it not been for the fact that Imperial Tobacco benefited from the brand acronym JPS, and the JPS Lotus team became not only easy to say but also very easy to spot thanks to the very effective application of its black and gold identity to the Lotus 72 cars.

It was another Imperial Tobacco brand, Gold Leaf, which is traditionally regarded as Formula One's first truly commercial sponsor, its red, gold and white colours gracing the Lotus 49s of Jim Clark and Graham Hill in 1968. Prior to that, sponsorship came in the form of patronage from car manufacturers, oil companies, tyre suppliers and companies manufacturing car parts such as brakes and spark plugs. Ford, Honda, Castrol, Dunlop, Ferodo and Champion were the racing brands of the 1960s.

Gold Leaf Team Lotus marked a new era and, when Imperial opted to replace it with JPS in 1971, Formula One fans and the media were introduced to a dramatic, classy and exciting new look. The way in which the brand was integrated with the team and car showed the extent of Imperial's ambitions, and in many respects paved the way for the manner in which Marlboro brought its red and white chevron into the sport in 1972, first with Frank Williams's Iso, then with BRM and finally at McLaren.

By the time I started working with Marlboro the company had been leveraging international motor racing as a core part of its global marketing for a decade and a half. It was a well-oiled machine.

The brand, and its application to everything from the cars to the transporters, team support vehicles, motor homes and hospitality units, was simple, consistent and impressive. Everything was red and white, in the correct proportions and with the right angles applied, irrespective of the shape of the surface, to communicate the roof top. The lettering, in black, ensured that Marlboro could not be missed.

They also understood the media, the photographers and the television broadcasters, so the Marlboro identity was writ large on the areas where that was most effective in maximizing exposure, and scaled to size in accordance with its presence in other locations. Drivers' uniforms, T-shirts and jackets featured the Marlboro identity in the same location on the left breast, on the collars where the Velcro straps would be pulled across on drivers' overalls, or on the peak of a baseball cap worn on the podium or when undertaking television interviews.

Part of my role involved working with drivers in a variety of formulae, including the 'training' series such as Vauxhall/Opel Lotus, Formula 3 and Formula 3000, where Marlboro insisted drivers understood the importance of keeping their overalls zipped up, the collars closed and the baseball hats on when conducting interviews. By the time any of those drivers made it to Formula One they were trained in the art of being a Marlboro brand ambassador. It was nothing more, nothing less.

Frustrated with the lack of success achieved by McLaren in the latter part of the 1970s and early 1980s, Marlboro used its clout to engineer the takeover of the team by Ron Dennis's Project 4 organization. Project 4 had been a successful team in other categories, most notably in winning the BMW Procar series that accompanied Formula One events in 1981. The Project 4 cars were sponsored by Marlboro, and in Ron Dennis Marlboro knew they had an ambitious winner.

Thirty years later Ron Dennis continues to head the McLaren Group, and his singular achievements in leading the team to multiple World Championship titles owe much to the early foundations created by him and his partners from Marlboro.

Attention to detail, to almost obsessive levels, is a personality trait often used to describe Ron Dennis. Sometimes it is levelled as a criticism, but if you had worked with Marlboro in the 1980s you quickly appreciated that everything to do with the brand, its presentation and promotion featured phenomenal attention to detail. Beware the team, driver or agency who applied the brand identity in the wrong location, with incorrect spacing, shoddy embroidery or an ambitiously applied key-line that was unrecognized by the bosses in Lausanne, Switzerland.

Brand guidelines and brand manuals have become commonplace for most companies and brands in the last 20 years, but in the 1970s and 1980s Marlboro was developing a clarity of brand promotion within Formula One that would become a template used by many in the sports marketing industry to the present day.

Marlboro underlined the strength of its commitment to Formula One to ensure that it spent the right kind of money to enable McLaren to achieve its ambitions – an obvious decision because, frankly, McLaren's success was inextricably linked to Marlboro's and there was no point in skimping. As a result of this approach McLaren had few other sponsors at the time: Shell, Honda, Courtaulds, Hugo Boss. And yes, there were others, but the point is that Marlboro recognized that taking primary ownership of the team from a brand perspective meant limiting the presence of other companies on 'their' cars and drivers. The issue of brand 'clutter' was on their minds as Marlboro sought to protect the purity and value of their investment. They valued their brand, and it was supported with the necessary resources.

At the 1988 Monaco Grand Prix, Philip Morris's CEO gave a speech in which he addressed the success of Marlboro in becoming the world's number one consumer brand. He addressed two aspects in particular, the success of Marlboro's advertising through the iconic Marlboro Cowboy ads, and the effectiveness of its Formula One sponsorship. It may have sounded like a CEO patting himself on the back, but on reading his words I knew he was right, because I had seen the effectiveness of Marlboro's sports marketing activities first-hand. They had every base covered; their positioning was to be number one in everything they did.

Marlboro always had complete faith in their brand, its value and the proposition it had developed over 30 years of successful sponsorship. Specifically they promoted core brand values of quality and flavour. If further evidence was needed of their confidence, that has come since the EU, WHO and major economies embraced a complete ban on tobacco advertising and sponsorship after 2005. While brands such as Lucky Strike, Benson & Hedges, Gauloises, Mild Seven, Camel, Winfield and Rothmans would never again be seen in Formula One, one company opted to buck the trend and remain fully committed to the sport and the brand association it had created over the previous three decades.

Somewhat controversially, Marlboro remains the main sponsor of Ferrari, removing its identity where required, but maintaining the red and white livery and the right to advertise the brand in non-aligned territories such as Monte Carlo where the most famous F1 race of all takes place. While its competition ran out F1's exit door in the wake of the ban on tobacco sponsorship, Marlboro remained fully engaged, careful to adhere to laws, but showing such brand confidence that the red and white identity of the Ferrari team will continue until at least 2015. Few people realize that the red and white logo of the Scuderia Ferrari team owes anything to the most famous tobacco sponsorship our sport has ever seen, but even from the point of view of subliminal messaging Marlboro continues to promote the products that remain legally manufactured and sold worldwide.

The Marlboro story is worth telling because, putting aside the moral and ethical debate surrounding tobacco advertising and sponsorship, it is a benchmark brand and its activation of Formula One sponsorship demonstrated some fundamental principles. Keep it simple, keep the messaging consistent, and never accept second best for a brand that aims to be number one.

It's telling that Marlboro's final home within the Formula One paddock has become Ferrari. Its logos had appeared on the overalls and helmets of Ferrari drivers during the 1980s, and it was perhaps inevitable that the world's number one consumer brand at the time would settle on an exclusive partnership with the world's most famous automotive brand. Both have a fierce passion for their brands, a desire to be seen as the very best in their respective fields.

Ferrari is the only team to have competed in Formula One in every season since the World Championship was founded in 1950. The Ferrari car business was only three years old at the time, for, although Enzo Ferrari had progressed from humble Alfa Romeo mechanic to starting his Scuderia Ferrari racing team in 1929, it was only in the post-Second World War era that he decided to commit to producing road cars bearing his name.

The prancing horse logo, an essential part of the Ferrari brand, went back to the First World War when an Italian fighter ace, Count Francesco Baracca, carried a black prancing horse symbol on the side of his Nieuport and SPAD aircraft as he developed into a fighter ace with no fewer than 34 kills to his name. The insignia was in tribute to his former cavalry regiment. Baracca's luck ran out on 19 June 1918, less than four months before the end of the war, when he was shot down. He was buried in his home town of Lugo di Romagna.

His mother, the Contessa, kept the prancing horse identity from her son's aircraft and, in 1923, presented it to a 25-year-old Enzo Ferrari, who was racing an Alfa Romeo in Ravenna. As Enzo had also lost immediate family during the First World War, his father and brother having died as a result of the flu pandemic that took advantage of the conditions at the time, there was much in common.

The prancing horse insignia would be added to the side of Ferrari's race cars after he created the Scuderia (literally 'stable') Ferrari in 1929, and red paintwork was the adopted colour, as it was the national racing colour of Italy in the interwar years. The brand's name, a single word, its colour and its emblem were fixed.

Over the last 60 years Ferrari has become the most famous automotive brand, and the world's most powerful consumer brand, as a result of being associated with certain values: Italian design ethos, a hand-built engineering quality, guaranteed high performance with a price to match, and a passionate racing heritage that permeates every activity. Although the car business often struggled, and indeed had to be rescued by Fiat in 1969, the select clientele who did order Ferraris played a role in building the prestige of the brand. In a time long before brand ambassadors had been created, it did Ferrari's reputation no harm to have movie legends such as James Coburn, Steve McQueen and David Niven seen at the wheel of their products.

The message was, again, simple: if you want to drive a car that has a racing pedigree and is ultra-cool, drive a Ferrari. The red, the prancing horse, that Italian passion: it made for a heady cocktail.

Ultimately, though, there were brand attributes that continued to elude Ferrari, particularly during its first two decades in the hands of Fiat when it continued to be a loss-making subsidiary and something of a hobby business for the major shareholders, the Agnelli family: quality and reliability. Its road cars became well known for being not only expensive to buy but very costly to run, with short service intervals. And it wasn't as if potential customers had no alternative, particularly when manufacturers such as Porsche could offer similar performance, race-bred technology and much higher levels of longevity for both the product and its customer's cash.

Similarly Ferrari's on-track capabilities failed to match its status, most notably as Enzo Ferrari entered his twilight years and the F1 team became managed by people drafted in by Fiat for a 'tour of duty' in their loss-making prestige brand. Although never completely out of contention, and sometimes right in the thick of the championship battle, the fact was that Ferrari's F1 team was consistently beaten throughout the 1980s and early 1990s by smaller, specialist, British teams such as McLaren, Williams and Benetton (originally Toleman).

It was very much as though Ferrari had everything on paper required to become a great team in F1, and a truly great automotive business, but was failing to live up to its brand reputation. Part of the problem lay in the management, but from a brand perspective the issues of consistency, quality and reliability remained.

Then, starting in the early 1990s, change was forced upon it, and proved to be the making of both the business and the brand. Luca di Montezemolo's appointment as president of Ferrari was Fiat's move to try to curb the losses and put in charge someone who could turn the business around. For the next few years Montezemolo did precisely that, driving Ferrari's road car business with a new range of higher-quality, more reliable products with a wider audience appeal, and setting the parallel goal of making the Ferrari F1 team the ultimate promotion of the brand by winning the World Championship.

By the mid-1990s Ferrari's automotive and F1 businesses were embarked on a step-change in quality control and efficiency in production, invigorating the brand and paving the way for the business to thrive.

Customers like products and services that are reliable, consistent and dependable, and it doesn't matter whether this comes from something costing $5 or $500,000. So Ferrari proved, for not only were its road car customers able to witness better product quality, reliability and customer service, but so too the F1 team began to unleash its potential and attract some of the largest commercial sponsorships yet seen in the sport.

By 1999 Ferrari was selling over 3,700 cars a year, a record for its business, while in Formula One it was on the cusp of astonishing success with well-designed, utterly reliable and high-performing cars, which

Michael Schumacher would drive to five consecutive World Championship titles in the first half of the next decade. As I often point out, what was remarkable about Schumacher's success was that, whilst the media focused almost exclusively on his personal achievements as he broke record after record, the simple fact was that Ferrari's team of several hundred factory-based personnel in Italy had given him the best-engineered and best-supported product in Formula One.

Suddenly the Ferrari brand not only had its appeal of design, performance and aspiration, but offered that with a bedrock of quality, reliability and customer service that no previous generation of Ferrari buyers had been able to enjoy. By 2012 its road car sales had almost doubled, whilst its brand licensing division, including luxury Ferrari-branded outlets in major cities and international airports, was pumping in the profits earned from selling a wide range of merchandise featuring Count Baracca's prancing horse emblem.

The Ferrari legend was no longer a myth, but a reality in terms of dollars, profits and growth for a business that its founder had struggled to develop. His bright red sports and racing cars, driven by champions and Hollywood stars alike, injected with that unique passion that Italians are world famous for, had always attracted a global following. Now, as a modern brand, it is attracting a global customer base.

Only one Formula One team has a proper name for its fans; Ferrari is followed by the Tifosi (literally 'fans'), and they had always ensured that, at the Italian Grand Prix in Monza or San Marino Grand Prix in Imola, the grandstands would be a sea of red. From the mid-1990s onwards that sea spread in a tidal wave of merchandise, reaching its zenith during the Schumacher era, when over 80 per cent of all Formula One merchandise sold worldwide had Ferrari's logo on it. For the other nine teams it was quite literally a case of being left with the crumbs from Ferrari's table.

At the relaunch of Lotus Cars in Paris in 2010 the master of ceremonies invited Stirling Moss on-stage and asked him what he thought of the new range of Lotus cars, and the return of the business to its heyday. Moss, succinct as ever, replied that Lotus had never had a heyday, had never really been that great a car company. And there is something similar in the Ferrari story. While its history and heritage built in the 1950s, 1960s and 1970s are highly romanticized, the reality was that the products seldom lived up to the brand's billing, and it has only been in the last 20 years that Ferrari as a brand and a business has truly come of age.

Sitting on board a private jet from Barcelona to Madrid, I was studying some paperwork in front of me while Dietrich Mateschitz, co-owner of Red Bull and driving force behind its global expansion, sat opposite giving an interview to a journalist. He was in full flow, swapping between German and English, talking about his plans for the Formula One team he had just bought, Jaguar Racing.

Mateschitz had stepped in and bought the team, saving not only some 600 jobs for the staff in Milton Keynes, but sparing Ford Motor Company its blushes should it have had to close down the business it had bought from Jackie Stewart in 2000. Branded as Jaguar, it was notable mainly for its turnover in management, interference from the bean counters in Detroit and spectacular lack of success on the race track. In terms of brand promotion, Jaguar's Formula One team had done nothing to promote positively a brand that had one foot stuck in the past. I know of Jaguar executives who still look back and blanch at the memory.

Red Bull's acquisition of a Formula One team came after a decade and a half of the brand sponsoring a variety of entities within the sport, commencing as a personal sponsor to Austrian driver Gerhard Berger and progressing through team sponsorship of both Sauber and Arrows. Its marketing had always been high-profile, but Mateschitz seized the opportunity to create an F1 team that would project Red Bull's brand values as never before.

As covered in Chapter 2, Mateschitz's entrepreneurship is a story of single-minded vision to create and dominate the energy drinks marketplace, and by the time he bought the Jaguar Racing F1 team he had already achieved that goal. Annual sales were over 2.2 billion units, they had just broken into Japan, and a new production facility was being constructed in Switzerland so that exports to the United States could meet demand and not fall foul of US rules on imports from EU countries.

I admit to being among those who wondered just what kind of team a 'Red Bull' F1 team would be like. In his address to the factory staff he had promised the investment necessary to make the team a winner and said he wanted to bring the values of Red Bull to bear, including that we would have a good time and more fun. Having fun wasn't something Jaguar had ever worried about, but it resonated with me thanks to my experience of 10 seasons working with a 'fun' and competitive team, Jordan. Not for the first time I would reflect that Red Bull Racing often resembled Jordan, but with a championship-winning budget.

The building of the Red Bull Racing team from the ashes of an unloved Jaguar Racing gave insight into what the Red Bull brand was all about, and why its business was such a success. The brand was everything, and from that all else flowed.

One of the first things I was able to observe was the creation of Red Bull's hospitality unit. At that time hospitality units in the Formula One paddock were traditionally trailer units or buses with awnings and floors attached, sometimes two or three per team, and still referred to as 'motor homes', dating back to the days when a driver or team might bring their Winnebago. McLaren had taken things a step further with its 'Communications Centre', which was more of a portable building, and paved the way for an even more impressive Brand Centre, which is used to this day.

But if the Communications Centre reflected McLaren's brand, and Ron Dennis's passion for millimetre-perfect presentation with its darkened windows, uber-corporate colour scheme and sometimes frosty reception staff, Red Bull's approach was about to stand everything on its head.

Red Bull was not going to have a hospitality unit, a motor home or a communications centre. It would have an 'Energy Station', a three-level transportable unit with team meeting rooms, restaurant, bar, nightclub, jacuzzi and, at the Monaco Grand Prix, even a swimming pool. It was all about energy: energy to work hard and play hard. Oh, and it was open house. Everyone could come: its own team personnel and sponsors, the media, any fans who happened to be in the paddock and, yes, even members of other teams and their sponsors too. As I said, it reminded me of Jordan, only 'go large'.

The Energy Station was also the largest unit in the paddock, thanks to a carefully crafted negotiation with Bernie Ecclestone. Staffed by glamorous young women and men, it also became party central for anyone beautiful or cool or rich or famous, preferably all four. Going to the

Energy Station became the 'must do' on the checklist of anyone lucky enough to be attending a Grand Prix with a relevant paddock pass, and before long there were stories of other teams upset with the fact that their sponsors, and sometimes even personnel, preferred the Energy Station to their own humble unit.

Energy, vitality and a passion for having fun: these were values important to Mateschitz and his Red Bull brand. Think about the way he used winter sports, garnered from his Austrian roots, later expanding that philosophy into extreme sports, and then the way he used his love of aviation to create the Red Bull Air Race and sponsor base jumpers, free fallers, and anything and anyone cool enough and mad enough to reflect high energy in what they did.

Even the Red Bull can was different from other soft drinks cans at the time; not for Red Bull the same cans used by countless Pepsico and Coca-Cola brands and their rivals the world over. The Red Bull can was part of the brand: slim, tall, more 'energetic' even on the shop shelves. Its colours, blue and silver, said 'cool'. It was as recognizable as the original Coke bottle or Toblerone chocolate's triangulated packaging.

The brand was also authentic, an important value that was protected very carefully. Not long after the Red Bull team was created, an agency representing a major vodka brand spoke to me about becoming one of the team's major sponsors. It was well known by 2004 that one of Red Bull's major successes was in being used by nightclubbers as a mixer, most often with vodka. Asking for an Absolut Red Bull or similar was commonplace, so the prospect for this particular vodka brand of having Red Bull's Formula One team promote its brand was too good an opportunity to miss – except the word came back from Red Bull executive Dany Bahar, at that time Mateschitz's right-hand man in Formula One, to the effect that Red Bull could not tolerate being presented as a mixer for someone else's alcoholic product. More than that, Red Bull was all about energy; alcohol is a depressant, and there was no room for both. The authenticity of Red Bull as an 'energy drink' was going to be protected.

More than anything, that made me realize just how serious Red Bull was about its brand values. In a sport where multimillion-dollar sponsorship opportunities did not exactly turn up every day, and where the ethics or morality of promoting certain products would have seldom been questioned, here was a new team owner making it clear that he had total confidence in his brand vision, and of course the cash to back that up.

I've seen Formula One sponsors that were thinly disguised fronts for less-than-savoury businesses. One such entity had a senior figure assassinated and found floating face down in a canal, prompting the team's other sponsors and engine supplier to demand the removal of the relevant brand on pain of contract termination. I have also seen a team approached by a global pornography brand, with a substantial eight-figure fee to support it, but once again the team's other sponsors and partners made it crystal clear that the 'disrepute' clauses of their contract would be activated.

Red Bull turning down the opportunity to relieve a vodka brand of several million a year showed a striking commitment to core brand values.

As with its other sports marketing activities Red Bull also made sure it underlined its commitment to youth and talent, bringing the young Christian Klien into Formula One with Jaguar and then with the re-named Red Bull F1 team. It also took over the Minardi team in 2005, renaming it Toro Rosso. The Italian Red Bull team had a specific task: to act as Red Bull's junior team and cultivate talent prior to selection for the main Red Bull Racing programme.

Early success in that tactic came from a young German driver who had been part of Red Bull's programme since he was 11 years of age, Sebastian Vettel. The precociously talented 19-year-old would win his first Grand Prix, and give Red Bull its first victory as a Formula One team owner, when he secured pole position and powered one of the Toro Rosso cars to victory in the 2008 Italian Grand Prix. It was a remark-able achievement, not only making him the youngest ever winner of a Formula One event, but setting him on a course that would see him promoted into the main Red Bull Racing team in 2009, where he would go on to win four consecutive Drivers World Championship titles be-tween 2010 and 2013.

Just as Red Bull had turned the Jaguar Racing team into a winner, and then given the former Minardi team – the minnows of F1 – a victory, so too it had developed a winning driver. Its philosophy of investing in people was paying off. Success was delivered consistently, and by 2010 it was reported that Red Bull was able to plot increased global sales directly against specific victories in Formula One; the winning effect was there to see.

Innovation was another brand attribute, as Red Bull Racing's increasing dominance in Formula One showed that its investment in people and technology was giving it a competitive advantage over automotive giants such as Ferrari and Mercedes-Benz. The sweet, fizzy drinks manufacturer from the foothills of the Austrian Alps was able to produce a faster, more reliable and more efficient Formula One car than the legendary brands from Stuttgart and Maranello.

It was evident that Red Bull Racing, under the technical leadership of Adrian Newey, was innovating so successfully in aerodynamics that everyone else was playing catch-up. The company whose long-standing marketing strap line was 'Red Bull gives you wings' was on top of the world of Formula One.

Parallel to its primary Formula One activity, Red Bull continued to use extreme sports, winter sports and aviation sports to drive home its messages about youth, vitality, passion for life and energy. Avoiding criticisms of being in any way elitist, its support for and promotion of inexpensive sports such as skateboarding showed that in the pantheon of Red Bull activities there was something for everyone. Key markets operated a range of activities across the arts, community events and charity.

Can Art invited budding artists to design sculptures from recycled Red Bull cans. Regional and national community events included the Red Bull soap box derby, where teams could build their own gravity-powered vehicles to race downhill, and Flugtag, which saw people from all walks of life build their own human-powered flying machines. Inevitably Flugtag was both comical – that 'fun' element again – and extremely popular with the media, since all entrants invariably would crash off the pier into the sea or a lake provided precisely to cushion the 'landing'.

On the charitable side, Mateschitz's own experience of seeing the brother and son of close friend Heinz Kinigadner paralysed in accidents led to the creation of the Wings for Life charity dedicated to raising funds for research into spinal injury. The high-profile charity not only contributed to this worthy cause, but added to the corporate social responsibility of a brand that could so easily have been construed as brash and arrogant.

Among the activities supported by Red Bull that further helped build its global brand, perhaps the best example outside of Formula One was its backing for Felix Baumgartner's high-altitude parachute jump, a world record. In a specially built capsule suspended below a balloon he rose to 39,000 metres, streamed live on the internet and on TV news channels the world over, and leapt to a cartwheeling 4-minute, 19-second free fall before opening his chute and landing safely in the New Mexico desert. The scale of the endeavour was one thing, but any concern that it might have been labelled merely a stunt was counteracted by NASA's interest in how someone might survive such a jump. In a public relations triumph, even Baumgartner's jump was seen to advance humankind's knowledge, exploring the edges of what is humanly possible.

It was a global event in every sense, a Red Bull-sponsored daredevil taking wing at a seemingly impossible vantage point above the planet, conveying the potential in humanity, its unstoppable development and its energy.

Young, innovative, authentic, fun, cool, friendly, successful, unlimited, passionate, invigorating, different and energy filled: Red Bull's brand values have been reflected in its business management, growth strategies and marketing communications. In Formula One its achievements have been nothing less than phenomenal, a testimony to a conviction in a strategy that has successfully steered it from its idiosyncratic beginnings to the global drinks giant it is today.

Marlboro, Ferrari and Red Bull have been, for me, the best examples from Formula One of how companies have built global brands by having an unerring belief in what they stood for and the values they represented. They have many traits in common: a commitment to quality; associations with attributes we all find appealing such as success, vitality and a passion for life; a consistency in the message about what their brand stands for; ownership of a name that is easy to remember; a colour scheme or identity that is repeated over and over; and packaging that is iconic, differentiated and easy to recognize – the red of Ferrari, the red and white Marlboro roof top, the coolness of Red Bull's blue and silver.

Against the backdrop of these successes, I have often been left wondering about the short-termism of two- or three-year sponsorship deals by brands that show little faith in a comprehensive marketing communications strategy. Or the corporates desperate to imbue their brands with some of the positive aspects of being involved in a sport like Formula One, with all the positive associations that can bring, only to apply their rigid brand guidelines and values developed in another time and another place. And finally, in the cut and thrust of negotiating sponsorship deals that carry with them the hopes and dreams of the brand marketeers responsible for the proposition their brand aspires to promote, the 'price-comes-first' negotiating mentality of some clients, and especially their agents, left me wondering how much they really understood about going out and developing real value for their brands. Cost and value often become confused.

If there was a central skill Ferrari, Marlboro and Red Bull showed in building their global brands, it was the understanding of value. They each understood that, if the consumer is to perceive the qualities inherent in their product, it deserved to have the very best value proposition built around it, and in each case that required investment – carefully considered investment, no doubt, and in none of these cases were the companies involved an easy touch for marketing spend. However, once they built a strategy around the product, its brand values and their vision for its development, they moved to implement it comprehensively, consistently and with conviction in the long term. In essence, they kept things simple and never wavered from the course.

LESSONS IN BRAND BUILDING

Studying the examples of Marlboro, Ferrari and Red Bull, there are significant insights into brand building. In each case they have created global brands, albeit in very different product categories and ranging from a commoditized product such as cigarettes through to the high-end luxury market for super-cars.

WHAT IS STRIKING IS THE COMMON APPROACH TAKEN TO LAUNCHING, BUILDING OR PROMOTING A SUCCESSFUL BRAND:

⟶ ***Keep it simple.*** Your market is only going to understand what you are saying if your message can be easily understood. This includes the brand name, the attributes and values you wish to attach to it and the ease with which your customers can spot it in an otherwise cluttered and competitive marketplace.

⟶ ***Small is beautiful.*** It's no accident that the global brand names that trip off the tongue are short – single or dual words or acronyms – and easy to recall: Apple, Google, YouTube. In F1 this has worked superbly for Marlboro, Ferrari and Red Bull. This is why you see Lucky GoldStar Electronics become LG, or GlaxoSmithKline evolve into GSK.

⟶ ***Own a colour.*** The Italian racing red of Ferrari, the red and white of Marlboro and the cool blue and silver identity of Red Bull are instantly recognizable. Owning a colour within your market is a very powerful tool, one that we learned at Jordan Grand Prix when we turned our team yellow. In a short time it became iconic.

⟶ ***Develop an instantly recognizable mark.*** Think about Ferrari's prancing horse, Marlboro's 'roof top' chevron and Red Bull's horned bull. Settle on an identity that means something to you or your business, industry or heritage, ally it to your colour and stick with it consistently. Be prepared to evolve it, particularly within an ever-changing media landscape.

➠ ***Have clear brand values.*** Brand values are the personality of your business, telling consumers what you stand for and helping to differentiate you from the opposition. Red Bull is 'energy'; Ferrari is 'passion'; Marlboro is 'strength'. Do you want to be 'exclusive' like Ferrari or 'inclusive' like Red Bull? Develop a brand value matrix including all the attributes that are important. But remember: your consumer will only recall the top two or three associations.

➠ ***Don't ignore the basics.*** It does not matter how fast a car Ferrari wants to produce, how energy-filled Red Bull wishes to make its consumers or how good Marlboro wants its cigarettes to taste to a dedicated smoker; major brands look after basic values first. Quality, consistency, dependability: consumers will value a brand they can rely upon.

➠ ***Be consistent.*** Successful brands can have very long lives indeed and, while the products or services will have to evolve over time to meet the demands of a competitive and innovative environment, consistency in brand messaging is essential. It gives your consumers an insight into your own faith in your business. Press home the message about the brand, its values and its associations consistently, relentlessly and over a long period of time.

➠ ***Drive value.*** Consumers want to feel good about the products and services they use. They may derive satisfaction from buying purely on price, but there always comes a tipping point where other values kick in, and this becomes the battleground for competitive advantage. So what are the values that you want customers to enjoy when they interact with your business? Once identified, drive them hard.

➠ *Be different.* In Formula One we have 11 different teams with 11 different cars, but although they are all designed to one set of regulations the key objective is to develop competitive advantage by differentiating your technology from the opposition. So too in brand building, differentiation is a key aspect. Red Bull didn't want a 'fat' can like Coca-Cola's or Pepsi's; they want a tall 'slim' can. So even in packaging they differentiated. Your customers are clever, they are discerning, and they are faced with multiple choices. Be different, stand out, and communicate why that is.

➠ *Have strong convictions about your brand.* Successful brands are owned by people who are intensely proud of the brand they represent. In F1 teams every member of staff is an ambassador of the business, and I strongly believe that employees of any brand business should see themselves in the same way. The management, too, owe it to the brand they own to proceed with conviction, invest in its future and show the strength of their support for it. How can you expect your customers to be passionate about your brand if you and your staff are not?

CHAPTER FOUR
BUILDING WINNING TEAMS

Getting people to work together in a manner that guarantees delivery, every time, is not easy. For that reason alone organizations around the world spend a great deal of time, effort and money on team building: constructing a bridge or raft from a selection of everyday items, or going on a military-style training course where leadership and team work will be essential to win – bizarre games and routines played out, well away from the workplace, to try to bond people together in the face of some concocted adversity or challenge.

Formula One is rightly regarded as providing good examples of team work even if, within the industry itself, there are good teams and bad teams, which means that not everyone is a shining example of excellence. Unquestionably world-class team work is a defining quality among those few teams who are strong, consistent competitors in the sport, and that sense of 'team', of collective responsibility to get the job done, is one of the great pleasures of working in this environment.

My first experience of team work came in late 1990 when Eddie Jordan asked me to help promote his fledgling F1 team, Jordan Grand Prix. It was growing out of his successful Formula 3000 team, this being the category of racing below Formula One at the time, and by the time I started providing press and media services to it there was a total of 33 staff.

By any standards this was a small team of people, even back then, and the task in front of them was truly colossal. As Eddie would go on to say some years later, if he had realized quite the extent of the challenge he might have thought twice about it but, as is so often the case with self-made entrepreneurs, ignorance of the pitfalls can be a good thing.

The first Jordan F1 car was designed by a team of four engineers: Gary Anderson, our technical director, with three young designers including Andrew Green and Mark Smith – both of whom are now F1 technical directors in their own right. Compared to the leading teams at the time, this was a tiny design group. Today a group of four design engineers would form a project team to produce a specific vehicle system or assembly.

A small group of individuals supported the design team, charged with buying, managing suppliers and ensuring on-time delivery. Everyone was multi-tasking. The mechanics from Formula 3000 formed the core of the new F1 team's race personnel, and as the new car progressed so they turned to building sub-assemblies and, finally, the complete car ready for testing in the autumn of 1990.

I organized a small gathering of the press in the modest business unit at Silverstone where the team would base itself for the first season at the highest levels of motor sport. One of those in attendance, the renowned French journalist Jabby Crombac, would famously write 'Why do they bother?' when he filed his copy. The tiny Jordan team, with its single F1 car built in a glorified garage, did not fill the key opinion formers in the F1 media corps with hope. They had seen it all before: dreamers hoping for F1 glory, soon to founder on the rocks of financial hardship.

As it transpired, that Jordan–Ford 191 turned out to be one of the most beautiful and effective Formula One cars of the early 1990s. A simple, neatly packaged product that featured some clever detailing that Gary and his guys had come up with. It was also easy to work on, a facet of Gary's design philosophy that he had carried with him since the days when he too had been a mechanic.

Powered by the powerful Ford Cosworth HB V8 engine, the car would go on to score its first finish in that season's Monaco Grand Prix, and its first points with a fourth and fifth for drivers Andrea de Cesaris and Bertrand Gachot in Canada, and drive the team into fifth place overall in the Formula One World Championship for Constructors. That was fifth out of an entry of 17 teams. Today such a performance in a debut season would be unthinkable.

How was that possible, given that our tiny design team was working with an unimaginably small budget and that the season was a first experience of Formula One for pretty well everyone involved?

Superb team work was at the centre of it, and we were able to undertake a giant-killing act by virtue of our small size. It worked in our favour. As the subsequent seasons would prove, it became very difficult to recapture the spirit and achievement of that first season, particularly considering that we came within a few laps of winning the 1991 Belgian Grand Prix only for the engine to fail. It would be seven years before we finally achieved that goal and, as luck would have it, it also came in Spa-Francorchamps.

Gary as technical director had a vision of what he wanted to achieve, and with a small group around him he was able to delegate the key systems on the car quickly and oversee progress in a typically hands-on manner. As someone who had previously designed his own Anson Formula 3 race cars he was very experienced at project-managing the design, manufacture and development of a car. The fact that this was Formula One didn't faze him, even if the pressure was intense.

So too with the rest of the team: the ability to learn quickly, relying on key relationships built between each other in the lower formulae, played a critical role. Of course, the team recruited some experienced F1 hands but, in the main, the Jordan team that embarrassed the likes of the works Ford-supported Benetton team did so because it was a small group of highly motivated, focused people determined to show the world what they could do.

No one in that team could click into cruise mode, or expect to be kept in the job without being able to deliver. The culture of the team was for everyone to work until the job was done, displaying a work ethic that ensured that Jordan punched way above its weight. The candle was burned at both ends, and all of the individual team members knew that they were being completely relied upon through to delivery. No one could shirk responsibility.

As the team grew in size, thanks in part to Eddie Jordan's ability to woo significant sponsors off the back of that first season's meteoric performance, it was noticeable how life became somewhat harder. The halcyon days of that first season began to fade.

The complexity of maintaining efficiency and strong team work in the years that followed taught us all some key lessons about business.

First was that you can quickly become a victim of early success, necessarily growing to meet the demands of sustaining that performance in an environment where the experienced competition have greater bandwidth and strength in depth. That growth often stretches the systems and processes that worked at the beginning, as few small businesses have the scalability required to step up to the next level.

The second was that people have strengths and weaknesses that come to the fore depending on team size. Someone who works superbly well in a small group may not necessarily flourish on becoming a smaller cog in a big machine. We certainly saw some of that at Jordan, where the complexity of building ever more sophisticated F1 cars during the latter part of the 1990s meant that the technical management would struggle to achieve the same level of delivery achieved in 1991.

The third was that, at every level of the business, the shortened lines of communication that we all enjoyed at the start became impossible to sustain later on, causing significant stress in the system. It became increasingly difficult to manage every aspect of the business as before, and that meant relying on a larger staff, often including new recruits who didn't have the same cultural approach to the task in hand. Ultimately we ended up with some personnel who regarded Jordan as 'just another job' and believed the salary at the end of every month was more or less guaranteed no matter how they performed. This kind of complacency is cancerous in any business.

Ultimately what saw Jordan through that difficult growth period was the leadership provided by Eddie and the relentless focus of a few key lieutenants who grew in their roles as the business progressed. Besides Gary as technical director, Trevor Foster grew from being an engineer and then team manager in Formula 3000 to directing operations for the F1 programme, assisted by team manager John Walton. A key lieutenant for Eddie was Ian Phillips, a highly experienced motor sports manager who had previously run the Leyton House March F1 team, while our former bank manager Richard O'Driscoll joined Jordan early on as finance director. Initially I worked on sponsorship with Eddie, and later joined the management board with responsibility for marketing and communications.

This tight-knit team of half a dozen individuals turned Jordan from being a giant-killing act in 1991 into the championship-challenging team we had in the period 1998–2000. By then we were employing upwards of 250 full-time staff, and empowering a new group of senior managers.

By then, too, we had suffered some casualties. John Walton had left the team in 1996, while Gary Anderson would depart in late 1998, almost in the very moment of winning our first Grand Prix. A strained relationship with Eddie had grown from the difficulties born of rapid growth and the increased expectation of our sponsors for the team to deliver on-track success. Growth also meant that Gary no longer led a small team; he could no longer single-handedly manage every aspect as he had done before without becoming a bottleneck. And among the young turks employed to bolster the team's capabilities were men such as Mike Gascoyne, Sam Michael and Bob Bell, people who would themselves go on to become technical directors of teams such as Benetton, Williams and Renault in the years ahead.

Our approach to the challenges of a fast-growing team and more complex structure was to attempt to keep the key disciplines each under a single leader and to join those leaders and their teams at relevant touch-points throughout the hierarchy: a classic matrix system. However, as ultimate authority within the technical, operational, commercial and financial side rested with individual leaders, they took full responsibility for their areas whilst ensuring that their staff were empowered and accountable. Cross-functional communications played a vital part in ensuring the right hand knew what the left hand was doing.

For me, this was central to Jordan's achievements and would later serve as an explanation as to why some of the very large car-manufacturer-backed teams that came into Formula One would prove incapable of matching that kind of success.

The classic example was Jaguar Racing, owned by Ford Motor Company and grown out of Stewart Grand Prix, itself partly funded by Ford. Stewart Grand Prix achieved a lot in its short three years of participation in F1 between 1997 and 1999, scoring a race win, a pole position and fourth place in the World Championship for Constructors in its final season. Founded by three times World Champion Jackie Stewart and managed with his son Paul, Stewart had similarities to Jordan Grand Prix in that it had developed from a team that had achieved success in the lower formulae.

Organic growth and the inevitable progression into Formula One were always going to be the outcome for a team owned and run by the well-connected, resourceful and ambitious Stewart family. Also in common with

Jordan, there was clear leadership from Jackie and a well-constructed management team of industry professionals tasked with taking responsibility for their area of the business, with clean, short lines of communication and a customer-first culture that owed much to Jackie's 30-year career as a global ambassador for brands such as Ford, Rolex and Goodyear.

The transition from Stewart Grand Prix to Jaguar Racing ought to have been a straightforward one: ideally, the same culture and structure bolstered by proper budgets and commercial clout.

Things did not work out that way, and between 2000 and 2004 Jaguar Racing achieved less than Stewart and ultimately became a case study in how not to run an F1 team. Talented staff found a top-heavy, burgeoning management that lacked clear direction and ultimately suffered from being a sub-division of Ford. It's always been my view that, once you take an entrepreneur-led, profit-centric and customer-focused business and squash it beneath a giant multinational that has little understanding of what made the acquired business thrive in the first place, you end up with a problem. That's what Ford got with Jaguar Racing.

The first indication that Ford had got it wrong was when Wolfgang Reitzle, head of its Premier Automotive Group, which included the Jaguar, Land Rover, Aston Martin and Volvo brands, assumed overall responsibility for the F1 programme, with Neil Ressler acting as team boss. Both highly capable managers and experienced automotive industry professionals, they soon found the going difficult. In F1, as in any business, it is vital that the leadership understands the industry inside out. There is no time to learn in a sector as complex, expensive and unforgiving as this.

Neither was given time to develop as the team was subsequently placed in the hands of US racing legend Bobby Rahal, then former F1 World Champion Niki Lauda and subsequently a British management consisting of CEO Tony Purnell and managing director David Pitchforth. These constant changes in management did nothing for company direction, leadership, morale or credibility with customers. By the time Purnell and Pitchforth started to make progress with the team, Ford had already tired of the project's cost and poor results, and the company was put up for sale in 2004.

It would be understandable if Formula One itself turned out to be simply a little too complicated for Ford's management. But as history would subsequently show, when the poorly performing businesses at Jaguar Land Rover and Aston Martin were subsequently sold, along with Volvo, their new owners made a great success of them. Indian group Tata was able to unleash the potential in the Jaguar and Land Rover brands, long held back by the dated culture of Ford at the time. Focus groups of existing Jaguar customers in the United States had dictated the continuation of product lines that owed everything to the Jaguar brand's leather-seated, wooden-dashboard past, and little to the technology-centric, design-focused younger audiences that it needed to lure.

Team work at the top of Ford had much to answer for in relation to the problems that beset the Jaguar Racing team, and with lack of leadership, empowerment and entrepreneurial culture it came as no surprise that the team underperformed and damaged the parent brand.

It is all the more ironic, therefore, that this same outfit would subsequently develop into the most dominant team in the sport between 2010 and 2013. Transformed under Red Bull's ownership, it would bring Germany's Sebastian Vettel four consecutive Formula One World Championships for Drivers.

It is striking to consider that Red Bull, an Austrian energy drinks company, had the ability to create a better Formula One team, and significantly faster Formula One cars, than Jaguar under Ford's ownership.

The tendency is for observers to view the Red Bull Racing story as simply that of a billionaire's obsession with Formula One and relaxed attitude at throwing hundreds of millions of dollars at his hobby. But, as we have seen in Chapter 2, Red Bull's Dietrich Mateschitz is no one's fool: an entrepreneur who understands that if you want to drive value from a business you have to invest in it with conviction, and find the right people to implement your strategy.

Considering the top-heavy nature of Jaguar Racing and its structure within Ford, one of the key factors in Red Bull's turnaround of the team was the way in which the reporting lines became much more simplified. With shortened lines of communications the ability to get a decision was much easier and ultimately the team was able to get support from the parent company rather than be viewed as a drain on resources.

The appointment of Christian Horner as team principal in January 2005 came as a surprise to many, but although inexperienced in Formula One he had run his own highly successful racing team in the lower formulae and in so doing won the confidence of Dr Helmut Marko, a key adviser to Mateschitz. Experienced in race team management, dealing with sponsors, drivers and officialdom, Horner represented an investment in the future, and he was soon supported by a small yet highly capable team of senior managers.

Another key appointment was David Coulthard, for when 'DC' joined the team he brought with him 12 seasons of testing and racing for two of the very best teams in Formula One: Williams and McLaren. And, unlike many drivers, DC also brought with him a strong intellect, an understanding of business and a vision of the key building blocks that would be needed to transfer the lacklustre Jaguar into the revelation that Red Bull Racing would become.

Thus it was Christian Horner and David Coulthard who played a pivotal role in convincing design genius Adrian Newey to join the team, and in ensuring that Newey would have the necessary financial support and empowerment to do his job. Ultimately this combination of Christian Horner and Adrian Newey, team boss and technical visionary, created the foundation for Red Bull Racing's emergence as a dominant force in the sport. In the same way that Frank Williams and Patrick Head created a powerful combination at Williams F1, or we experienced the benefits of a close-knit team at Jordan, so with Red Bull Racing part of the success came in the simplicity of its management structure.

I was very mindful of these lessons when, in 2005, I established Status Grand Prix along with Dublin businessman Mark Kershaw with the aim of entering an Irish team in the A1 Grand Prix World Cup of Motorsport. This was a new series, the brainchild of businessman Tony Teixeira and Dubai's Sheikh Hasher Maktoum al Maktoum, a relative of the ruler of that emirate.

A1 Team Ireland was born with the objective of creating a winning team, indeed a team that could prove the concept of A1GP where countries of all sizes could compete on a level playing field with the aim of winning a World Cup trophy.

The A1GP concept required that we used a standard A1GP car designed and built by Lola Cars in Huntingdon, Cambridgeshire, powered by a reliable and impressive engine from Zytek, a specialist in its field. As every team had the same car, same engine and even the same tyres, from Cooper Avon, it really came down to the 'team' of people to make the difference, and that was what really appealed to us.

To begin with, in the 2005/06 season – for the series ran to a 'winter' schedule in the northern hemisphere – we did quite well with an ex-Formula One driver Ralph Firman and rookie Michael Devaney supported by a highly experienced engineer in Andy Miller and a team of mechanics put together by a former colleague of mine from Jordan Grand Prix.

It was clear, however, that simply banding a group of experienced people together was not enough and, although we finished a creditable eighth in the series at our first attempt, we had a single podium finish to our name and more often disappointment than a sense of achievement.

For season two we made some changes. The budgets had overrun in season one, a lesson in itself as a result of having insufficient controls and systems in place, so we were forced to replace Ralph with Michael Devaney and subsequently Richard Lyons, both capable drivers, but from the outset performances were poor. Not only had we failed to make progress since year one, but the competition had improved and we were falling backward. Our changes, our lack of stability, did not help.

It led to the situation where a blame culture developed. The drivers were complaining about the car, the engineer was scratching his head because the decisions he was making were not having the desired effect, and the team of mechanics became frustrated that in spite of their best efforts to prepare the car immaculately we remained out of contention.

Again we went through changes. We temporarily worked with John Booth, boss of the Manor Motorsport team in the UK and later to become team head of the Marussia F1 team. Finally we replaced Andy Miller with my former colleague, the ex-Jordan F1 technical director Gary Anderson.

Michael Devaney was a good young driver, but we felt that our problems were so deep-seated that we needed the expert input of a much more experienced racer – and one who had worked with Gary Anderson before to good effect. Richard Lyons ticked the box, and so he was drafted in to help us get to the bottom of our issues.

Unfortunately things did not improve, although there was an initial surge of motivation brought about by making those changes and being seen to do something. Our problems continued; we finished the second year in a disastrous 19th place and had even gone as far as swapping our car for a new one, so sure were we that the issue might have belonged to some problem with the chassis. Ultimately we never really knew what the problem was.

What I did know, and what Mark and I realized from our first two years, is that we did not yet have a 'team'. Some were too ready to blame others for the problems, and there was a lack of accountability. I felt responsible, because after all I was the team boss and had recruited the team. It was all well intentioned, but for whatever reason it had not gelled. It really needed a new approach.

One of the big questions for me was our drivers. They had all possessed good qualities, but if we were honest with each other there were question marks. Was it a case of not enough experience, or perhaps too experienced and fixed in their ways? Was their motivation the right motivation for the job?

We decided to go out and employ the very best racing driver in the island of Ireland at the time, and there was no doubt that driver was Adam Carroll. He had been on the cusp of breaking into F1, even testing for the Honda team, but his career was stalling, thanks primarily to a lack of opportunity at the highest levels.

In taking on Adam I knew that we need not worry about the driver; this was a variable removed from the equation. Initially we partnered him with a young engineer named Dan Walmsley, with the bulk of the mechanics remaining the same and benefiting from two years of experience working together.

Immediately our results improved; in Adam's first race for us at the Czech circuit of Brno he finished on the podium. Three more podium finishes would come our way that year, and most importantly a victory. We won the A1 Grand Prix of Mexico on 16 March 2008, the eve of St Patrick's Day and a notable moment for everyone connected with A1 Team Ireland.

The race win was down to a lot of things: a great performance from Adam and a stunning pit stop executed to perfection by the mechanics, a pit stop that ultimately helped us to clinch the win. We had a *team*, and they were sharing in the success.

At the end of that year we finished sixth in the Championship and felt sure that there was more to come, but not before one final change. We again needed to find a new engineer. To my frustration we were still not finding it easy to keep our team stable from season to season.

This time I did things quite differently because I had learned from the first two seasons that just putting drivers and engineers together and expecting them to work perfectly was difficult. To achieve our goals we needed a team of people who trusted each other, had mutual respect and who, when faced with a problem, would simply put all their skills into finding the solutions.

As a result I asked Adam to help me by meeting our potential new race engineers personally, and effectively interviewing them from a driver's perspective. I wanted to be certain that Adam had an engineer he really felt he could work with. It was an interesting experience, because the engineer I thought might best fit the team was not the one Adam chose. Instead he selected Gerry Hughes, a hugely talented engineer with experience in Formula One at Jaguar Racing and Super Aguri, but with a personality quite different from Adam's.

It was the right decision, because what Adam had spotted was Gerry's unerring and relentless attention to detail and process. Adam felt confident that if Gerry said 'Do this' it would be the correct engineering decision, based in science. He could trust him, and trust is a vital aspect of efficient team work.

When he joined the team Gerry insisted on certain things being changed from an engineering perspective. Those changes weren't always appreciated, but he was very clear about what he wanted: that A1 Team Ireland would approach the new season with no stone left unturned to unleash car performance.

Our fourth season in A1GP started with two retirements from the Feature Race and Sprint Race at the Dutch round in Zandvoort. It was a disastrous weekend, and it was easy to feel we had taken two steps back. But in truth the weather was atrocious and it caught out even the most capable drivers, Adam included. It turned out that weekend had been an anomaly.

As if to respond in perfect style, Round 2 in China saw us win the first race, and more victories were to follow in Portugal and Australia, with a further three second-placed finishes setting us up for a decisive final round in the UK, at Brands Hatch. It turned out to be the perfect weekend; Adam qualified on pole position, and won both races. We had won a world championship, the World Cup of Motorsport.

I recall those years as being extremely challenging, mainly because of the combined pressures of managing the cash flow, the people and the complexity of what we were doing. It could be a lonely existence, but it was a project I felt passionate about.

It worked beautifully in the end, and I learned a lot about myself as a team boss, as well as about other people. I learned the importance of delegating, and making sure you surround yourself with the right people. I realized that learning from your mistakes and making sure that each time you perform you improve are essential; you have to plot a relentless, upward trajectory, and that can only come from being constructive and positive. We were constantly reviewing what went right, what went wrong, implementing improvements and moving on. We kept pushing forward.

I also learned that some people are not as good as they think they are, and you have to be honest with yourself and them when that happens. It's not about building a team of nice people whom you get along with; it's about building a team of the right people whom you can succeed with.

Looking back I also realize that there were some moments of truth that cut to the core of what I was trying to do with the team. Sacking a senior engineer and telling a driver he is no longer going to race for the team were not pleasant experiences, but I knew they were the right decisions at the time. As I explain in Chapter 6, it can be painful, and some people are prepared to understand it, while others won't, especially if they see only how it affects them in the short term. But I knew as team leader when change was needed, when 'more of the same' was never going to get us anywhere.

Telephoning suppliers to explain that we wouldn't be paying their bills that month because the cash flow wasn't as expected was another tough call. I saw it as an essential part of my role as team boss not to delegate the dirty jobs but to take responsibility and tackle them head on. In every case I resolved issues through this approach, and I am pleased to say I received good feedback for being honest, communicative and transparent.

As a footnote to this story, what few people ever knew was that even in the moment of ultimate victory there was a major problem to be solved. A1GP was itself in serious financial trouble as we headed to our final race in Brands Hatch and, when I was informed that the tyre supplier Michelin was going to withhold its tyres because of unpaid bills, I realized I had to act. If we were to win the championship, the race had to take place and that meant having tyres for us and our competitors to race on.

I called Michelin and, using a significant amount of our available cash, wired them a payment to partially cover A1GP's debt. The tyres were provided and we had competitors to beat, races to win and a title to clinch. When we stood on the podium and I lifted the World Cup trophy for Ireland, my emotions were running high as a lifetime of hard work, four years of dedication and a few days of tackling the intense problems facing A1GP leading up to that race came to the fore. It's not a moment I will forget, especially as I knew for certain that, behind it all, we had built a world-class team.

LESSONS IN TEAM BUILDING

Building winning teams is never easy, because it requires a group of people to achieve a collective approach to fulfilling a range of tasks, adhering to systems and processes, overcoming challenges and achieving goals. The individual has to work in a way that enables the group, and this invariably means accepting a degree of compromise as regards personal ambitions.

This doesn't mean that, to be part of a great team, individuals have to suspend their personal career development, since a successful team should always encourage its members to flourish, but the key principle is that the team comes first.

Formula One teams are not large organizations, being SME engineering businesses employing 300–600 full-time staff, but team work is required at every level in order to ensure that the company achieves its targets. To design, manufacture, build and operate Formula One cars requires the same skill sets as occur in any manufacturing business, even if we are talking about a very low-volume, prototype product category.

The operations of the business are global, sometimes with a long supply chain, everyone working within the context of immovable deadlines, strict rules governing compliance, and – as if there is not enough pressure already – always under the watchful eye of the world's media.

Winning customers requires everyone from the chief executive and drivers through to the mechanics and receptionists at the factory to be aligned with those responsible for securing the deals. Everyone has a role to play as an employee of the company, for each person is an ambassador for the business.

Across all the normal functions of finance, administration, travel, marketing, human resources, IT, facilities, procurement, supply chain management and so on, every member of staff has a key role to play. And in the sport of Formula One we see all too easily what can happen when an individual opts out; the effects can be catastrophic. A lack of responsibility and accountability can lead to a defective component or assembly failing during a race. At best a failure can cause retirement from a race. At worst it could cost the driver's life.

In the quest for success, winning races and World Championships or growing the customer relationships that provide the lifeblood of the business, these teams have to work together as effectively as possible, seamlessly delivering a world-class performance.

TO SUMMARIZE:

⟫ *Investing in people is the best way to create a winning team.* Everyone has his or her own personal traits, ambitions, strengths and weaknesses. By investing in our staff and providing equitable support to all we can build a cohesive, motivated team.

⟫ *Remember what motivates people.* Motivation is a cocktail, not a straight shot. Money is only one aspect, and often subsumed by other factors. At Jordan Grand Prix we did a giant-killing act because people were motivated to prove themselves at the pinnacle of the sport, excited by the opportunity to travel and compete against the best in the world, interested to enjoy new experiences and keen to stretch themselves. They also believed in the leadership's ambitions for the business, and wanted to share in that.

⟫ *Make the organizational structure as simple and practical as possible.* If the key lieutenants in the business have to manage the relevant disciplines effectively, they must be fully empowered to do so, supported by the senior team and given the resources necessary to do the job.

⟫ *Excellent communication means keeping the lines of communication open, short and filled with consistent, honest and credible content.* 'I did not know what was going on' is the one sentence you never hear in a high-performing team. Everyone knows what he or she is responsible for, and who is accountable for each aspect of the activity.

⟫ *Teams need to be led, so make sure your leadership is visible, communicative and genuine.* We cannot know all of our staff all of the time, but all of our staff should know us and what our priorities are for the business and all its stakeholders. And they should be inspired by strong, accountable leadership.

➡ *If you want to reach your goals in the time frame required, then not only invest in having the right people, but empower them to get on with their jobs, make decisions and be accountable for them.* This requires a positive culture, not one buried in fear of recrimination. Empowering competent staff creates an upward spiral.

➡ *We need to trust one another and have faith in our colleagues.* In a 2-second Formula One pit stop all team members are completely focused on their specific task. They have no time to check to see whether their colleagues have done their jobs; they must have complete faith in themselves and their co-workers to complete the task safely, reliably and in the fastest possible time.

➡ *Building a winning team is not about employing the nice people, but the right people.* You want to have people who are the very best at what they do, whose skills complement other people's skills, and who can all deliver in their respective areas. Even if there is some short-term pain, work hard to get the most talented people working together.

➡ *Remember that building a high-performing team is not easy.* If it were, every organization would excel. The reason why the world's top teams are so good at what they do is that they have worked extremely hard, over a long period of time, to build, sustain and continually develop a group of highly motivated employees who buy into the leadership's vision for the business. They are all pulling in the same direction.

CHAPTER FIVE
THE PIT STOP

Considering the millions of dollars spent on designing, manufacturing and developing a modern Formula One car, not to mention employing a driver capable of unleashing its potential, it's paradoxical that one of the most important parts of a Grand Prix comes when the car is stationary. Pit stops are mandatory, a critical moment in the race, and inevitably the time when teams can gain a competitive advantage or see it slip away. A pit stop undertaken at precisely the right time, and executed efficiently, can determine the outcome of the race, and there have been many occasions when this has happened.

For a few seconds the car sits at rest, the driver composed within his cockpit, while up to 22 ordinary mechanics, technicians and managers set to work and do something quite extraordinary: perform a pit stop during which all four wheels and tyres are changed, and the aerodynamics of the car adjusted.

I can't recall the last time I had all four tyres changed on my own car, but I doubt the garage answered the telephone within 3 seconds never mind provided me with the level of service that Formula One drivers have come to expect.

In those 3 seconds a Formula One pit crew is doing something remarkable, with all the members of the team knowing precisely what they have to do, taking responsibility and knowing that they are fully accountable. They have a fixed set of processes to follow using equipment and technology provided by the team to give them the best chance of success.

You really don't want to be the mechanic who drops the wheel nut and watches as it rolls across the pit lane, or fumbles with the wheel gun while trying to remove the wheel – with your colleagues looking on, a

World Champion Formula One passenger metaphorically tapping his watch, not to mention being in full view of the world's media and several hundred million television viewers around the world.

The car, the product of many thousands of hours of design and development, is the team's product, and the pit stop is effectively real-time product service. The driver is a fellow team member, but perhaps best thought of on this occasion in terms of being an internal customer, someone for whom the team has to deliver a world-class service in order for them to have any chance of achieving the goal they have been tasked with: winning the race.

Think about the task facing the crew.

Two are required to operate the front and rear jacks. The front jack man is standing in the pit lane waiting for the Formula One driver, who has been driving the car at 200 mph a few seconds earlier, to stop precisely at the required point: at the feet of the front jack man so that he can slide the specially designed jack under the centre of the front wing and lever the car into the air. The front jack has to be located precisely, engaged positively with the car and activated instantly.

The same front jack man must then watch as his colleagues perform their tasks. When the tasks are completed, with the hands of all crew members raised to signal that their jobs are done, the front jack man must drop the car back on to the ground and step out of the way, removing the jack from the path of the car to enable it to power its way back down the pit lane.

The rear jack is engaged as soon as the car is stopped and, since the operator has to wait for the car to enter the pit stop box, comes a fraction of a second after the front jack has been engaged. The rear of the car carries most of the weight, including the engine and gearbox, and with it being levered into the air the two rear wheels, larger in size than the front, can be slipped off and replaced. Again the rear jack man has to wait until he sees the rear wheels have been fully located on their hubs, the wheel men moving back, before he can drop the car on to the ground. For the rear jack man there is the added complication that the rear wheels are used to transfer the 780 bhp produced by the engine to the track, so it's vital that the wheels are back on the ground before the driver drops the clutch and wheel-spins his way into the pit lane. Dropping the car on to the ground with the wheels spinning is a recipe for disaster.

Then we have two personnel whose job it is to stabilize the car which, balanced on centrally mounted jacks front and rear, can be in danger of rocking on either side. They step forward, grabbing the central roll hoop, watching their colleagues changing the wheels before stepping aside as the jack men drop the car back to the ground.

Each wheel requires three personnel.

First comes the wheel gun operator, whose job it is to locate the powerful pneumatic gun on to the wheel nut. This has to be drilled off the threaded spline on the hub to enable the wheel to be removed, and then reattached and driven home into a locked position once the new wheel has been placed on the car. Engaging the heavy gun, with its thick pneumatic line running toward the overhead gantry, is by no means straightforward; you need to engage smoothly and squarely and press it fully home. The movement has to be very smooth and accurate.

The second member of the wheel crew has to step forward and grab the wheel, pulling it off the car in one seamless manoeuvre, and putting it out of harm's way. Loose wheels can cause havoc. Ideally the crew member will take hold of the wheel in the very moment it stops rotating. The tyre is hot, its surface of molten rubber at over 100 degrees Celsius, while the wheel itself has been heated by the hub and brake assembly, which glows red hot at 800 degrees.

The third crew member has the task of placing the new wheel and tyre on to the hub, locating the wheel perfectly first time in order that the wheel gun operator can set to work and re-drill the nut on to the hub. Locating the wheel squarely on the hub, considering the all-up weight of the cumbersome wheel and tyre comes to 9 kilograms, is never an easy task. The wheel man cannot afford to position the wheel on the hub wrongly, as this will either complicate matters for the wheel gun operator or necessitate taking a second attempt at locating the wheel itself.

For each wheel, therefore, these three technicians have four tasks to perform inside 3 seconds: wheel nut off, old wheel off, new wheel on, wheel nut on. That works out at 0.75 second per task. When people talk about split-second team work, this is it in action.

When you multiply that operation by four, you have 12 personnel each facing the same extraordinary challenge. For those working in the most competitive teams in Formula One, they fulfil their task with the added pressure that their performance really does make the difference between winning and losing.

Finally we have the crew responsible for making small aerodynamic adjustments. This is carried out by means of quick-release mechanisms on the front wing flaps that allow for the angle of the wing to be increased or decreased, while on the rear wing a Gurney flap, which is a long thin vertical addition to a typical wing, can be altered and even removed entirely. Again, as with the wheel change, the time frame is 3 seconds, with the objective of improving the aerodynamic balance on a car that relies heavily on finely tuned aerodynamics to optimize performance.

The pit crew's 3-second window to carry out a 'normal' pit stop can turn into something much more complex if the car has sustained damage or a technical failure that requires more than the four wheels to be replaced and the wings adjusted. A damaged nose section, which includes the front wing and its protruding wing endplates, is a frequent occurrence, and teams plan accordingly. A significant structural component accounting for around 20 per cent of the car's structure, the nose sections come equipped with a quick-release mechanism. This enables the crew to change them in around 12 seconds. In some respects this is even more impressive than the achievement of changing four wheels in 3 seconds. It increases the number of personnel working on the car and involves additional processes including jacking the car up from the side whilst the front wing jacking point is replaced.

Other potential reasons for lengthy pit stops include the need to replenish the compressed air unit that powers the pneumatic valves in the high-revving engines, as the air valve system can develop leaks that could lead to potentially terminal failure if left unchecked. It is also not uncommon to see the steering wheel replaced if the team suspects that its electronics have developed a fault whether through component failure or some rain water getting into the system during the torrential rain that can afflict races. Open cockpits filled with electronics and rain water are not a happy combination.

In 2012 there was much comment made when Lewis Hamilton drove his McLaren to a strong fourth-placed finish in the Indian Grand Prix in spite of a pit stop for all five wheels: four new tyres and a new steering wheel. The speed of that change was 3.1 seconds. While the four wheels and tyres were being replaced Hamilton disengaged the steering wheel using its quick-release mechanism while a mechanic slid the new wheel into place. Hamilton was able to flick the car into gear instantly, ready for the off.

While the crew is primarily the focus of everyone's attention as to whether a pit stop goes well or not, the driver too has a pivotal role to play. It's yet another example of why F1 drivers have to recognize their place within the team.

Drivers first of all have to fulfil the team's race strategy requirements, whether conserving their tyres and/or fuel or ensuring they get their car to its optimum position with the race. Naturally their starting position determines the degree to which they may be helped or hindered by traffic during the race, and becoming trapped behind a slower car can play havoc with the best-laid plans. Weather is another variable that has to be taken into consideration, for a fundamental change in conditions will again necessitate a strategy rethink, and then of course there is the competition. You can guess what the competition's strategy might be, but you have to allow for the fact that a clever or unexpected move on their part might necessitate an instant response from you. Flexibility is vital.

From the moment the race starts, the best strategies are the ones that can adapt to circumstances, particularly since no strategy can predict the opposition's tactics with 100 per cent accuracy.

Good two-way communications with drivers is essential, for although they are driving the car they are by no means in possession of the full picture – in fact, quite the opposite. Looking out of the narrow visor of their race helmet they can see relatively little apart from the information on the steering wheel read-outs, a few hundred metres of tarmac directly ahead, and fleeting glimpses of the car behind in the tiny, vibrating wing mirrors situated on either side of the cockpit.

Faced with a paucity of information about how the race is playing out, drivers are totally reliant on their race engineer, data analysis technicians and strategists to advise them as to what is happening: to their car, the competition and the big picture of how the race is unfolding and the variables that are coming into play.

Once a pit stop is called and drivers know they are going to be making a stop, they start working through a procedure. It starts with them making sure that any natural instinct to begin to slow down during the 'in' lap is resisted. The drivers will push hard on the 'in' lap to ensure that they maintain maximum performance over the first and second sectors of the three-sector lap, knowing that in the third sector they will necessarily lose time when they peel off the track and into the pit lane. They are often reminded by their race engineers to 'push' over this all-important 'in' lap.

Even then, driving into the narrow, often twisty, pit lane entrance, drivers have to maintain performance, because they do not have to slow to the pit lane speed limit until they reach a designated line within the pit lane itself. Driving the initial part of the pit lane as though it is a continuation of the race track is essential in order to minimize lost time. Although the team knows the car's position on the track, and can see from the data its reduced speed as it enters the pit lane, a back-up procedure of having drivers radio a short 'I am in the pit lane' message also prepares the team for what is to come, particularly if a stop has been hastily rescheduled in reaction to some unforeseen event.

Once in sight of the pit lane speed limit zone, drivers have to be ready to brake hard, engage the pit lane speed limiter by using a button on the steering wheel, and then motor down the pit lane looking for the correct 'box' where the pit crew will be waiting.

The crew will themselves have been advised via the race engineer and team manager that the pit stop is about to happen. They will not rush into the pit lane immediately, thereby giving the competition additional information about their strategy plans, but wait until they hear over the pit crew radio channel that the driver is now in sector three and about to come into the pit lane. The crew now know they have 20 to 30 seconds to prepare for their all-important 3 seconds of high-performance team work.

Obviously drivers should know precisely where their pit stop box is located in the pit lane. After all, they will have driven the car in during three practice sessions and qualifying. However, the pit lane can become confusing to drivers during pit stops, particularly with the 11 pit crews and all of their equipment blocking the normal line of sight. For this reason the teams will have a set of visual aids that drivers will look out for.

At the 2013 Malaysian Grand Prix the importance of the driver's role within the pit stop process was brought sharply into focus when Lewis

Hamilton forgot that he was now driving for the Mercedes-Benz team and steered his car perfectly into the McLaren team's pit stop box. They had been stationed in the pit lane waiting for their driver, but Hamilton saw them and appeared to forget that he had changed teams the previous winter. Cue much amusement, but some significant embarrassment for Hamilton.

To assist drivers in locating their team's pit box a member of the crew will stand on the pit wall, often the driver's own pit board man, and hold an arrow or marker board out into the fast lane of the pit lane to remind of the pit box location. The team manager or crew chief who has overall responsibility for managing the pit stop will hold what is known as a 'lollipop' – a long pole with a flat sign on one end – out from the pit stop box to give a second location marker. And the team itself will have designed both the pit lane gantry and coloration of the markers on the pit lane surface to provide further visual guidance.

Once they have found their box, drivers have to swing the car into location, taking care to avoid the pit box of the competitor immediately adjacent to their own pit garage, and ensure that they line the car up straight and squarely to stop 'on the marks'. These 'marks' are the lines marked on the pit lane surface, using tape or paint, which illustrate precisely where all four wheels should stop and the front wing line up so as to match the body positioning of the front jack man and the four wheel gun operators. A few centimetres either way can make all the difference, adding tenths or hundredths of a second to the commencement of the wheel change.

Getting drivers who have, only half a minute earlier, been racing at 200 mph to guide their car to a very specific stopping point is a challenge. Stopping doesn't come naturally. The cars and the drivers are built for speed, yet tactically the key part of the race comes when they are stationary. Judging the car's braking to be inch-perfect is part of a driver's skill set, and the team will have practised stopping 'on the marks' throughout practice so as to ensure drivers know precisely how much grip there is on a piece of tarmac, or sometimes dusty concrete, that has not had the benefit of any of the rubber build-up that occurs on the race track itself. It is also for that reason we see drivers asked to perform a fast pull-away during practice in order to spin the rear tyres within the pit box where they must make their stop during Sunday's race. This is sometimes mistaken by fans for showing off, but in reality the drivers are performing a wheel-spinning burnout in order to layer as much rubber as possible on this vital few metres of pit lane.

Once the car is halted, correctly positioned in its box, then and only then can the pit crew swing into action. The half-tonne piece of aerospace and automotive precision engineering, components red-hot from half an hour of searing performance at the hands of the driver, is awaiting its service. The clock is ticking.

It's all too easy to get it wrong, and over the years we've seen pretty well every combination of how not to do it: wheels not ready when the driver comes into the pits; the wrong set of tyres prepared or still in their tyre-warmers; jacks misaligned and requiring a second or third attempt to jack the car up; a driver unable to stop 'on the marks'; and drivers missing their pit box entirely or even, as we have seen with Hamilton, stopping at the wrong team.

At the 2011 Chinese Grand Prix Jenson Button relinquished the lead of the race when he was distracted after flicking the wrong button on his steering wheel and accidentally steered his McLaren into Red Bull Racing's pit box. It was a mistake his team boss Martin Whitmarsh called 'fairly disastrous'.

Then you have the really serious mistakes, with cars released from the pits before the crew have completed their task, always dangerous and never more so than when F1 pit stops include refuelling. A car accelerating with the fuel rig still attached can lead not only to a fire but to physical injuries suffered by crew from flailing wheel guns, refuelling rigs pulled out of position and even the refuelling line itself ripped away from the gantry entirely.

Then there are the moments when the wheels have not been reattached correctly, as with Nigel Mansell's Williams in Portugal in 1991, when I recall having to jump out of the way as his right rear wheel bounced towards the Jordan garage, ending his race in ignominious fashion. It turned out to be a pivotal moment in that year's championship.

What can be more damaging to the reputation of a world-class team than the wheel literally falling off the car? And all because of a failure of team work and process. If the wheel nut hasn't been put on the car properly, there's no point in the car being released, and yet this is what we have seen happen on more than one occasion. In the case of Mansell's race in Portugal, one of the tyre men on the wheel had indicated to the team manager that their 'wheel' was fine by raising his arm, when in fact his colleague was still trying to drill the wheel nut home. The process wasn't adhered to, and the result was terminal.

It can also be comical. In the early 1990s I recall one of the smaller F1 teams in the next garage to ours, its crew of raw recruits looking panic stricken as their car came in for an unscheduled pit stop. As one of the rear tyre men pulled the wheel from the car he flung it over his shoulder into the path of the new wheels that were being rushed from the back of the garage. Sure enough, one of his colleagues got rather confused and put the old wheel back on the car. Cue the sight of a car with three new tyres, one very old one, behaving like a table with one leg shorter than the others.

The point is: pit stops require perfect team work in order for the team to have any chance of success. Get it right, and it can give you a competitive edge, even if usually no one notices. Get it wrong, and the results can be a failure that is public and usually very embarrassing. Get it badly wrong, and someone could be injured, or worse. It's not a job for the faint-hearted or anyone hoping to get away with their mistakes.

When I started Status Grand Prix I recall one of our promising young mechanics being quite unable to execute a pit stop properly, and not for want of being motivated and trying his hardest. He simply couldn't do it consistently, and the more frustrated he became the worse things got. His task was to act as wheel gun operator and, although he had all the physical attributes you would imagine could be of real value, the reality was that he wasn't placing the gun on to the hub squarely enough and this was causing the gun to spin off or, worse, jam the nut on the splines. As the physical errors mounted, the psychological effect became evident as he could see that all eyes were on him. His composure was gone, and his focus moved from calm analysis and implementation of what needed to be done to rushing the procedure.

'Less haste, more speed' isn't a bad mantra in these circumstances, and as a team we found that, the more you got the crew to relax and focus on their tasks, breaking it down and putting it back together again as a clear procedure, the better things got. In the end our team became among the very best at pit stops, and it was just such a perfectly executed stop that brought us our first victory in the A1GP World Cup of Motorsport in Mexico City in March 2008.

At Jordan Grand Prix I witnessed our dedicated crew raise their game steadily, aiming to match the very best teams in the world, Ferrari and McLaren. Between 1991 and 1997 when we had been a young pretender, a pit stop mishap might have cost us a points position, at that time a top-six finish. But by 1998, with former World Champion Damon Hill on board, to be joined the following year by race winner Heinz-Harald Frentzen, the pressure was on. Winning was the aim, the very clearly stated aim for Eddie Jordan and our management team, for we had major customers to keep happy in the form of brands such as Benson & Hedges, MasterCard International and Sony PlayStation.

As Damon Hill pointed out, our Jordan Mugen-Honda 198 was basically a good car, with a decent engine and strong potential. It wasn't a McLaren and Ferrari beater in a straight fight every weekend, but on the right day it could challenge them. This was when the pit stops would go from being important to critical. In the event that Hill could somehow manage to position himself in front of McLarens driven by Mika Hakkinen and David Coulthard, or the Ferrari steamroller of Michael Schumacher and Eddie Irvine, the Jordan crew would have to produce as good a pit stop time, or better, as these two world-class performers.

The right day came, and with it came faultless team work including four pit stops for Damon Hill and Ralf Schumacher during a 1998 Belgian Grand Prix affected by torrential rain. It was also a race restarted after a first-lap pile-up triggered by David Coulthard spinning his McLaren out of La Source, the first-corner hairpin bend on the classic Spa-Francorchamps circuit.

Fans and media remember our famous 1–2 victory in that race, the first ever maiden 1–2 by a team in Formula One history. They remember it for the dramatic start accident, the restart and a collision between Michael Schumacher's Ferrari and David Coulthard's McLaren, which sent the German into a rage. It is also recalled for the team orders voiced by Eddie Jordan over our radio system requiring Ralf Schumacher to hold station behind Hill in the closing stages of the race.

But I remember that weekend for two things: the first was a formidable performance by Hill in qualifying, which saw him outperform Michael

Schumacher over the same lap, the cars split by a few hundred metres. On the same track and in the same conditions, Hill squeezed more performance from the Jordan than Schumacher could manage with the Ferrari. It was a World Champion's performance, and positioned Hill perfectly to challenge the two McLarens into the first corner the following day.

The second reason I remember the race was the team work, all weekend. But it climaxed with the race performance, in dreadful conditions with the pressure really on, and I felt that day our victory was a team effort. Best of all, our factory staff had decided to make an outing to that Grand Prix, the first and only time that many of them had attended a race, and they were joined by our fan club at its annual Belgian Grand Prix trip. And, as if that wasn't enough, we had all of our major customers present, senior personnel from Gallaher PLC, owners of Benson & Hedges, MasterCard, Lucent Technologies and Pearl Assurance. The team work represented by Jordan's pit crew that day delivered not only a memorable victory, but delivery for key stakeholders across our business.

McLaren, Ferrari and Red Bull have been the dominant teams in Formula One in recent years, and they have pushed pit stops to a new level, gaining significant advantages at a time when competitive advantage through technical innovation has been squeezed.

With the abandonment of pit stop refuelling in 2009, it was evident that Formula One's pit stops were about to become much faster. The limiting factor had always been the length of time it took to refuel the cars, for the FIA-regulated refuelling rigs delivered fuel at the rate of 10 litres per second. With the average stop requiring 55–60 litres of fuel, the context within which the stop had to be made was 6 seconds, even if the wheels could be replaced in less time.

At that time, therefore, the wheel men could effectively take their time, as a 5-second wheel change set against a 6-second refuelling window meant it was fast enough. But, with refuelling banned, suddenly it was the wheels that became the focus, and the realization that there was a new battle to be won.

I remember analysing a 3-second pit stop executed by the Ferrari team in the Korean Grand Prix in 2011. By then the top teams had found a number of ways to reduce the stop time. It came down to people, process and technology; all three were examined and revised and changes implemented.

Take the front jack, for example. The front jack man not only has to stand in the pit lane and wait for the car to arrive at his feet, but on completing the stop has to disengage the jack from the car and then step out of the way to avoid being run over. Ferrari's elegant solution was to have the jack redesigned in such a way that, once the car had been jacked up, the operator could move out of the way by swivelling the handle and then use a quick-release trigger to drop the car on to the ground before he pulled the jack out of the way. This small change meant that the stop became faster whilst also reducing risk.

Another aspect of the stop was the way in which the Ferrari mechanics engaged very directly on to the car, trusting the driver to stop on the marks, and how their training meant that the 3 seconds witnessed one seamless movement. The front wings were adjusted, using the by-now familiar quick-adjusters, which required a simple click up or down depending on the wing angle required. The Gurney flap on the rear wing was removed entirely during the stop; the need to reduce downforce had been condensed into a neatly designed rip-off strip.

With 3-second stops now de rigueur it was interesting to see the targets shifting even higher in 2012, with the McLaren team using the talents of newly signed operations director Sam Michael to create the technology, process and training needed to break into the 2-second bracket. During the first half of the season we witnessed several issues with the McLaren pit stops, but as with many step-changes in performance you cannot expect everything to go smoothly. Change is never easy, and in the arena of Formula One mistakes are not only very costly but extremely public.

At the German Grand Prix, however, everything clicked perfectly into place, Jenson Button's McLaren benefiting from a 2.3-second pit stop en route to a second-placed finish. McLaren's target was a sub-3-second pit stop every time, and the times were dropping inexorably towards the magical 2-second marker.

Red Bull Racing, not content with dominating Formula One in terms of race victories and Championship titles in the period 2010–12, decided to redouble its efforts to regain the high ground in the pit stop battle in 2013. This is a typical behaviour among winning teams: it's never enough to be the best in most areas; they tend to aspire to being number one in every single area of activity.

Just as Ferrari and McLaren examined every detail of the human performance, process and technology used within a pit stop, Red Bull Racing did the same during the winter. On lap 9 of the second round of the 2013 season in Sepang, Malaysia, Mark Webber pitted from the lead and we witnessed his wheel changed in an astonishing 2.05 seconds, a full quarter of a second faster than McLaren's record. A replay of the stop shows that trust is again an important part of team work, the four mechanics responsible for removing the wheels grabbing hold of them as they complete their final rotation as the car comes to a halt. As they begin to pull at the wheel their colleagues responsible for the wheel nuts have already begun to drill them off. Reducing the number of turns required by the wheel nut to remove it from the hub has helped to speed up this task enormously, and it also means that the nut can more easily relocate and spin back on to the stubby, deeper splines.

Suddenly 2 seconds was the new benchmark, making the 3-second stops that we were admiring back in 2011 seem decidedly second-rate – a full 50 per cent slower!

For the balance of the 2013 season Red Bull Racing, McLaren and Ferrari continued with their average stops around 3 seconds and their best-in-class stops in the mid- to low 2-seconds bracket. Surely this was the moment of peak performance for Formula One pit stops?

Not everyone thought so. McLaren made it clear they were continuing to seek the next step, to 2 seconds or less. I must admit that it seemed unlikely anyone could jack up a car, change four wheels and tyres and return it to the ground in less than 2 seconds.

But no one told Red Bull Racing; not satisfied with their World Record performance in Malaysia back in March, nor winning their fourth consecutive World Championships for Drivers and Constructors, the team achieved a 1.923-second stop for Mark Webber on lap 28 of the United States Grand Prix. On-board cameras, notably one mounted forward of the front right-hand wheel, picked up the detail of the first ever sub-2-second stop, and as with Malaysia it reinforced the message about training, process, trust and team work – everyone operating at peak performance, with no room for error and everyone utterly confident in their own ability and that of their colleagues to get the job done. Mission accomplished.

CHAPTER SIX
THE IMPORTANCE
OF CHANGE

Most people don't like change, and certainly not the thought of it. How many times have I heard the mantra that 'It's always been done this way' in some aspect of business, and inevitably one of the attributes of the great leaders and innovators is their use of change as an effective business tool. As I cover in Chapter 8, all the major step-changes in Formula One design technology have driven new levels of performance, even if this has meant legions of production staff, engineers and mechanics coming to terms with new technologies or entirely new ways of doing things.

I am quite sure that, when John Cooper decided to put the engine behind the driver, or McLaren's John Barnard raised the prospect of making a chassis from carbon, there would have been a few raised eyebrows.

From my experience change is a good thing, mainly because change comes hand in hand with continuous improvement and innovation. Formula One cars are changed by means of relentless development season to season, race to race, and even from one practice session to the next. So the mindset of people working in Formula One is that avoiding change, trying to keep everything just as it is, is a guaranteed way of failing. The moment we aren't changing, be it evolving our product, adopting new technology or improving our processes, the competition will leap ahead.

The ability to manage change and make the most of new challenges can deliver great rewards. When I look back at the changes within Formula

One, it is striking just how much has changed and why, and the effective way in which it has been managed.

The changes wrought by Bernie Ecclestone on the sport during the 1970s dragged Formula One into the modern era of commercialized sport. He was the trailblazer, and not everyone could see the big vision Bernie had for the sport. Today he is renowned for building Formula One into a global sports business and, although his style has sometimes courted controversy, his strengths are clear. He recognized value, and he knew how to develop a sustainable and highly profitable business model around it.

At the time of writing, in 2014, he has been embroiled in a number of court cases resulting from the purchase of Formula One by private equity giant CVC Capital. This includes a criminal case in Germany but, whatever the outcome, nothing will diminish his achievement in developing Formula One. It has been a story centred on constant evolution.

When he bought the Brabham F1 team and realized that Formula One didn't actually have a viable business model, his strategy became based on change. Getting all of the teams to commit to compete in all of the races was a start. Back in the 1970s not all of the teams competed in all of the races.

Having all of the races on a Sunday was another step, because events had evolved to take place on Saturdays, Sundays and even public holidays during the week. When combined with the lack of guaranteed attendance by all the teams and drivers, it meant the sport was more difficult to follow from the point of view of the media and fans and, perhaps most importantly of all, for TV broadcasters.

For Bernie Ecclestone this meant changing the relationship with TV broadcasters to offer them the opportunity to purchase the rights to the sport on long-term, lucrative contracts, and effectively using the same tool to convince race promoters to pay fees to stage F1 events. Organizations that in previous years had been suppliers suddenly found themselves transformed into customers; the money flowed in the opposite direction.

All these changes took time and encountered resistance, but in the case of the TV broadcasters and race promoters they knew that Bernie had it within him to take his show elsewhere if they were not prepared to pay for it. He understood the value of the business better than anyone else at the time. There are those, such as McLaren's Ron Dennis, who are critical of Bernie's actions, and maintain that he effectively robbed the Formula One teams of their birthright to the sport's commercial control under the terms of the Concorde Agreements between Ecclestone and the FIA commencing in 1981. I have some sympathy with that view, but ultimately no one else was able to deliver the changes that Bernie drove through, and his main crime seems to have been the ability to out-think all the other stakeholders.

Changes large and small are important to building and evolving a business. If you accept that innovation is vital to business success, then you are also accepting that change is an inevitable part of business life. And it is, because, even if you make the decision to try not to change, to maintain the status quo and resist progress, eventually events will overtake you, because change is inevitably forced upon us by outside sources. There is always someone innovating and changing, and you cannot strategize based on anything other than change. There is also the issue of compliance and regulation, factors that affect most businesses – F1 included.

Among the apparently small changes made by Bernie's organization was the requirement for each Formula One team to field two cars – not one or sometimes three as happened in the past – and for the design graphics on team cars to be the same. This gave each team a strong identity, created a better platform for sponsors and gave the made-for-TV F1 show a more polished finish. Today it is not even questioned, but moving to a two-car-per-team format was yet another step in evolving the F1 sports entertainment show.

He also introduced fences around the Formula One paddocks to keep the general public out and applied security systems to limit who entered. Only passes issued by Formula One Management to the teams could permit access, the exception being the credentials issued by the FIA to the media and race officials. A controversial move from the point of view of the paying spectators, limiting access to invited team guests only raised the value of becoming a sponsor, positioned Formula One's inner sanctum as the elite place to be seen, and created a more rarefied atmosphere for the drivers and teams to go about their business untroubled by autograph hunters.

This change remains a bugbear for fans, and some marketeers with teams and sponsors, as it made Formula One inaccessible, limited driver–fan interaction and has given the impression that Bernie does not care for the spectators keen to catch a glimpse of their heroes. Once again, it is an understandable view, but Bernie recognized that the value lay in exclusivity, and that, for the corporate customers keen to gain privileges for their guests at events, paddock access would be a key selling point. And, quite frankly, the fans are not Formula One Management (FOM)'s customers; they are the customers of the event promoter. Formula One's job is to lay on a spectacular show.

By the time I joined the management board of Jordan Grand Prix in July 1998, paddock passes issued by FOM had become so highly sought after by sponsors that we could effectively apply a simple rule of thumb: for every $1 million spent by a sponsor with the team on an annual basis they could have one pass. As Eddie Jordan said to me at the time, every negotiation with a potential Formula One sponsor would come down to two things: the size of the logo on the car and the number of paddock passes. He wasn't wrong.

Large sponsors like tobacco giant Benson & Hedges might secure 10 passes per weekend for the season, in return for their overall US$25–30 million deal, while a modest sponsor such as Brother Industries would be offered four passes at only selected races or even at certain times of the race weekend. Having an FOM-issued sponsor guest pass meant you would be among the elite of Formula One, and that was the positioning Bernie strove to create.

Other small changes included FOM's insistence on each team parking its truck and mobile hospitality units within a defined space, each unit equidistant from the next such that the Formula One paddock area is immaculately laid out and presented. One of the most frequent comments I have had from clients has concerned this attention to detail, the fact that the truck and support vehicles are just as immaculately presented as the Formula One cars themselves. It all helps to woo customers seeking to promote their brands by associating them with a world-class activity.

As the sport of Formula One found its commercial feet in the 1980s, the Ecclestone business model developed further. The fact that television companies were by now spending a lot of money on the TV rights meant that those same broadcasters had to elevate Formula One to the top of the sports schedules to ensure they drew in the largest audience possible, while the race promoters were also more motivated than ever before to sell as many tickets as possible in order to meet the financial demands of their contracts with FOM.

With vastly increasing television audiences and well-promoted events, the teams found it possible to attract a larger and broader range of commercial sponsor. The tobacco industry, for so long a staple source of revenue, continued to pump hundreds of millions of dollars into the sport, while sectors such as clothing, electronics, IT, telecommunications and energy arrived and developed, so that by the 1990s to walk through the Formula One paddock was to gain an insight into the industries, sectors and brands that were making good money and confident of their global ambitions.

At Jordan Grand Prix between 1995 and 2000 we saw tobacco sponsorship from Benson & Hedges augmented by significant multimillion-dollar deals from brands such as MasterCard International, Pearl Assurance, Hewlett-Packard, Lucent Technologies, Infineon, Deutsche Post, DHL, Danzas, Brother Industries, Total Oil and Repsol: global payments systems, insurance companies, IT, telecommunications, computer chips, freight logistics, computer printers, and oil and gas companies.

But change was coming, and it would require a great deal of management.

A number of things began to happen at the same time. The campaign against tobacco advertising and sponsorship was gaining pace. As covered in Chapter 3, France's Loi Evin in 1991 effectively curbed tobacco and alcohol sponsorship within that major European economy. This had a devastating effect on France's place in world motor sport, effectively surrendering the future growth of the Formula One-based high-performance engineering and technology sector to the UK.

With tobacco coming under threat it was also noticeable how commercial sponsors were beginning to evaluate and monitor their sponsorships within Formula One more carefully, for it was no longer one of a few global sports entities. In the 25 years since Bernie had taken over the reins of Formula One, sports such as soccer, golf, rugby, cricket, snooker and sailing had carved out their own significant offerings. Our customers were facing a lot of choice, and were becoming more discerning.

We were also seeing that, with the previously cast-iron tobacco revenues coming under threat, we could not rely on our other types of sponsor to be as committed. Indeed, we began to see that not every new sector had the fundamental strengths of the cash-rich tobacco sector.

Around the turn of the century what is now referred to as the dot-com bubble came home to bite us. Sponsors such as Lucent Technologies, MCI WorldCom and Nortel Networks, which had come in with a bang, suddenly upped and left. The NASDAQ exchange had taken a dive, which led to an exodus of marketing dollars. Here was external change, and we had to cope.

We also saw some sponsorships end because an increasing emphasis from shareholders around the world on good corporate governance exposed some of the old-style deals whereby a CEO had driven sponsorships simply because he liked Formula One. At Jordan we saw one sponsor embroiled in a corruption scandal, and another pull out in the wake of inappropriate behaviour by a senior executive who was accused of using the Formula One activity for his own personal gain. In neither case was Jordan party to what took place.

With stock markets uncertain, the new technology sectors under pressure and commercial sponsors becoming more selective by the day, Formula One teams in general retrenched and moved back towards tobacco – at the very moment when it was under threat as never before.

In 2000 British American Tobacco started its own Formula One team, acquiring the entry previously owned by Tyrrell Racing, while Benson & Hedges remained with Jordan, Mild Seven sponsored Benetton, Gauloises supported Prost, West backed McLaren, Marlboro remained with Ferrari, and Winfield had just completed its activity with Williams. That was seven teams beholden to tobacco.

In July 2002 it was announced by the European Union that legislation had been agreed that would see an end to tobacco sponsorship and advertising in three years' time. Formula One's single largest source of revenue would end on 1 July 2005. Here was a classic example of change coming from outside; either you prepared for it, accepted it was coming and did something about it, or you stuck your head in the sand and hoped somehow to get through. The latter strategy didn't seem particularly appealing.

I recall sitting in my office in 2002 and wondering where on earth Formula One teams would find a replacement for tobacco. It didn't seem easy, and it wasn't.

Vodafone's arrival with a title sponsorship of Ferrari in 2004, a deal that moved to McLaren in 2007 partly because of the continued demands of Marlboro as Ferrari's long-term partner, gave some light. But even more hope came from the next sector to be targeted by the Formula One team sales departments: banking.

HSBC had been involved since 1998 thanks to Jackie Stewart, but in the mid-2000s ING, Credit Suisse, Royal Bank of Scotland, Santander and UBS would come into the sport, eager to promote their brands globally and associate them with a sport renowned for its following among the international business community. To some, it looked as though we had found our tobacco substitute.

As we now know, some of those associations would become relatively short-lived thanks to more external tremors, this time from the financial crisis of 2008 and the subsequent bank bail-outs. Royal Bank of Scotland, now a global player, was a particularly high-profile victim, its CEO Fred Goodwin a Formula One fan whose ambitions for RBS and close friendship with Jackie Stewart had led to a title sponsorship of the Williams team. ING came and went in three years. Credit Suisse followed suit. Only UBS and Santander stayed in, the former as a key partner, not of a team, but of Formula One itself. In Santander's case they had avoided the worst of the financial storms and cleverly used Formula One's popularity in the UK to make the most of rebranding of the recently acquired Abbey National Building Society with the help of brand ambassadors Jenson Button and Lewis Hamilton.

What was evident within the commercial sponsorship arena was that Formula One was having to endure not only the boom-and-bust waves of natural economic cycles, but the rigours of the modern business world and the inability of many companies to take anything more than a short- to medium-term view. Brands that Formula One attracted and lost, such as Nokia, felt burned by their experience. Not only that, but those major brands that were attracted by the global audience and associations with Formula One were, more than ever, only interested in supporting top teams with a winning record.

For the teams lower down the order, the end of the first decade of the new century proved to be a disheartening time, as they had to rely even more on the revenue from FOM, sponsorship generated by their drivers and, in many cases, shareholders' funds paid directly or indirectly through associated businesses dressed up as sponsors.

As if the dot-com bubble, tobacco legislation, the banking crisis and economic turmoil in F1's heartland of Europe were not enough, the sport also witnessed a sharp correction as four major car manufacturers exited with little notice. The decisions by Ford (2004), Honda (2008), Toyota and BMW (2009) to turn their back on the sport were a further hammer blow. And if that was not enough, demands for better corporate governance in relation to sponsorship deals and growing concerns about F1's image in a world where environmental awareness was increasingly important only added to the mix.

The behaviour of car manufacturers, who fall in and out of love with Formula One in a bizarre cycle of appraisal, investment, reappraisal and withdrawal, added to the view that for many teams the traditional commercial model was likely to remain broken, or at least never regain reliability.

Changes brought about by external factors such as economic cycles, legislation and revised business priorities among customers are an inevitable part of the cut and thrust of business. To Formula One's credit, across the spectrum of the commercial rights holder at FOM, the regulator in the FIA and the leading teams, meeting the challenges presented by these changes has been more or less successful, even if it hasn't come without a degree of collective hand wringing along the way. Change is seldom easy, but faced with Hobson's choice the option of doing nothing is likely to be terminal.

For the teams facing a much more demanding sponsorship environment the winners, at teams like Ferrari, McLaren, Williams and Benetton, were those that offered ever more diverse services to existing customers and repackaged their offerings to new ones. The old model of selling sponsorship based primarily on the brand awareness generated by TV coverage combined with corporate hospitality at events was replaced by a much more sophisticated offering that provided the customers with value 365 days a year.

Factory visits, team-building events, the presence of the F1 car and drivers at trade and consumer shows and exhibitions, product launches and internal staff motivational programmes: these have become the day-to-day nature of sponsorship activation within Formula One over the past 15 years as the sector has had to change its customer proposition.

Bernie Ecclestone's response to growing the revenues of Formula One at a time of increasing uncertainty over the traditional business model was to begin a process, in the late 1990s, of harnessing the power of the sport's appeal to an entirely new type of customer, which would include governments and sovereign funds. Just as he had understood the potential in packaging Formula One for the television age in the 1970s, introducing competition between broadcasters and race promoters, so he recognized that governments were increasingly interested in using global sporting events to promote their nationhood, communicate that they were open for business with international markets, and promote tourism.

Compared to the ritual of the International Olympic Committee and FIFA awarding the rights to stage the Winter or Summer Olympics and the Football World Cup to a different country ever four years, the appeal of Formula One was clear. Generating a global audience whose cumulative figures each year could stack up favourably against the quadrennial Olympic Games and World Cup, here was a sport that didn't have to run a long-drawn-out raffle to award an event. Build a Formula One track to specification, with sufficient hotels and transport infrastructure nearby, and a multi-year contract can be had to stage a premier World Championship sporting event in return for a substantial rights fee – but one that was significantly lower-cost than the offering from either FIFA or the IOC.

Malaysia was the first to come to the table, its government under Dr Tun Mahathir undertaking to build a state-of-the-art Formula One facility adjacent to the brand new Kuala Lumpur International Airport and sign up to a long-term contract. I remember arriving at the Sepang Circuit for the first time in 1999 and wondering in awe at the sheer scale of the place, ultra-modern garages, enormous paddock, covered grandstands, well-equipped media centre and medical facilities.

Not known as major followers of Formula One, the Malaysian people did not exactly flock to those initial events, but then they were not the audience being sought. For Malaysia the benefit of having Formula One was to put the country and its capital city at the centre of the world sporting map for a week or two every year. As F1's media corps jetted into town, a generation of sports fans from London to Tokyo, Montreal to Sao Paulo, were introduced to the reality of Malaysia as host nation, and Kuala Lumpur as our base.

Malaysia worked well for Formula One, so much so that the model was repeated within three years and contracts signed with Bahrain and China. By 2004 they had built their venues and were staging the inaugural Formula One races in the Middle East and most populous nation on earth respectively, and from then on a surge of new markets and venues burst upon the sport: Singapore, Abu Dhabi, South Korea, India and ultimately Russia, President Putin rather ironically opting to have Formula One help ensure the sporting legacy of the estimated US$50 billion spent on creating the infrastructure at Sochi for a single Winter Olympics. That must have struck Bernie as being ironic.

This drive eastwards for Formula One helped meet the challenge of the changes impacting on the traditional business model of the sport, not only generating new revenues directly from the host venues and their promoters, but potentially creating a wealth of new commercial sponsorship opportunities from among companies eager to reach those markets. The fact that the indigenous populations of some of these countries were not avid followers of Formula One was an early concern but, as the trends have shown in China and India, their growing middle classes and wealthy elite become drawn to Formula One as their aspirations grow and consumerism takes holds.

As an example, Ferrari opened its first dealership in mainland China in a downtown Shanghai location in 2004, the same year as the first Grand Prix was staged just outside the city. With some 25 per cent of China's trade being driven through that one city, it came as no surprise that the Shanghai dealership provided to be a success, and by 2012 Ferrari had expanded to add more than a dozen around the country, by now the Italian marque's most important market in terms of growth. Out of a total of 7,138 cars sold worldwide during that year, 734 were sold in China, making it second only to the United States in terms of Ferrari sales.

In 2013, at the 10th Formula One race to be held in Shanghai, the race attendance was among the highest yet seen, with over 80,000 spectators on race day alone. If ever there was an indication of the long-term game plan of Formula One playing out, that was it.

The flip side of Formula One's expansion eastwards has been a reduction in the number of events held in Europe. In 1997 there were 16 Grands Prix, of which 12 were in Europe and four 'long-haul' in Australia, Japan, Canada and Brazil. By 2012 that balance had shifted, with 20 events featuring only eight in Europe and 12 in the Americas, Middle East and ASEAN countries. At a time of economic difficulty in Europe this change, although controversial with the media and fans sorry to see traditional venues disappear, helped drive up the value of remaining core events such as the Grands Prix in Monaco, Italy, Britain, Germany and Belgium. It also gave enhanced credence to Formula One's status as a true *World* Championship.

Change in the organization and structure of Formula One's business has also seen parallel changes in its priorities, technologies and processes. Each met with resistance; each resulted in improvements in key metrics including safety, performance and spectacle.

The changes brought about in terms of safety have been profound, ending the all-too-regular fatal accidents that killed drivers, spectators and track marshals during the first five decades of the sport's history. It is remarkable now to reflect on the fact that Jackie Stewart was pilloried by some for his campaign for improved safety including questioning the validity of racing Formula One cars around the Nurburgring's Nordschleife circuit, which was built in the 1930s.

From seat belts to full face helmets, fireproof clothing and, much later, the more recent innovations such as the HANS device, the changes met with suspicion and questions, but it's only as a result of these changes that the safety record of Formula One has improved to become the benchmark of motor sport worldwide. The remarkable thing now is just how few other series have embraced the holistic view Formula One has taken to changing its priorities.

Processes have changed too, from a time when pit stops were something to be avoided through to the modern era where they are not only mandatory but embraced by all the teams as a key aspect of race strategy. A grainy video on YouTube shows a 22-second pit stop by Brabham's Nelson Piquet in 1982, the mechanics hurriedly trying to replace all four wheels and tyres and refuel the car as fast as possible. Thirty-one years later that same process was no longer a novelty, and the time taken for the performance-enhancing stop had dropped to 2 seconds, admittedly without the refuelling element. At the 2013 United States Grand Prix, Red Bull Racing set a new benchmark of 1.923 seconds for a pit stop with driver Mark Webber.

Along the way countless teams of mechanics had to wrestle with the improved performance demanded of them by the team bosses, examining the processes, technology and training involved in producing year-on-year improvements against a backdrop of ever increased safety demands. Performance and safety have had to work hand in glove.

Technological change within Formula One has been an inevitable part of this techno-centric sport, but the rate of change has increased dramatically over the years, particularly with the arrival of data-driven engineering and the information technology age.

When I started working in the sport, engineers in the 1980s still drew designs on paper, the draughtsman's job unchanged significantly since the industrial revolution. Clipboard in hand, race engineers would carefully make handwritten notes during practice, qualifying or a race in order to discuss the subjective feedback of the drivers afterwards. More often than not engineers were using their eyes, ears and noses to detect problems with a car, for without data systems only the tell-tale plume of black smoke from the rear of the car, drip of fluids on to a garage floor or grating sound of an engine misfiring on one cylinder would warn of mechanical failure.

The IT revolution required existing engineers to retrain and an investment in talented young personnel for whom the new technologies were familiar. There were those who changed, and those who didn't, and it was the former who thrived. Neither experience as an engineer nor utilization of the new technologies could win on its own, but combine the two and it was a powerful tool.

To start with, cars were fitted with rudimentary systems that enabled engineers to download basic performance information using an umbilical cable connected to a laptop when the car came into the pits. This gave us a chance to look at what had happened in the minutes and laps driven beforehand. During the 1990s this developed further with wireless networks giving teams the opportunity to monitor both the car and driver performance in real time, allowing for instantaneous decisions on mitigating technical risks, optimizing performance or changing tactics during an event. And now we have systems that are sufficiently sophisticated for us to be able to predict outcomes by analysing trends and mining the data. Big data has become a powerful new tool in Formula One's armoury.

At Jordan Grand Prix we made management decisions based on two principal questions: will it make the car go faster, and will it improve the business? Everything was about the product and the bottom line. Change invariably became part of the week-to-week discussion, because in deciding to purchase new technology, revise a process or alter a priority we had to undertake the most crucial aspect of this philosophy: communication.

You cannot expect to force change on customers, staff or suppliers without undertaking a rigorous analysis of the challenge or opportunity and then communicating the background to the decision in such a way that everyone is aligned. Enforced change is possible, but seldom smooth; it's more effective to explain the reasons for the decisions and allow a period of constructive discussion and development ahead of implementation.

The speed of change in Formula One is necessarily fast because of the complete focus on delivery against immovable deadlines, relentless performance reviews and intense competition from our rivals. We don't have time to debate change at length, so evaluation, decision making and implementation or rejection are rapid.

At Jordan our design office moved from drawing boards to 2D design and finally 3D computer-aided design and computer-aided manufacturing in a matter of five years and, being responsible for the IT partnership with Hewlett-Packard, I was closely involved in managing those changes. As our technology partner Hewlett-Packard was able to advise us of new developments in hardware, software and solutions management, while on our side the technical leaders within our business were constantly looking for new opportunities to improve performance, speed and efficiency within the design, manufacturing and development processes.

Naturally on the management board we had to factor our supplier's encouragement and our personnel's desire to acquire the latest technology against the business's needs to manage available resources. In the case of Hewlett-Packard we initially had US$1 million a year to 'play with' in relation to their sponsorship of the team, above which we had to pay cash. Eddie Jordan, an entrepreneur ever keen to protect and enhance the bottom line, was not overly keen on blowing the sponsorship allocation and starting to hand over cash, so we had to balance our desire for adopting and adapting to new technologies against the priorities of the business to manage its finances.

This is why decisions on expenditure relating to the business, including changing technologies, processes or people, always came down to answering that question about either making the car go faster or making the business more profitable. An ideal answer was both.

A key moment came for us in 1998 with the opening of our 'new' wind tunnel in Brackley, Northamptonshire, which was in fact the refurbished wind tunnel left derelict following the collapse of the Leyton House March Formula One team back in 1991. A new technology, that of stereolithography, or 3D printing as it is more commonly know, was sought by our design department, but it represented a significant investment in terms of cash, change in R&D processes and people. This technology appeared to be straight out of the world of science fiction at the time, enabling us to design a component and print a three-dimensional model of it in resin, a model with sufficient structural integrity for it to be installed on a wind tunnel model and tested immediately. What had taken weeks in terms of prototyping was reduced to days, sometimes hours, and, although this represented significant change, the benefits for our business and to our employers was very clear: it had the potential to make the car faster and improved the bottom line because we could fast-track developments much more efficiently.

The advent of rapid prototyping required investment, retraining, and a change in car development. The benefits became clear very quickly, and in a highly competitive team like Jordan everyone was eager to see those benefits translate into a faster, stronger, safer, more reliable car on the race track.

Customers can drive change and, so long as we are listening to them, create significant opportunities to retain and grow relationships. When

Formula One saw the anti-tobacco legislation of 2005 and financial crisis of 2008 cause an exodus of customers, it needed to do everything in its power to sustain those that remained, and find ways to develop new ones.

During the period of 2008–09 it became clear that one of the sport's major customers, the Renault Nissan group, was demanding that the gas-guzzling V8 engines that were the mainstay of F1 should be replaced with much more energy-efficient power units. Within two years Renault, Mercedes, Ferrari and Cosworth agreed with the FIA a step-change in technology, with a tiny 1.6-litre V6 engine mated to a powerful electric motor and two sophisticated energy recovery systems. This major change was extremely costly, and met a lot of resistance, but it was driven by customer demand; Renault's CEO Carlos Ghosn painted a picture of an automotive future where hybrid and all-electric vehicles would make up his company's product range, and Formula One had a choice to make. We would either be road-relevant, and benefit from Renault's continued custom, or continue with our outdated technology and become irrelevant to their business.

Fuel efficiency lay at the heart of Renault's power train strategy, and when we discussed this matter with Mercedes-Benz they confirmed that small hybrid engines would indeed form an important part of their future product planning. Ferrari was initially highly sceptical, but even for a luxury sports car manufacturer the need to meet emissions legislation and fuel economy targets in key markets reflected the need for Formula One to take heed.

The decision to move to an entirely new set of technologies demanded a great deal of resources, but the objective was to keep Formula One road-relevant in order to maintain these key customers, as well as to attract new ones. Honda's decision to return to Formula One in 2015 has been driven by their enthusiasm for the new power train units, vindicating the advice given by Carlos Ghosn, and the decision by Jean Todt at the FIA to legislate for their mandatory introduction in 2014.

The wider implication of this significant change was also to address another complaint from existing and potential customers about our sport: that it was ecologically damaging and did not promote environmental sustainability. Burning large amounts of fossil fuel in front of a live global television audience was not going down well with multinational companies whose own corporate social responsibility and environmental programmes were regarded as sacrosanct. The new power trains, producing the same performance with a reduction in fuel consumption of almost 40 per cent, not only address that issue head on, but arguably promote the capability of Formula One to engineer energy-efficient solutions that can benefit wider society in the longer term.

Considering the initial resistance within our industry to these recent changes, the advantages are very clear, even if for many people the positive effect has only become evident with hindsight.

I have also seen the resistance that comes from major changes in process such as the adoption of an enterprise resource planning (ERP) system such as that offered by SAP or Microsoft Dynamics. At Cosworth this added several layers of bureaucracy, it seemed, and, since not everyone was prepared to input the data required within their area, not surprisingly the output data were neither accurate nor useful. Staff used to working with manual systems, or at most using spreadsheet planning, resisted the adoption of an ERP system because of the complexity and 'clunkiness' that it added to an environment where we were already working on time pressure to fixed deadlines.

The reality, however, is that an effectively implemented ERP system can be enormously effective in driving efficiencies, reducing costs and achieving precisely the outcome from which everyone will benefit. But without the necessary engagement, education and communication of such a system's adoption it is impossible to get staff to accept such a change and optimize its use.

So this is the key thing about change: getting people to accept it, understand the reasons for it and embrace it. If you can show a Formula One team that a change will produce a winning car, making their lives richer in the process, naturally it's not such a hard sell. But a change such as happened following the 2008 financial crisis included having to downsize some of the teams and, in some cases, close entire departments. That's a much harder sell, especially for those being made redundant. But for those remaining in the business isn't it better to change and survive than to do nothing and risk complete collapse? Again it comes down to how the communications are handled; change should only become a problem if poor communication means that a change of course comes as a nasty surprise.

LESSONS IN CHANGE MANAGEMENT

Considering the complexity of modern business life, effective change management is an important ingredient for any successful company, and 'change' in all its forms needs to be embraced and understood. It is striking how often change is resisted, although this is often driven by fear: employees frightened at the prospect of a new technology, system, process or organizational structure that might upset their happy routine.

Technology is ever evolving, and as we accelerate towards the mid-part of the 21st century that is going to continue unabated. Wave after wave of technological developments and innovations will continue to crash over us. We either stand up, watch for them coming, and ride the waves of change, or we turn our back on them and receive constant surprises and shocks to the system.

Consider how the internet has revolutionized commerce, forcing industries to reappraise every aspect of how they work internally and externally, and creates a world where 'mobile' is no longer the generic term for a device, but the means of production, delivery and consumption. Those who saw the opportunities, seized them and met the challenge have thrived. Those who resisted, were complacent about their current capability and found it hard to innovate into the future struggled.

In Formula One we have seen how change has driven success, starting with the way that Bernie Ecclestone repackaged the entire sport in the 1970s and 1980s to build a made-for-TV offering that would attract sponsors and car manufacturers in their droves. This resulted in a raft of internal changes to meet the goals of attracting, sustaining and developing customers.

We have also seen how an external factor such as the anti-tobacco advertising and sponsorship legislation came about and forced a seismic shift in the commercial realities of our industry. Legislation and compliance commonly bring about change, and in Formula One we have had to learn how to adapt our business accordingly.

WITH RESPECT TO THIS TOPIC, MY TAKEAWAYS ARE AS FOLLOWS:

→ *Change is not an option.* Whether we like it or not, change is not only inevitable but in fact an essential part of business. The debate should not be about its merits, but how to evaluate, drive and embrace change for the betterment of our business and its employees, suppliers and customers.

→ *Avoid a bunker mentality.* In an ever shrinking world, and whether we are 'local' or 'global', our businesses will be affected by what happens elsewhere. We need to keep our eyes on the horizon, looking for the changes that are coming from within our industry, competitors, suppliers and of course the wider economy.

→ *Plan for continuous technological innovation.* Technology is going to continue evolving at a meteoric rate, giving our customers ever greater choice, enabling new processes and systems to be developed, and empowering new competitors. Our use of technology cannot be a static condition; plan for evolution and improvement, but expect revolution.

→ *Compliance, like quality, is a foundation stone.* It's essential if we are to compete effectively; we all have to meet the same sets of rules, whether governed by industry-specific regulation or by legislation. And since this can vary from country to country, region to region, we have to build flexibility into our strategies to accommodate changes when they come.

⚡ **Resistance to change is natural.** That negative reaction among staff, suppliers and customers needs to be understood. People like predictable outcomes, and fear uncertainty. So in managing change we need first of all to put ourselves in the position of those affected, and understand what is going to drive their objection.

⚡ **Engagement, education and communication are key to generating buy-in and securing alignment from those affected.** This is especially the case when management wants to implement changes to technology, systems, processes or structure, and thus has the opportunity to plan. But, even when change is enforced, sudden or unexpected, management should work hard to create the time for effective communication.

⚡ **Customer-driven change – such as when key automotive clients demanded Formula One put energy efficiency at the centre of its future technical regulations – requires special sensitivity.** In a customer-centric business, make time to listen to what customers want, examine how their demands are changing and find out where we can add future value.

⚡ **Change needn't be frightening.** By listening to those around us, particularly our customers and suppliers, and watching the competition closely, we can take much of the fear factor out of future plans.

CHAPTER SEVEN
FORMULA ONE'S
SAFETY REVOLUTION

The car behind us was clearly anxious to overtake. My driver, Keith Wiggins, owner of the fledgling and struggling Pacific Grand Prix team, was in no mood to let him past. We sped up. Our car, a Honda as I recall, leapt forward, but our pursuer remained fixed to its tail, matching each manoeuvre, jinking this way and that, trying to find a gap to pass. It was no easy task. The road into the Autopolis circuit in Japan was a single track, winding its way through the low hills, neatly terraced crop fields either side, smoke rising from the modest rural homes dotting the landscape.

We were there, coincidentally, for the Pacific Grand Prix, so named because the owner of Autopolis had convinced Bernie Ecclestone to grant him a race even though the well-established Japanese Grand Prix at Suzuka was also on that year's calendar. Never one to miss an opportunity, Bernie had elected to grant him his race, and give it the 'Pacific' title.

The eponymous race team was to be rather like the race: a journey of hope, one man's dream, short-lived and soon to become no more than a distant, unloved memory. But on this morning, with 'Wiggy' anxious to get to the track and see his cars driven by Bertrand Gachot and Paul Belmondo take part in practice, the mood was light and he was not about to let the driver behind beat us to the track.

The dice continued. As we entered the circuit the guards checked our passes and we were directed into the car park marked 'Formula One Team Personnel'. The driver behind tried to follow us, but the attendants blocked his path and directed him into the overflow car park; we'd taken the last available slot. An irritating diversion followed for him, into an unpaved, pothole-strewn and waterlogged section of ground.

It wasn't hugely surprising when, a few minutes later, the door to our office in the paddock burst open and the driver of the car we had beaten to the last parking place stood there, fuming and cursing us. He was shouting, hands outstretched, remonstrating with us for daring to block him and, worse, take the last place. What was surprising was his identity. Ayrton Senna, three times Formula One World Champion, wasn't happy.

I'd seen an Ayrton Senna rant before, also in Japan, when he had railed against the FIA president, Jean-Marie Balestre, in the post-race press conference at Suzuka in 1990. Unhappy about his treatment by the FIA at the 1989 and 1990 title-deciding races at the same circuit, he had let fly in front of a stunned media – it wasn't often that you heard a newly crowned World Champion using the F word in relation to the FIA president. And he was at it again, asking Wiggy what the f*** he was doing blocking him on the way into the circuit. We looked at each other, and Wiggy was beginning to formulate an explanation when we noticed something change in Senna's demeanour; he was smiling, and then laughing. He wasn't angry at all. This was one of his little jokes; he had thoroughly enjoyed the 'race' into the track.

We chatted for a few minutes, Ayrton asking us how things were going with the team, and he offered to come and meet any potential sponsors we had in order to endorse Wiggy's efforts in F1. They had known each other for a dozen years, for Wiggy had been one of Senna's mechanics in the Rushen Green Formula Ford 2000 team back in 1982. The young Brazilian had been living near Snetterton Circuit in Norfolk, having becoming good friends with Ralph Firman, owner of the Van Diemen racing car business, and he knew all the local racers well. For him, Wiggy was part of his enjoyable early years in racing.

To have Ayrton Senna offering to provide a helping hand whenever needed, to endorse the efforts of the Pacific team, an underfunded, uncompetitive back marker, was remarkable – an insight, if ever one was needed, into the nature of a man who could give no quarter when racing at 200 mph, yet be among the most sensitive and compassionate when outside of the cockpit.

Two weeks and two days later Ayrton Senna was dead, killed in a 190 mph accident when his Williams-Renault FW14B speared off the track and into the wall whilst leading the San Marino Grand Prix. Formula One had lost one of its greatest ever exponents.

In front of a live, global television audience estimated at 115 million, the only multiple World Champion still racing in Formula One at that time, arguably the greatest natural talent of his generation, had been killed in an accident that would not only change the sport, but contribute to far-reaching changes in car safety design that reverberate to this day.

For those of us who have made our career in professional motor racing, none will forget that event nor fail to wonder at its legacy. Senna's death continues to influence the sport today, mainly because it led to a step-change in attitudes to safety and technology such that not a single Formula One driver has been killed during an event in the 20 years since. Considering that, including non-Championship races, events open to F1 cars and the occasions when the Indy 500 counted towards the World Championship, Senna was the 47th driver to have been killed at the wheel of a Formula One car since the inaugural series in 1950, it could so easily have become another tragic milestone. Instead, it marked a turning point in a business that finally determined safety should come above all else.

San Marino 1994 was Formula One's Lehman Brothers collapse, BP's Deepwater Horizon or Costa's *Concordia*. Risks were taken, processes incomplete, attention on other priorities; in each example the outcome was catastrophic. In the case of Formula One it generated a deep desire to ensure that such an occurrence would never be repeated.

The ability of the sport to react to this one death in such a dramatic fashion as to totally eliminate F1 driver fatalities stands as testimony to what can be achieved when people reset their priorities. In Formula One safety was elevated overnight into being the number one priority within the regulations concerning car and circuit design. Everything would now be done to provide the technology and support infrastructure required to ensure that those competing in this sport would have the physical risks mitigated as far as humanly possible.

As tragic as Senna's death was, it is sad to reflect on the fact that none of the 46 drivers to have died before him triggered the wide-ranging changes that had been needed all along. The Swiss driver Jo Siffert was killed in a non-championship event at Brands Hatch in 1971, for example, his car failing as a result of accident damage. He died of smoke inhalation, none of the circuit's trackside fire extinguishers working correctly, and this prompted a review of extinguishers, fireproof overall design and provision of oxygen supply to drivers. This was one of a multitude of accidents that resulted in changes, but it was often a case of too little too late.

Senna's accident resulted in a step-change because it brought to new depths a San Marino weekend that had already produced appalling accidents and fatalities. There was also the cumulative effect of this together with the serious accident that befell Austria's Karl Wendlinger in Monaco two weeks later, which galvanized the leadership of Formula One into taking action. Wendlinger suffered serious injuries when his Sauber crashed at the chicane following the famous Monaco tunnel, causing him a significant concussion. Although he would return the following season, he never returned to form, and few doubt that the Monaco shunt took a heavy toll.

But it was San Marino two weeks previously that forced the safety overhaul that would now begin in earnest. On the Friday the Circuit Enzo e Dino Ferrari had witnessed Rubens Barrichello suffer a horrific accident when his Jordan was launched into the air by a kerb, clearing the safety barrier. It was only prevented from entering a public area by the presence of high-level debris fencing. The Brazilian suffered a concussion, swallowed his tongue and was fortunate to have received emergency treatment at the track prior to being airlifted to hospital.

The Saturday brought disaster in the form of the fatal accident that befell Austria's Roland Ratzenberger in his Simtek during qualifying. The 34-year-old from Salzburg was a popular driver, enormously charismatic and talented. I had met him first in 1987 when he was competing in Formula 3 in the UK, but we got to know each other better still when he raced in the British Formula 3000 series in 1989, in which he finished third. Tall, good-looking, with an infectious smile and ready wit, Roland was at the beginning of a promising career. He had everything to live for.

As with so many F1 hopefuls he had been underfunded, but had worked hard to establish his career in the sport, and in 1994 he had signed an initial five-race deal to drive for Simtek in Formula One. This was his big chance and, although the car was not competitive, he was determined to prove himself. This determination to make the most of the opportunity may have contributed directly to his accident, for he had gone off the track on the previous lap, possibly damaging the front wing. The usual protocol, now universally understood in racing, is to return to the pits after an off-track excursion in order to check for signs of damage.

On this occasion, however, Ratzenberger elected to continue on to the next lap, pushing hard. On the fast section through and beyond Tamburello corner the front wing appeared to fail, sending the Simtek into the barriers at 195.68 mph (314.9 kph). Suffering a basal skull fracture, Ratzenberger died instantly, television cameras broadcasting images of his head lolling in the cockpit, the driver lifeless as the car slithered to a halt.

Naturally there was a horrified reaction to Ratzenberger's death, particularly from Ayrton Senna, whose deep compassion had been seen before, notably when Northern Ireland's Martin Donnelly suffered a catastrophic accident in his Lotus during practice for the Spanish Grand Prix in Jerez in 1990. Catapulted from his disintegrating car, Donnelly's body lay in the track, his shattered legs bent at impossible angles. Senna was one of the first on the scene, and he was affected by what he saw. Donnelly would recover from the worst of his injuries, but never race in F1 again. There is no question that this accident played on Senna's mind for a time and now, in San Marino, the knowledge that Ratzenberger had given his life seemed to have a profound effect on the Brazilian superstar.

The events of the next day have been well chronicled; another accident occurred at the race start when JJ Lehto's Scuderia Italia stalled on the grid and was hit from behind by Pedro Lamy's Lotus, sending a wheel high into the crowd, debris injuring eight spectators and a policeman. A safety car was deployed and the field, led by Senna, who started from pole position, circulated for five laps while the debris was cleared.

When the race got under way again Senna pushed ahead to maintain, even extend, his lead over the coming man of Formula One, Michael Schumacher. Entering Tamburello on lap 7, Senna's Williams appeared initially to turn into the high-speed left-hander before stepping out of line, hopping on to a different trajectory, one that took him off the track at 190 mph (310 kph) and, after braking, into the wall at 135 mph (218 kph). Naturally the impact was severe, but the right front wheel slammed up and back, a piece of suspension piercing the former World Champion's helmet, causing fatal injuries.

Senna's life, and death, can be witnessed in the award-winning documentary *Senna*, directed by Asif Kapadia and written by Manish Pandey, an extraordinary piece of film making that gives an insight into a driver, a man, who almost 20 years later is still revered as Formula One's benchmark talent and sporting icon. 'The next Senna' is an overused but oft-quoted term for any fast up-and-coming driver these days.

I was not in San Marino on the day Senna met his end. Instead I was in Nice en route to a round of the World Rally Championship in Corsica. That night my wife and I headed to Monte Carlo for dinner, and as we wandered along the streets of the principality I pondered on how the world of Formula One would react to the day's events. I considered too how appropriate it was to be in Monaco, a venue Senna made his own, winning the Grand Prix five times, securing six pole positions and famously beating team mate Alain Prost to pole in 1988 by 1.4 seconds, an unheard-of margin around the 2.068 mile circuit, the shortest track in Formula One.

Some of the initial reactions to the deaths of Ratzenberger and Senna, though the former is too often forgotten, were both understandable and predictable: an outpouring of grief within the sport among fans world-wide, and for Senna at a national level in Brazil to such an extent that he was afforded a state funeral.

The Williams team found itself under scrutiny, Italian prosecutors keen to apportion blame. Senior team figures including Frank Williams, Patrick Head and F1 design legend Adrian Newey found themselves at the centre of a protracted legal investigation that only ended in 2007. A team with a hugely impressive track record, who prided themselves on achieving success through world-class engineering, found themselves quite literally in the dock and answering questions about their product, the integrity of components such as the steering that was alleged to have broken, and their management's approach to safety.

Much as occurred on the many previous occasions, many in the sport expected the furore over Senna's death to subside over time, until the next fatality. Had that happened, Formula One would have been no better than, and certainly no different from, the many human activities where safety issues rear their head from time to time but remain an 'accepted' fact. It becomes all too easy to say that accidents will happen, and fatalities are inevitable in a high-risk arena such as this.

It was not so on this occasion, and that can be attributed to a small group who took it upon themselves to change Formula One for ever and in doing so provide a template to the world on how to address the fundamental question of safety management and risk mitigation. That this author can write at a time, 20 years later, when there has been not one single further driver fatality in an event[1] is a testimony to what was achieved: how a culture can be changed, priorities reconfigured and the intellectual capabilities of its stakeholders focused on one area that in relative terms had been pushed to the margins.

As covered elsewhere in this book, Formula One teams have an overriding ability to focus on delivery. Whether it is on the delivery of a winning performance, introduction of new developments, or the achievement in ensuring that 30 tonnes of equipment are in the right part of the world at the right time in order to compete, F1 has long embraced a 'can do' culture.

What was achieved in the wake of the Senna and Ratzenberger fatalities was that the FIA, under president Max Mosley, set out to harness the brainpower of Formula One, tie that into its ability to deliver results and combine them under a clear target for the industry, namely to put safety at the top of the agenda and to eliminate fatal accidents. This objective remains difficult to recall without the feeling that it is nothing other than a worthy sentiment, except that in the case of Formula One the target was indeed achieved – initially for drivers, and more recently for all the other audiences involved. Team personnel, media, fans, trackside marshals: all have come to benefit from the FIA's decision to 'innovate to zero' the likelihood of people losing their lives in the course of attendance at a Formula One event.

The process by which the FIA improved safety took into account not only the technology within the cars themselves, but the environment within which they raced, and this led directly to the creation of Formula One venues where the design of the circuit took into account the certainty of accidents and set out to mitigate the risks associated with them.

Mosley was joined in his quest to revolutionize safety by Bernie Ecclestone, the sport's commercial rights holder, and together they empowered a team of people to develop the systems, processes and technology necessary to make the step-change. This included people such as Charlie Whiting, Formula One's race director and safety delegate, and medical delegate Professor Sid Watkins. Supported by a range of able lieutenants and expert advisers, they were at the vanguard of the revolution that unfolded in the months, years and decades ahead.

Whiting's overarching role as technical delegate meant that he was already at the epicentre of creating the rules and regulations governing Formula One car design, so when safety was pushed to the forefront of the agenda he was able to effect the changes needed.

Watkins, a neurosurgeon at the Royal London Hospital, had worked in and around racing since the 1960s, including when he lived in Syracuse, New York, attending races at Watkins Glen. But it was in 1978 that he started a new role helping Bernie Ecclestone to improve the medical facilities at Formula One races, commencing at that year's Swedish Grand Prix and witnessing the organizational debacle surrounding a serious accident at the Italian Grand Prix that claimed the life of Ronnie Peterson.

In the years that followed, Watkins worked tirelessly to ensure that rapid response teams were on hand at each Grand Prix, including the mandatory presence of air ambulances to transfer injured drivers to local trauma centres, which he personally checked in the days before each event. He made sure that the right skills were available: trauma specialists and anaesthetists instead of the nutritionists and psychologists who simply wanted to work at their local F1 event.

Watkins passed away in 2012, but part of his legacy is his two excellent books, *Life at the Limit* and *Beyond the Limit*, which tell the story of his role in the safety revolution, starting with treating the effects of these awful accidents, but moving in the post-Senna era to injury prevention. Accidents in Formula One are inevitable, so the achievements of Whiting, Watkins and their associates have been to ensure that the drivers walk away, and that team personnel, media and spectators do not get caught up in the incidents when they occur.

It is Watkins who recalls how the FIA harnessed the expertise of Dr Harvey Postlethwaite, a noted Formula One designer, who reviewed all the circuits used by Formula One. A total of 27 high-risk corners were identified, particularly those where lateral G-force exceeded a factor of 4. Through changes to car design regulations alone, slowing the cars by around 3 seconds per lap, the number of high-risk corners was reduced to 13, and these were then tackled by other means including corner redesign and the implementation of improved safety systems.

In some ways it is amazing that these kinds of profound changes were not made earlier.

Formula One, as with all forms of motor sport, has always been dangerous, and for decades we lived with fatal accidents and life-changing injuries as though it was a terrible but nevertheless inevitable outcome. The list is long, and some of the accidents so horrific that you can only wonder what today's rolling news channels would have made of them. Lorenzo Bandini was burned to death in his Ferrari in Monaco in 1967, and a similarly fiery fate befell Roger Williamson at the Dutch Grand Prix in 1973. The film of Williamson's car, upside down, with ineffective fire marshalling and fellow driver David Purley desperately trying to tackle the blaze, is the stuff of nightmares. Tom Pryce, another great British hope, was killed at the South African Grand Prix when two marshals elected to run across the track. One, a 19-year-old volunteer named Frederik Jansen van Vuuren, was killed instantly when hit by Pryce's car. Van Vuuren's 18-kilogram fire extinguisher then struck Pryce in the face, causing fatal injuries including partial decapitation.

This catalogue of horror was accepted, even if deeply regretted. Adjustments were made, proposals discussed, rule changes tweaked, but there was never the step-change in overall approach to the risk.

Risk was not only accepted; to some it was even part and parcel of life as an F1 driver. I recall meeting the late Innes Ireland, a six times Grand Prix winner in the 1950s and 1960s, in a bar in Brazil. He regaled me with stories of his era, including the time when he realized his Lotus had suffered a failure at 120 mph and was going off track.

'That got my attention, because there was a huge earth bank and wall in front of me and I didn't fancy hitting it,' he said. 'So I stood up in the cockpit – we didn't wear seat belts in those days – and I simply jumped out at about 80 mph. Best decision I ever made; broke a few bones, you know, but the car was destroyed and that could have been my last day on earth.'

So there you have it; risk mitigation 1960s style involved jumping out of a Formula One car. Interestingly, it was Ireland who was later credited with suggesting in 1979 that a medical car driven by a professional driver should follow the opening lap of each Formula One race, statistically the time when most accidents will occur.

In Ireland's era the cars were regarded as a death trap in certain accidents. Made of steel and aluminium, they often featured a cockpit that sat between the fuel tanks; crashing in a bathtub of fuel was something to be avoided. If the fuel didn't ignite then the car would concertina around you, sending the steering column into your chest, the wheel and dashboard towards your face, and the pedals up against your legs. Head, face, chest and internal injuries were the inevitable consequence, never mind broken limbs.

Interviewing Stirling Moss in his Shepherd Market home in central London in 1987, I couldn't help but notice the mangled steering wheel of his Cooper car mounted on the wall of his office. This was the wheel that had buried itself against him in the accident that ended his professional motor racing career at Goodwood in 1962, the nation watching and waiting in the days and weeks that followed to see if the sport's greatest hero would survive his injuries. Survive he did, but he would never race in the top flight again.

If death or permanent disablement was to be avoided, the simplest solution was to retire early, even if few had the luxury of being able to make that decision. One such was Jackie Stewart, three times World Champion, who stepped from his car during qualifying for the 1973 United States Grand Prix and called it a day. He had just witnessed the aftermath of the fatal accident that befell his team mate and close friend Francois Cevert, a prodigious talent with film star looks, whose Tyrrell submarined under an Armco barrier, killing him instantly. For Stewart, who was personally able to count over 50 drivers killed during his career, it marked a watershed. He would never race again.

Stewart's decision was the culmination of years spent lobbying for safety improvements, but his pleas often fell on deaf ears and were at times characterized as showing fear, a quality unbecoming of a Formula One driver. Nothing could have been further from the truth. The Scottish ace, regarded by many as the pre-eminent driver of his generation, lacked for nothing in skill, courage and focus on winning, but he added to that an intellectual understanding of the risks being taken and the need to manage them. His campaigns for mandatory seat belts, full face helmets, improved fireproof clothing and race track safety did not make him popular, but in reality he was simply a man ahead of his time.

The trajectory of a racing car in an accident is something that can be forecast. The angle of attack of a car veering off the track during an accident, whether as a result of component failure such as a punctured tyre, hitting a kerb that might deflect its path or a collision with another vehicle, can be predicted to a high degree.

As a result, circuits are now designed to have walls as far away from the track as possible or, where this is impossible for reasons of topography and track boundaries, the likely impact points are designed to ensure that the car will hit at as acute an angle as possible. Head-on collisions with walls are to be avoided, so the task for the last decade and a half has been to ensure that the cars slow down as much as possible and only impact with walls at a speed and angle that optimize driver protection.

Among the earlier initiatives to de-risk accidents included the catch fencing, sand and gravel traps that we saw introduced from the late 1960s onwards. These initiatives brought their own problems, however. Catch fencing designs involved netting strung between poles imbedded in soft ground, the idea being that the cars would become caught, bringing them to a controlled halt. In reality, the prospect of drivers being trapped by netting, marshals finding extraction more difficult, and catch fencing poles striking drivers on the head during impact made such a solution counterproductive.

Gravel traps became de rigueur during the 1970s and 1980s but, while they did indeed cause cars to slow down and become bogged in the loose shale used to fill the traps, lateral impacts with the gravel often resulted in cars being overturned. Famously this happened to Ayrton Senna at the 1991 Mexican Grand Prix when in the long, fast Peraltada Parabolica the Brazilian lost control of his McLaren, which spun backwards into the gravel trap and then flipped upside down when its wheels dug into the very material introduced to improve safety. It was a shaken Senna who emerged, but this was only one of many such incidents in motor racing.

Ultimately the FIA's holistic approach to improving safety meant that circuits would have to be adapted to allow for the most obvious ways of mitigating risk during a high-speed incident. This included creating more room for the cars themselves to slow down thanks to their powerful brakes and the high grip levels afforded by their racing tyres, and ensuring that when they did hit the walls they encountered absorbent material.

In relation to car design there was a wide range of changes brought about by the FIA's subsequent analysis of accidents together with the teams, and discussions with the technical brains across the sport. Front suspension mountings were altered to prevent them from folding backwards towards and into the cockpit. Wheels were fitted with extremely strong Kevlar ties to reduce the likelihood of them flying into the crowd, as happened during the fateful 1994 San Marino Grand Prix.

Side impact protection was introduced as one of many measures to strengthen the carbon fibre monocoque, or safety cell, within which the driver sits. The seating position was lowered to reduce the potential for the driver being hit by debris, and the driver's head was protected by the introduction of deformable structures mounted on the cockpit either side of the helmet. This Confor foam, covered in Kevlar skin, was demonstrated by the Motor Industry Research Association in the UK to dramatically reduce the effects of impacts to the head and neck. Seat belts were widened to help spread the loads involved in an accident more evenly across the torso of the driver involved.

The invention of the head and neck safety device, known by its acronym HANS, was another significant development. Imported from the United States where it had been developed by Professor Bob Hubbard at Michigan State University for use in power boat races, it tackles the issue associated with significant rotational, whiplash-style injuries and the more serious concussions caused by the brain impacting on the inside of the skull as a result of high G-force accidents.

What was perhaps more impressive than the design changes carried out on F1 cars was the manner in which the race car's environment was altered to ensure that, when the inevitable accident occurred, the circuit would itself help to protect the driver. This was achieved through adopting a wide range of initiatives based on the lessons learned, and the hard data collected, from multiple accidents.

Given the manner in which a car's trajectory during an accident can be calculated, circuit design has evolved since the Senna era. Gravel traps have been abandoned in favour of very large tarmac run-off areas that enable drivers to slow the car using the best device available: its own brakes and the tyres in contact with the ground. As a result, all the new circuits designed by Formula One's lead architect Hermann Tilke feature wide run-off zones and walls set far back, angled away from the likely trajectory of cars losing control in an accident.

Gravel traps do still exist, notably at older, traditional tracks where the topography makes it difficult to relocate walls back several metres, but the size of the gravel is carefully calculated so as to slow the cars and make it more difficult for them to dig in sideways and roll over. Handled correctly, a driver can drive across a gravel trap and rejoin the race, but in the event of a significant accident the trap will degrade the car's speed before it can impact the circuit wall.

The walls themselves have changed, of course, for the old-style Armco barriers have long lost their appeal because of their unforgiving nature. Surprisingly a much more traditional basis of wall has continued to deliver safety: towers of old car tyres, bound together and clad in a protective, unifying cover.

Debris fencing has been a feature of motor racing track safety for decades, but the height, location and construction have been greatly improved in the last 15 years to prevent spectators, media and track marshals from suffering from race car debris, or indeed the cars themselves, being able to fly beyond the track.

Senna's death was not the last fatality at a Formula One event, three track marshals being killed in tragic accidents at the 2000 Italian Grand Prix, 2001 Australian Grand Prix and 2013 Canadian Grand Prix. In the first two cases the marshals were struck by wheels flung from cars during accidents, whilst the 2013 fatality was more typical of an industrial accident, no less serious and just as alarming.

In Monza in 2000 an accident involving my own team's Jordan cars, driven by Heinz-Harald Frentzen and Jarno Trulli, resulted in a rear wheel being violently ripped off at right angles, striking a marshal, Paulo Gislimberti, who had left the safety of his marshal's post to find a better vantage point from which to watch the start of the race. In Melbourne it was the BAR Honda of former World Champion Jacques Villeneuve, which suffered a high-speed accident after colliding with the Williams driven by Ralf Schumacher. Launched into the air, Villeneuve's car slewed to the left and slammed into the wall and debris fencing, a wheel passing through a gap in the fence, normally left for photographers to have an unimpeded view, but resulting in fatal injuries to track marshal Graham Beveridge.

What both these incidents showed was that irrespective of how safe the cars had become for their occupants, including the safety measures implemented track-side, third-party risk had not been fully mitigated. This resulted in wheel tethers, which had already been in use, being increased in size and strength, and the location of marshals' posts and gaps for photographers being reviewed.

In Canada in 2013 marshal Mark Robinson succumbed to injuries caused when he stumbled and fell under the wheels of a crane being used to recover one of the Formula One cars after the race. He had dropped his radio, but fell when he stooped to pick it up. The crane driver, unsighted, was unable to avoid running over him. It was the kind of incident that could occur on any industrial site, but it shocked the F1 world that a volunteer track worker should meet such a fate. It was a reminder that safety procedures and guidelines extend far beyond the most obvious dangers in any environment.

Changes to process, including that of the manner in which competitors actually race against one another, have been implemented in an effort to reduce risk further. It is one thing to address the potential outcome of an accident, but better still if the accidents are avoided completely.

Strange as it may seem in an adrenalin-filled sport where drivers race wheel to wheel at 200 mph, stringent efforts have been made to make drivers understand that some risks are unnecessary, unacceptable even, and that their intellectual ability and lightning reflexes can be used just as much to avoid an accident as to find the competitive edge needed to win.

By and large the drivers have welcomed this, since the benefits of accident avoidance are many. Not only do drivers want to survive accidents, but more than that they want to avoid them entirely so that they can keep on racing, complete the distance and give themselves the chance of a good result. Just as it works in relation to reliability, so in the context of safety does the adage 'To finish first, first you have to finish' speak an important truth.

Complacency was always going to be the enemy of safety in Formula One, and so it has proven, as the increased safety of cars and circuits has enabled a new generation of drivers to avoid injury entirely and walk away from the kinds of accidents that often resulted in serious injury or death. This is particularly the case since the FIA ensured that many of the safety lessons learned in Formula One were cascaded into lower formulae of racing, meaning that today it is more often the case that drivers can race cars from the age of 16 or 17 and never once encounter a truly life-threatening accident.

This has led in some cases to a deterioration in driving standards, with drivers taking more risks safe in the knowledge that the worst that could happen would be retirement from the race and the annoyance of a non-finish. It is natural that some veterans of the sport, including Jackie Stewart, have pointed out that drivers today can take risks that would have been unthinkable in the 1960s.

The problem for the FIA, therefore, has been to find ways to penalize poor driving standards and police the drivers in a manner that does not prevent high-quality racing, but at the same time ensures that the competitors remain mindful of their obligations to others, if not to themselves.

The way in which races have been conducted has also been reviewed, with the use of the safety car now commonplace when the race director decides that the risks associated with racing at full speed are too high. As a result, safety cars are used when cars are abandoned in a dangerous location, an incident occurs that requires the medical teams and marshals to be in attendance, or heavy rain causes the track conditions to deteriorate as a result of standing water, which can promote aquaplaning. Halting a race is also more commonly used, as in the Canadian Grand Prix in 2011 when torrential rain forced a mid-race delay of 2 hours 20 minutes. Frustrating as that was for all concerned, notably a hard-pressed media and worldwide television audience, the reality was very clear. Unable to guarantee the safety of the drivers, the sport preferred to wait for better conditions to arrive. Nothing is so important that safety should be compromised.

The safety car has been just one means of controlling events, reducing risk and promoting safety. Equally important is the presence of the medical car, driven by a professional driver accompanied by qualified medical personnel and able to reach the scene of an accident within 20 to 30 seconds.

In *Life at the Limit* Sid Watkins relates the story of how Wilson Fittipaldi, brother of former World Champion Emerson, was asked to use a saloon car race on the Saturday afternoon of the Brazilian Grand Prix to practise his technique for following the opening lap of the Formula One event at the wheel of Sid's medical car. Wilson obviously didn't quite understand the concept, because the Mercedes medical car was up to 16th position at the first corner and leading the race at the end of the first lap.

An unexpected outcome of the death of Ayrton Senna was what happened when the FIA turned to the car industry, hopeful of finding that it had a sophisticated crash-testing and vehicle safety approval system in process. Adopting best practices from other industries can be a quick way to shorten a learning curve.

What Max Mosley and his colleagues on the FIA Safety Committee discovered, however, was a car industry that regarded safety legislation as a necessary evil, an additional cost likely to erode the bottom line. Crash-testing procedures had not been reviewed since 1974, when car technology and speeds were very different indeed.

Successfully lobbying for support within the EU, and gaining the support of key automotive executives including Renault's CEO Louis Schweitzer, the FIA suddenly found itself at the forefront of a safety initiative that went far beyond Formula One motor racing. Using the knowledge gained from accidents including Senna's, and developing robust crash-testing procedures for racing cars, the FIA became involved in developing the European New Car Approval Process whereby vehicles are tested and awarded a rating.

Mosley recalls that it was as a result of selling the commercial rights of Formula One to Bernie Ecclestone's organization for €350 million that the FIA Institute was founded and later, in 2001, US$300 million was used to create a charity, the FIA Foundation, that has been a pivotal organization in relation to Euro NCAP and its successor, Global NCAP, working alongside a multitude of other organizations and NGOs. The Euro NCAP tests rate cars in a crash test on a scale of 1 to 5. Few cars were initially able to rate higher than a 3, but as Schweitzer's Renault discovered, a high safety rating was a useful marketing tool when targeting a car-buying public rather keen to avoid being killed in accidents. A step-change occurred, the automotive industry buying into a new safety protocol born as the result of that fateful day in San Marino, 1994.

That Formula One has not witnessed another driver fatality at an event since 1994, and that the track marshals who died created further safety initiatives in an already risk-averse industry, is a testimony to what can be achieved when humans decide to alter the priorities and apply their considerable brainpower to adopting a new culture.

The average person does not associate Formula One motor racing with safety, so it comes as a surprise to many to discover that in the new era words such as 'safety' and 'reliability' come before performance. Unfortunately it took the death of Ayrton Senna to force upon us the wake-up call that led to a change in philosophy. The flip side is that the fatal accident that befell Roland Ratzenberger 24 hours earlier probably would not have had the same effect. The death of a relatively unknown driver with little track record in Formula One would have prompted some short-term hand wringing, but overall the response was not likely to have changed much.

Such is life, and the lessons from Formula One's safety crusade are very clear.

If safety and risk management is going to be priority, take a holistic view and address all the elements. Making cars safe was one thing, but there was no point in doing that without making the circuits safe to drive on and putting in place the rules, regulations and processes around the sport to mitigate further the likelihood of a negative outcome.

More difficult, of course, was getting all of the individuals involved in Formula One to adopt a new culture. The fact that everyone present in San Marino needed no reminding of the importance of safety is one thing, but as the years have gone by new generations of mechanics, engineers, team managers, officials, track marshals and drivers have had to be introduced to the systems necessary to avoid fatal accidents.

When safety is compromised and we experience injuries and fatalities, it becomes an intensely personal matter. San Marino in 1994 made safety a priority because that weekend was an intensely personal experience not only for those directly involved, but for the entire world audience of Formula One. The scale of that incident has ultimately made it easier to educate future generations about the importance of safety and why we do things the way we do.

Getting the technical and sporting regulations modified to put safety first was, in reality, the easy part. Much more difficult was the cultural change in an environment that sees an influx of young, talented staff year by year, anxious to work in the exciting world of Formula One, with the risk factor adding a certain frisson to the daily routine. Injuries continue to occur, particularly during the frantic sub-3-second pit stops that we see today, so as the tempo of world-class team work has increased so too the opportunity for mistakes and risks has increased.

What is clear, therefore, is the need for regulations and processes to be backed up by training, and by the example set by the senior staff whether at the factory or out in the field at events. When safety is uppermost in everyone's mind, top down, the new recruits quickly adapt and it becomes second nature to them. Safety leadership requires setting an example, practising what we preach. There can be no exceptions.

Ultimately my conclusion from Formula One's experience of safety and risk management is that technology, processes and systems can go so far, but ultimately the cultural change across everyone involved in the industry was key. The leadership identified the need to change, and the clear message was cascaded down throughout the sport, its constituent teams and its stakeholders. Once the need for change was experienced, and the decision made to do something about it, it became a question of developing the systems and processes to effect that change and then – most importantly – sustain the benefits.

The fact that F1 was really serious about managing risk was evidenced when all the teams, normally ultra-competitive, came together with the sport's governing body to come up with an industry-wide approach that gave us best-in-class solutions. Looking outside Formula One was also an important part of that journey, for, whilst we were unable to learn from the automotive sector, the airline industry gave us an appreciation of the advantages of using on-board computers as accident data recorders to help to build knowledge about accidents and their causes.

Formula One's success in eliminating driver fatalities over the last two decades is testimony to what happens when safety is put at the centre of the agenda, the leadership gives a very clear vision of what the target is, and the systems and processes put in place to deliver it are backed up by the most important thing of all – the culture of the people involved.

In 2014 the Red Bull-owned Toro Rosso Formula One team had a rookie driver from Russia, Daniil Kvyat. His debut season in the sport came 20 years after Senna's death; Kvyat was five days old at the time.

We now have a generation of drivers who have no experience of fatal accidents in Formula One, so the next challenge facing the FIA, teams and stakeholders across the sport is to reinforce the messages about safety, educate the new generation about why we do things the way we do, and protect them from the C word that threatens anyone working in a high-risk environment: complacency. This alone will ensure that Formula One's leadership will continue to place safety at the centre of the sport.

LESSONS IN SAFETY AND RISK MANAGEMENT

Success in Formula One is as much about risk management as it is about optimizing performance. We spend a great deal of time managing the risks inherent in our business. We mitigate commercial risk by maintaining and growing a diverse portfolio of sponsors. We aim to avoid financial Armageddon by managing budgets prudently, controlling costs, and keeping our eyes firmly fixed on the bottom line.

The operational risk involved in shipping many tonnes of precious equipment to 19 venues across the planet is significant, not to mention the dozens of race team personnel who are working in a high-pressure environment in spite of the relentless travel.

Then there are the risks we have to manage during a Formula One race itself, when thousands of components and dozens of systems on board the car have to be managed effectively, performance optimized and issues resolved in real time. The telemetry systems enable us to fine-tune the performance of both the car and its driver, but during a race we are looking for the anomalies, the degradation in performance, and the systems failures. For, if we want to finish first, first we have to finish, and so mitigating risk during the race is all about managing a wide range of variables, some of which are not under our control, and developing the ability to react instantly to issues when they arise.

But 'risk' and 'Formula One' usually bring to mind a very personal risk associated with young men driving light, high-performance cars at 200 mph and battling wheel to wheel. The risks are very clear, the potential for tragedy all too obvious.

In an industry where fatalities were all too common, the change in culture, technology and systems associated with safety has been the most profound. For all the glitz, glamour, technology and money that Formula One has attracted in recent decades, its most significant achievement has been in managing the risk associated with racing. In 2014 the sport was able to commemorate 20 years since the last driver fatalities in a race event – those of Ayrton Senna and Roland Ratzenberger at Imola in 1994 – and redouble its efforts to maintain its safety record in the face of a new generation for whom complacency is the biggest enemy.

FORMULA ONE'S SAFETY RECORD IS A WORTHY CASE STUDY IN HOW WE CAN TACKLE RISK HEAD ON, AND THE LESSONS ARE VERY CLEAR:

➠ *Make safety and risk management a central pillar of your business.* This is precisely what Max Mosley, president of the FIA, and Bernie Ecclestone, chief executive of Formula One Management, did in the wake of the Senna and Ratzenberger fatalities.

➠ *Communicate your objective very clearly, and make it a high ambition.* The FIA's decision to 'innovate to zero' the likelihood of further fatalities within Formula One was a brave target, but it provided the overarching context of all the changes that took place in the years that followed.

⟫ ***Remember that safety and risk management is all about people.*** Systems, processes, checklists, regulations and legislation are important. But they mean nothing unless every person involved believes in them, commits to the culture and sustains it every day. Performance is all about team work. So too is safety. You cannot divorce the two.

⟫ ***We know the risks, so be realistic and robust in tackling them.*** In Formula One we know that accidents will happen, cars will break, or they will collide or crash through driver error. We also know what happens to the trajectory of a car in an accident, and so we can plan for that. We have to prepare for all the negative scenarios and work backwards to eliminate or reduce their effects.

⟫ ***Recognize that, as with performance management, the truth is in the data.*** Not only do we know what types of accidents occur; we usually know when. In Formula One, for example, most major pile-ups are likely to occur on the opening lap. For that reason the medical car follows the field at the start in order to provide the fastest-possible reaction in the event of a serious accident.

⟫ ***Take a holistic, thorough view of the risks and the steps required to mitigate them.*** In Formula One we addressed the cars, the tracks, the personnel, the equipment, the emergency services and the trauma facilities. Attention to detail in every area enabled the whole industry to move to an entirely new level of safety performance.

⟫ ***Accept that accidents will happen.*** It is a fact of the human condition. It is an inevitable consequence of what we do that accidents are going to occur. Put just as much energy into mitigating the effects of an accident as to ensuring that they don't happen in the first place.

⟾ *Use the power of regulation, legislation and enforcement.* People must understand that the organization is serious about managing risk and promoting safety; therefore the flip side is that sub-standard practices cannot be permitted. A Formula One driver's safety equipment is clearly specified and mandatory; so too is the safety performance of the car. Adherence is non-negotiable.

Note

1 Spanish Formula One test driver Maria de Villota suffered a serious accident during a private test session for the Marussia Formula One team at Duxford airfield on 3 July 2012 when her car ran into the back of the tail-lift of a support vehicle parked in the car's holding area. The team was using the airfield for 'straight-line' testing, and it is not an accredited Formula One venue. It was also her first time in a Formula One car, although she was a very experienced and capable racing driver. She suffered serious head and facial injuries, which led to the loss of her right eye. In spite of making a good recovery, 15 months later she was found dead on the morning of 11 October 2013 in a hotel room in Seville, and an autopsy found she had suffered a cardiac arrest. Her family was informed that this might have been caused by the brain injuries suffered in her testing accident.

CHAPTER EIGHT
INNOVATING
TO SUCCEED

Victory in Formula One requires many things: a good budget, the best technical resources and of course a great team supporting a fast driver. But if there is one aspect of winning teams that stands out time and again it is the ability of top teams to innovate constantly in their relentless quest for competitive advantage.

Innovation fuels success in our sport, driving a culture founded on the understanding that we can never stand still and rest on our laurels. We are only as good as our last race and, even if our last race produced a victory, the need to push onwards and develop even better results remains the same. You can never stop and say 'This is it; this is as far as we have come and we have no need to develop any further.'

As with risk management, developing a culture of innovation necessarily means that you are going to embrace change continuously. The two go hand in hand. My experience is that if you aim to be the best then it's essential to evolve constantly, learn from past mistakes, look for new opportunities and have the flexibility to implement improved processes and solutions along the way.

I often point out that early Formula One cars, though sophisticated for their time, had not advanced much since the internal combustion engine replaced the horse as the mode of transport. Look at a 1950s F1 car and you see the horsepower still at the front, four rather spindly wheels, and somewhere for the driver to sit at the back.

I remember attending a fascinating seminar by the US vehicle designer Chris Bangle, at that time head of design for the BMW Group, in which he sketched the evolution of the car from horse-drawn carriages. He demonstrated how designers took ideas from sleek boat designs and later jet aircraft to develop some of the iconic design features of the interwar and then post-war years. Innovation was coming thick and fast in automobile design, ultimately taking its cue from a multitude of design influences.

In 1950, the inaugural season of the Formula One World Championship was more impressive for its ability to stage an international motor racing series so soon after the Second World War than for the technical sophistication of its cars. However, innovation was there, fixed in its DNA, from the very start.

Those big, powerful, front-engined Grand Prix cars from Ferrari, Lancia, Maserati and Mercedes-Benz were in for a shock, however, when a British design engineer called John Cooper decided to innovate in a rather fundamental area. Recognizing that the engine sitting in front of the driver, and over the steering wheels, was less than ideal he decided to take a radical approach. The standard design philosophy tended to promote poor handling characteristics given that the heavy mass of the engine up front was transmitting all its raw power through to the rear wheels and in so doing playing havoc with the car's inherent stability in corners. The centre of gravity was simply too high and weight distribution poor.

His solution, his innovation, was to put the horse behind the person, moving the engine to the middle of the car. It was not an obvious decision, but then he realized that, as this kind of horsepower could be situated anywhere, situating it rearward and yet in front of the rear wheels would give the car a better-located, lower centre of gravity and more neutral handling style – good for the driver, better for tyre and brake wear, and faster.

Cooper's innovation was a resounding success, embarrassing the giants of Formula One and not only changing race design for ever, but ensuring that all 'super-cars' of the future would feature predominantly race-bred mid-engined design layouts. To use modern parlance, mid-engined race car design was a game changer.

From the 1950s and into the 1960s innovation continued, with constant development, and more often than not coming from the smaller businesses run by visionaries. In 1967 Ford Motor Company agreed to sponsor the Cosworth engineering business to develop a new Formula One engine, a V8 engine, which would be known as the DFV, standing for double four valve. What made this engine so unique was that Cosworth's founders, Keith Duckworth and Mike Costin, elected to design it to work as a chassis member. While all other racing engines were held in a metal frame within the chassis of the car, Cosworth realized that this not only added weight and complexity, but also promoted flexing as a result of poor torsional strength.

Their solution was to remove the frame and make the engine immensely strong in itself, literally holding the entire car together. The front section of the car, including cockpit, front suspension and wheels, would be bolted to the engine, with the gearbox, rear suspension and wheels attached to its rear. That the DFV was also a powerful and very efficient engine, its 90-degree V8 configuration being topped by cylinder heads containing two inlet and two exhaust valves per cylinder, added to its potential.

First time out, in the Lotus 49 of Scotland's Jim Clark, the Cosworth DFV powered to victory at the 1967 Dutch Grand Prix in Zandvoort. Its performance stunned the opposition, and Clark would go on to win four Grands Prix that season en route to third in the Championship, while team mate Graham Hill would win the 1968 World Championship outright. The Cosworth DFV was the tool to have, and its technological innovation became copied by all its opposition in the seasons that followed. Ultimately the DFV would go on to power 152 Formula One race winners, carrying Jackie Stewart, Emerson Fittipaldi, James Hunt, Mario Andretti, Alan Jones, Keke Rosberg and Nelson Piquet Sr to World Championship titles in its various derivatives up until 1982.

When I took over running Cosworth's F1 business in 2009 I salvaged an old, framed photograph of Keith Duckworth, Colin Chapman and Jim Clark taken in 1967 and put it on the wall of my office. It was there to remind me that the very essence of Cosworth's success lay in a commitment to innovation as well as working with partners who share the vision to succeed.

With mid-engined cars thanks to Cooper, and fully stressed engines invented by Cosworth, the performance of Formula One cars moved on to levels never seen before. So fast were they that, in some cases, they literally began to fly, the crests and brows on the public road courses such as Germany's Nurburgring and Belgium's Spa-Francorchamps witnessing Grand Prix cars becoming airborne.

Engineers began fitting wings to their cars in the late 1960s. The aim was the keep the cars firmly fixed to the ground and enable them to make better use of the tyre's contact patch with the race track.

Initially these were mounted high in the airstream, at the tips of improbably tall and flimsy wing mounts, and sure enough they suffered some frightening failures. But the point had been made: placing wings on the cars could generate 'downforce', harnessing the power of aerodynamics in a way that had only previously been touched upon in racing circles.

These wings operated precisely like the wings on aircraft, the difference being that they were inverted, pushing the cars into the ground as opposed to generating lift. The advent of wings was an innovation that paved the way for the principal area of design development of the next 40 years, as Formula One embraced the complex principles of aeronautical engineering and found ever more sophisticated ways to use airflow to maximize performance.

I often point out that the modern F1 car owes more to aerospace than automotive technology, since we have spent the last four decades flying our cars into the ground as fast as possible. Rather like putting the horse behind the driver or turning the engine into a chassis member, flying upside down at 200 mph seems counter-intuitive, but as with so much innovation the most interesting developments come from questioning standard thinking. Just because something has been done in the same way for years doesn't mean it's the best or only way.

As wings became de rigueur within Formula One, it was engineers such as Peter Wright and Lotus boss Colin Chapman who looked to unleash the next step-change in performance, and the latter's fascination with aerodynamics led him toward the next major innovation. Realizing that a front and rear wing could generate only a certain amount of downforce, a new generation of F1 aerodynamicists opted to take a more holistic view of the car and treat it as a single, massive wing. The car's upper surfaces could act as the top of a wing, while its underbody could be designed in such a way as to accelerate the airflow travelling beneath the chassis, effectively sucking the car on to the track. The era of 'ground effect' technology was born.

The 1978 Lotus 79 made full use of this innovation, and Chapman's solution to the problem of airflow leaking out from underneath the sides of the car was simply to create vertical walls, known as skirts. These sealed the gap between the side of the car and the ground, helping to ensure that the airflow under the chassis would accelerate up and out of the rear of the car through a swept diffuser. The car, a 200 mph wing on four wheels, was astonishingly fast, taking cornering speeds to unheard-of levels. The Lotus 79 swept all before it, winning both the World Championship for Drivers and the World Championship for Constructors.

This was such a sophisticated technological step, a radical innovation, that many teams struggled to understand how to copy and compete. Ferrari, with their powerful but wide Flat 12 engine, had difficulty implementing a design to mirror the Lotus philosophy, but ultimately joined everyone in chasing the benefits to be had from making the most of ground effect technology.

Unable to replicate the efficiency of Chapman's Lotus design, another innovator came up with a fascinating and slightly comical solution, which also proved to be a winning alternative. Gordon Murray, chief designer at Bernie Ecclestone's Brabham team, decided that, if the best way to create performance was to have the car sucked on to the ground, he would build the world's most powerful vacuum cleaner.

Arriving at the 1978 Swedish Grand Prix in Anderstorp, Brabham drivers Niki Lauda and John Watson found themselves at the wheel of a Brabham BT46B modified to carry a huge fan driven from the gearbox and channelling the airflow from under the car at very high speed. It was effective, and in ways beyond those intended by Murray, because not only were the Brabhams sucked on to the track like a 200 mph Dyson, but they fired all the dust and debris out of the back, rendering it impossible for anyone to follow even if they had managed to keep up. The car duly won the race, Lauda triumphant, and the design was promptly banned by the sport's governing body; it wasn't illegal, because no rule maker had ever thought of such a thing, but it was clearly taking a route the sport's governing body didn't want anyone to follow.

Murray's approach to Formula One design owed much to a relentless quest to innovate in every area. Ahead of the 1978 season, months before the 'fan car' had been conceived, Murray appeared on the BBC Television's *Sports Personality of the Year* show and unveiled a Brabham BT46 design featuring a surface cooling system rather than traditional radiators. Radiators have always been a necessary evil, providing cooling to the engine and gearbox whilst requiring a large surface area to be presented to the airflow, so Murray's innovation would undoubtedly have had a profound effect on performance, had it worked. In this case the innovation failed, the heat exchangers incapable of providing sufficient cooling, but it showed how he was thinking. For him performance and innovation were bedfellows.

This wonderful insight into the mind of an innovator such as Gordon Murray keeps us on a trail that leads to today's top innovator in Formula One, Adrian Newey, technical director of Red Bull Racing. His cars not only won four World Championship titles for Red Bull between 2010 and 2013, but his previous designs at McLaren and Williams had amassed 12 titles over the past 20 years. As with the innovators such as Murray, Chapman, Duckworth and Cooper before him, Newey's edge comes from looking at every aspect of product performance and questioning defined wisdom.

Consider, for example, that Newey's design teams have taken wing design forward by engineering a degree of flexibility into these previously rigid devices, enabling the wings to bend towards the race track at speed, harnessing the power of Chapman's ground effect. Wings can be made to flex along their length, or breadth, returning to their static shape when the car reduces speed and returns to the pit lane. In this way, a car's wings may pass all the necessary tests for minimum height above the track surface when measured in scrutineering, yet once they are on the race track they can alter shape into an altogether more aggressive and aerodynamically efficient design configuration.

One of Newey's criticisms of contemporary Formula One has been the stifling of innovation through the creation of rules that leave fewer and fewer opportunities for designers to introduce ground-breaking ideas. As the FIA has sought to improve safety, limit costs and prevent teams from incorporating technologies or materials that will prove increasingly difficult to police, so designers are left with a prescribed list of rules and regulations.

Compliance is as important in F1 as with any other regulated business, but for the innovator it is often seen as the enemy. It can prevent exploration, blunt inspiration and resist lateral thinking. But there is evidence that, even in this era of strangled compliance, opportunities for innovation remain. It all comes down to how you read the rule book, not for what it says, but for what it doesn't say.

In 2009, as Red Bull Racing began to exert its position of dominance within Formula One, we became aware of a new innovation. Once again it came from the design office of Adrian Newey, this time in close collaboration with engine supplier Renault Sport, and again it took the form of rethinking established practice.

A Formula One engine's principal purpose has always been to provide the motive power and, since 1967 and development of the Cosworth DFV, act as a fully stressed chassis member. Its efficiency has always been important; an engine that requires less cooling or has lower fuel consumption is seen as beneficial, as is smooth delivery of the power and torque available to the driver.

Engine exhaust gases were first used to enhance aerodynamic efficiency in the early 1990s when exhaust tailpipes were integrated into the diffusers sweeping up from the underbody of the car, the exhaust gases being used to help accelerate the airflow. This was beneficial, but somewhat limited by the fact that the speed of exhaust gas flow was naturally related to the speed of the engine. At lower speeds the exhaust flow would reduce, and with it the aerodynamic benefit diminish.

Newey's design team worked with its engine supplier at Renault to come up with an innovation whereby the engine's role as an 'air pump' would be enhanced such that, even in slow corners, the exhaust flow would be maintained, increasing downforce and enabling the car to corner much more quickly. Initially this was achieved simply by keeping air flowing through the engine even when the driver would come off the throttle as he approached a turn; this would be known as cold blown diffuser technology. Later enhancements would see the engine's ignition timing adjusted so that it would continue to fire without generating torque: 'hot blown' diffusers were born.

Red Bull Racing and Renault's use of this innovation gave them a significant advantage, for, even though the Renault F1 engine produced less power than rivals such as Mercedes and Cosworth, its smooth power delivery and lower fuel consumption allied to hot blown diffuser technology delivered an important advantage. Combined with the ever efficient aerodynamics of its Newey-inspired cars, Red Bull dominated Formula One in 2010 and 2011.

Even when blown diffuser technology was banned in 2012 – thanks to compliance again – Red Bull was able to recover some of that performance after a tough start to the season and re-establish its competitive edge in the latter part of the year thanks to further innovations introduced at the Singapore Grand Prix in September 2012. Developing a configuration that allowed the Red Bull cars to run a much more pronounced front-to-rear rake, harness the remaining exhaust flow and its interaction with the diffuser, and create intricately detailed aerodynamic tweaks at the front of the car helped the team maintain its advantage. The team's domination was reasserted, not only clinching the title for a third time in 2012 but establishing the edge that carried Red Bull Racing and driver Sebastian Vettel to four successive titles in 2013.

Whilst Newey is not wrong to point out that innovation has been stunted to some extent by the FIA's list of proscribed technologies and materials combined with rigid rules applied to car dimensions, weight and so on, it remains the case that innovation remains fundamental to achieving success within the sport. This is particularly the case in respect of the strategy, now employed by several top teams, to diversify their businesses and utilize the innovation culture of Formula One in new markets.

Good examples of this come from McLaren, Williams and Caterham. McLaren's Applied Technologies Division takes innovative technologies and processes, applies them in new fields and creates value for its customers by bringing Formula One's culture of deadline-driven delivery to bear on complex solutions. Williams Hybrid Power and Williams Advanced Engineering have seen that team move to the forefront of hybrid powertrain solutions, developing know-how that has attracted automotive customers including Porsche, Audi and Jaguar Land Rover. Caterham, one of Formula One's newest teams, has taken its investment in carbon composite technology and applied it in areas as diverse as carbon fibre racing bikes and sailing yachts.

Innovation is not just driving these Formula One businesses on track; it is directly helping teams to generate new revenue streams and develop a more robust business model at a time when the traditional sources of funding such as commercial sponsorship have come under threat. With major commercial sponsorship more difficult to secure owing to the fact that these customers have more choice than ever before, and are more rigid in their evaluation of sports sponsorships, the need for Formula One teams to create a range of new revenue opportunities has never been greater. Applying their natural innovation culture to adjacent markets in automotive, aerospace, defence and renewables is opening a new chapter in this sports industry's development.

Understanding the core competences of a Formula One team, and then applying those skills and cultures in new areas of business, is turning out to be a formidable weapon for those teams with the leadership and vision to create a diversified engineering, marketing and business services organization.

McLaren has long held ambitions to outdo Ferrari off the track as well as on it, and their move into becoming a mainstream automotive company began back in 1990 with the creation of the iconic three-seater McLaren F1 road car. Applying an F1-bred approach to vehicle design, the McLaren F1 featured widespread use of lightweight materials including a carbon fibre composite monocoque. McLaren had been the first team to employ carbon fibre in chassis construction, partnering with the Hercules aerospace company to develop the 1982 McLaren MP4/1. The innovation of using carbon fibre to construct the driver's cockpit safety cell delivered a multitude of benefits, being not only extremely light and rigid but very strong. In one fell swoop, performance and safety took a step forward, and eight years later it was being employed in a road-going super-car.

McLaren's prowess in applying its Formula One know-how in road car designs, exemplified by the F1, soon landed them with the opportunity to develop the McLaren Mercedes SLR, including establishing its production facility at the team's new headquarters near Woking. And, when McLaren's ambitions diverged from those of partner and shareholder Mercedes-Benz, the McLaren Group went its own way, with the development of a new range of McLaren sports cars commencing with the MP4/12C launched in 2011.

McLaren's relentless quest to use its Formula One know-how and innovation led it to create a multitude of businesses within its group, including McLaren Electronic Systems, Applied Technologies, McLaren Marketing and high-end hospitality business Absolute Taste. Hard to believe that a Formula One team can be employed to host a corporate event, manage a product launch or provide hospitality services at the Olympic Games.

Innovation in products, operations and delivery is ensuring that McLaren can expand into areas of business apparently unrelated to Formula One. Through this approach the organization is unleashing its future potential and sustaining growth. I often like to describe this as the moment when a company stops thinking in mono and starts working in surround sound, by taking stock of its total capabilities and the intellectual property it commands and applying them to adjacent markets.

Rather in the manner that Apple stopped being a computer company and focused on producing beautifully designed and engineered consumer products for a wide range of customers and market segments, McLaren is no longer merely a Formula One racing team, but a group applying the know-how gleaned from being a consistent winner in Formula One to create high-end engineering, technology and business services solutions.

In the case of Williams, the advent of kinetic energy recovery systems (KERS) in Formula One in 2008 led to the company developing a separate business, which set about developing advanced carbon fibre flywheel energy recovery systems. This division of Williams went on to develop systems installed in high-end sports cars, including the first hybrid car to win the Le Mans 24 Hours endurance race in France. The Audi R18 e-Tron that won the event may have been a great advertisement for Audi, but the flywheel technology that enabled it to clinch victory in a head-to-head battle against the hybrid entries of Toyota were entirely the result of investment in innovation by Williams. The company subsequently successfully sold this technology business to GKN in 2014.

The use of telemetry in Formula One has been widespread since the 1980s, and developing robust, high-performing systems that can cope with the intense heat, vibration, electronic noise and impacts inherent in Grand Prix motor racing has given suppliers such as McLaren Electronic Systems (MES) and Cosworth Electronics a capability now being employed in a variety of new areas.

In partnership with Microsoft, MES produces the standard electronic control unit (ECU) now fitted to every Formula One car, while in 2011 they also won the contract to supply the standard ECU to every competitor in NASCAR, the United States' top form of motor sport. It's ironic to think that NASCAR, with its reputation for focusing on entertainment value over technology, relies on one of Formula One's most capable organizations to provide the control system for each vehicle.

Cosworth Electronics' long-standing reputation for producing data acquisition and monitoring systems was born out of Cosworth's acquisition in 2004 of PI Group, formerly Purnell Instrumentation. Its racing telemetry systems have now been applied in areas as diverse as defence, renewables and sailing.

The UK's Ministry of Defence, faced with the challenge of improvised explosive devices in battlefields such as Afghanistan, identified an urgent operational requirement to instrument military vehicles involved in such incidents and use data acquisition to gather data about explosions and the manner in which injuries and fatalities were being caused. Rather like the path Formula One went on in the post-Senna era, the military is understanding the benefits of taking data systems previously used solely for operational performance and applying them in understanding what it is that is causing fatalities. A roadside bomb may cause a fatality through direct impact on the occupant of the vehicle but, if the data system can teach that more fatalities and serious injuries are being caused by loose ammunition cases and weapons being thrown about inside the vehicle, a route opens up to reducing unnecessary casualties.

Developing a culture of innovation requires management to create the environment within which it can flourish. This is often a challenge when the more mundane requirements of producing a product strictly on time, and within a strict set of rules, appear to leave little room for creativity.

As a result, the ongoing development of the product is divided into three clearly identified phases of design innovation and development. The first phase is the design, development and manufacture of the base product, which has to be produced against a rigid time line so as to make the start of pre-season testing in February each year. Normally this process starts in early summer; at Jordan Grand Prix we would kick off the following year's design in earnest in June, with the new-car designers having used the previous months to look at some overall concepts.

With the base car under way to meet a January build schedule, in the second phase the team starts to look at opportunities to bring further development to the table, some of which may be able to be incorporated within the initial product when it is launched, while others require further analysis prior to being committed. As a result, when the new car is finally launched, there will already be a raft of future developments planned, and these are then rolled out during pre-season testing and into the start of the season, optimizing the performance of the car and hopefully taking its performance on an upward curve.

The third strand is the long-term development of innovations that require more intensive research and development, evaluation and testing to ensure that they meet the requirements of being robust, reliable and of course safe. This is particularly true when you have a significant innovation that will require a step-change in technology, processes or operations.

A good example of technological innovation has come in the form of the 2014 Formula One powertrain regulations. Producing almost the same amount of power as the 2.4-litre V8 engines they replace, these new units feature an extremely small 1.6-litre, single turbocharged internal combustion engine mated to a pair of motor generator units, an electrical energy storage system and control system. The benefit is a reduction in fuel consumption of over 35 per cent, and the development of an impressive petrol–electric power unit, which ensures that Formula One technology remains not only innovative but road-relevant for the automotive companies investing heavily in the sport.

In this instance the driving force behind the innovation was the FIA. It listened to the automotive industry's plea for Formula One to use its research and development capabilities to innovate solutions to the problem of developing powerful but extremely fuel-efficient power units. The 2014 power units answered that demand, and demonstrated how an innovation culture can drive solutions to complex problems.

The advent of the 2014 Formula One powertrain is the latest in a long line of technical innovations that can be plotted back more than six decades, each illustrating the benefits of applying our brainpower to find new, more efficient ways of achieving improved performance. It has been an essential ingredient in the success story of the winning teams and their technical partners, as they continue on their quest for race performance on track and business performance off it.

LESSONS IN INNOVATION

Whatever business sector you look at, be it manufacturing or services, from technology products such as the mobile phone and tablet computer through to low-cost air travel and the convenience of online shopping, innovation is a central driver for all successful companies.

During Formula One's 65-year history we have seen one innovation followed by another, and the legendary names within the sport are associated with step-changes in technology, the radical integration of systems or creating entirely new ways of doing business.

Whether it was John Cooper putting the engines in his cars behind the driver, Cosworth creating an engine that was part of the chassis, or Colin Chapman's Team Lotus turning an F1 car into an inverted aircraft, innovation was driving the continuous quest for competitive advantage.

This has required creativity, courage, lateral thinking and the confidence to question the accepted ways of doing things. If we all do the same as the competition, what will differentiate us or our performance?

To get ahead we need to be prepared to be different, and to innovate without compromising the central pillars of quality, reliability and performance.

Formula One teams innovate with entirely new products each year in order to meet the revised regulations that are constantly being evolved in order to limit performance and enhance safety. Once produced, a Formula One car is then developed, race by race, and this mentality of innovation and continuous improvement is what drives the teams to achieve success. It is a relentless quest for the next performance improvement.

WE CAN SUMMARIZE AS FOLLOWS:

➠ *The winning teams throughout the history of Formula One have tended to be those who innovate in design and the way they integrate technologies into the final product.*

➠ *Innovation can only take place where the culture permits it.* This means incubating ideas, enabling creativity, and encouraging a flow of ideas that question established practice and look at new possibilities. The leadership of an organization has to create an environment where innovation is encouraged and can flourish.

➠ *The process of innovating may involve one person, a team working together or even the entire supply chain.* Suppliers can bring their ideas to the table to help the team develop new approaches. Think Renault and Red Bull Racing.

➠ *The innovators in Formula One often took one technology and integrated it with another to create a better solution:* an engine used as part of a chassis, another engine used as an air pump, or a car using aerodynamics to unleash greater performance.

➠ *Sometimes when the competition innovates and achieves a competitive advantage it may not be possible to duplicate the idea precisely, but replicate the outcome through a separate innovation.* Gordon Murray's Brabham 'fan car' was just as fast as a Lotus 79!

➠ *It is often argued that regulation and compliance stifle innovation.* In reality the real innovators are those who can interrogate the rules and exploit the opportunities, whatever their context. At a time of huge regulation in F1, Red Bull Racing's Adrian Newey has emerged as the industry's greatest ever innovator.

▸ ***Our know-how is our biggest asset.*** In Formula One it has become increasingly common for the innovations developed in one area of the business to be applied in new markets, driving growth and profitability. McLaren's Applied Technologies Division and Williams Advanced Engineering are two such examples of innovation-driven businesses.

▸ ***The 2014 F1 power units have shown how innovation can not only respond to the demands of customers, but address wider challenges.*** Highly efficient, and revolutionary in design, these new units not only have answered the demands of automotive manufacturers but as a result of using 35 per cent less fuel have gone a long way to tackling the challenges of environmental sustainability and social responsibility.

CHAPTER NINE
PERFORMANCE
MANAGEMENT

In Formula One the objective is to try to win, pure and simple. Managing the performance of the car, the driver, the team, and its systems and processes is a never-ending task. There can be only one winner, and for everyone else the outcome is measured by the degree to which you lose. It is often said that finishing second means you are the first of the losers.

There are 11 teams in Formula One, and each of these engineering companies is trying to design, manufacture, develop and operate a pair of Formula One cars with the objective of winning – or, at least, they should. In reality there are teams that aim to win and others that, whether publicly or privately, accept that winning is not a realistic prospect and therefore their objectives become something quite different: surviving as a business, finishing races, scoring points, reaching the podium.

This is fair enough were it not for the fact that in my experience the moment you set a target other than winning you automatically build in an acceptance of not winning – or of losing – and in that decision you fix a compromise that will be hard to shake. One of the aspects of working with Eddie Jordan was the knowledge that the team had won in Formula 3 and Formula 3000, stepping stones to Formula One, and 'EJ' was determined to win in Formula One. These things become self-fulfilling in my view. If you put enough energy into visualizing success and working out what you need to achieve it, it becomes a lot more likely that you can make it happen.

Performance management is important because if your goal is to reach the top the only way you can do that is constantly to review progress, alter tactics along the way and accept that you will have to improve continuously until you win. And, even when you do win, the next task becomes sustaining that success, which means that reviewing performance and reforming where needed are key attributes behind a winning culture.

In Formula One performance management and review are relished, because every time we look at how things are going we have an opportunity to improve. And that's what we want: improvement to the point of winning.

I've been fortunate to work directly with a large number of racing drivers and, no matter what their talent, fame or achievements, their awareness of the need to review performance at every step makes it an intrinsic part of their job. David Coulthard likes to tell the story of how Sebastian Vettel, fresh from winning his World Championship title in Suzuka, Japan, in 2010, went straight into an engineering debrief: to discuss what went right, what went wrong, how they as a team could learn and what could be implemented next time out to sustain their success. Even in the moment of outright victory, the emphasis remained on performance management.

When Irish golfer Paul McGinley won the BMW Munich Open golf championship in 2008 he gave great credit to Eddie Jordan, who had caddied for him and applied some of the techniques we use in Formula One to review performance, fix targets and understand what we have to do in order to win. Speaking to the *Sunday Times*, McGinley described how Eddie reviewed their performance as they progressed, breaking the golf round into sections, explaining what was required next if they were to be on target. This was Eddie bringing well-honed skills from Formula One to bear on the golf course; and it worked.

A Formula One car is our product, and in order to monitor the performance of both the product and the driver we instrument it with up to 200 sensors and a sophisticated telemetry system that enables the team to monitor the performance of every technical system and human input in real time. To some extent this is the driver reduced to the role of machine operator. Given that we need the machine to be operated in a very specific way in order to derive optimal performance then we want to ensure that the car, the driver and the way they interact are fully measured.

When I started working in Formula One in the 1980s teams did not have data systems to provide raw information on what was happening to the vehicle's systems, or indeed what the driver was doing. Systems to monitor performance were rudimentary.

The most obvious performance monitoring system was the humble stopwatch. Armed with a few of those, you could still do quite a lot.

The first thing was to monitor the performance of our drivers by timing them over a single lap, giving us a base metric. Then we can time them over a sequence of laps, giving an insight into the consistency of performance of driver and car. This can be further extended to time them on an 'out lap', when they are leaving the pits, or an 'in lap', when they are returning: important information to have when planning pit stop strategies and their effect on total race time.

When we also time drivers' team mates, we double the amount of information available, allowing us to compare driver performance over the course of a lap or multiple laps, to see whether one is quicker than the other, more or less consistent. As a general rule if a lap time of two Formula One drivers armed with the same car and identical settings varies by more than 0.15 second, then one of them is likely to come under scrutiny.

The stopwatch can also be used to time the drivers around individual sections, or 'sectors', of the track, and even specific corners. Monitoring the performance of sector times and corner times was commonplace during the pre-data age, and remains an important way of gauging driver and car performance when you want to take it to the most basic level.

Measuring a corner time is very useful. Most race tracks have key corners where a lot of performance can be won or lost, and to start with it is important to get it right here before going on to look at the corners that offer much smaller increments of performance improvement.

Using a stopwatch to monitor corner times means selecting two fixed points on the track prior to the braking area for the corner and after its exit, and then timing the car and its competitors between those points. The observer with the stopwatch can not only record the total time it takes to complete the corner, but also watch the behaviour of the car under braking, cornering and acceleration – effectively the three 'phases' of each corner – as well as the racing line or trajectory through the corner that the driver steers. With a second stopwatch it can even be possible to time one or more of those phases.

With a set of corner times and observations on how a driver brakes, changes gear, steers and accelerates, an experienced observer can glean a significant amount about a driver's performance, that of the driver's team mate and of course that of the competition.

This technique of timing a car and driver over a specific sector of track might appear odd at first, but in Formula One the way to win is to deconstruct the overall performance required to win over 60 or 70 laps and break it down into ever smaller units of measurement. A 300-kilometre race ends up being measured in centimetres, 100 minutes of performance reviewed in tenths and hundredths of a second, and laps broken down into sectors, corners and their constituent parts.

Most race tracks have certain characteristics, whether being a low-, medium- or high-speed circuit featuring certain topography, types of corners and so on. If you take a circuit like Monte Carlo, for example, it is unique in having the shortest lap of any F1 track, at 3.34 kilometres, and doesn't have a single 'straight' – it is essentially twisty across its entire length, which means the drivers have to cope with constant, finely balanced changes of direction. This means the track requires intense focus, with little time to 'relax'.

Monte Carlo can be broken into three sectors. The first sector takes drivers across the start–finish line down to the right-handed corner at Ste Devote, then up the steep hill, curving left–right–left–right as it goes, before the fast left-hander into Casino Square and then right, downhill towards the Mirabeau hairpin. The timed sector 1 ends just before Mirabeau, which means that an analysis of that sector involves three corners, with the relevant stages of braking, cornering and acceleration. Comparing your two drivers over that single sector will show you where the opportunities might arise to improve performance; one might be quicker than the other at turn 1, or the roles might be reversed in turn 2. If you can review those performances, drill into the details of what is happening, you may be able to help both achieve a better performance, whether from within themselves or from a change to the set-up of the car.

A very different style of track is Monza in Italy, which is 5.793 kilometres in length and high-speed in nature: long straights separated by a series of three chicanes and fast-flowing corners. Here is a track where drivers do have time to 'relax' on the straights, and in the case of Monza sector 1 features far fewer changes of direction than for Monte Carlo. A long straight leads into the first chicane, a tight right–left taken in second gear, and then a long acceleration around the curving right-hander known as Curva Biassono, ending sector 1 before the entry to the Della Roggia chicane.

As a result of there being 'less to do' in sector 1 of Monza compared to Monte Carlo, with only a single braking and/or downshift in gears as opposed to three, it is easier to see immediately where the difference in performance – or performance delta as it's called – is coming from.

Measuring and managing performance in Formula One is all about taking the overall target, working out what you need to get there and then breaking it down into smaller increments until ultimately you are looking at individual bits of data showing how a specific aspect is working at a precise moment in time.

We start with the goal of completing a race of 300 kilometres in distance at the fastest possible speed. Considering the pit stops are mandatory and that you will therefore make at least one pit stop, factors such as weather, track temperature, tyre degradation, fuel consumption, lap length and pit lane time are just some of the variables taken into account in determining the optimal strategy. In the event that two pit stops are chosen, this means that the 300 kilometres are already divided into three parts, namely a first, second and third 'stint'.

Each stint will consist of a predicted number of laps, and on a 5-kilometre track the 300-kilometre race will therefore consist of 60 laps divided into three stints, with the performance over each stint combining to determine the race outcome. Consistency of performance over each lap, and across each stint, is key, so lap times need to be managed effectively by the driver and the team to ensure that, whilst there may be peaks and troughs according to variables such as tyre wear and fuel load, the cumulative effect is to achieve the fastest time over the course of the race.

Starting position is an important variable, of course, since clearly those starting from pole position, first place on the starting grid, have a theoretical advantage over the remaining 21 cars and their drivers. With a clear track ahead and no one in front to take into consideration, the driver starting from pole position has a greater range of options than any other competitor. But to start from pole position requires getting the most out of the car over a single lap during qualifying the day before the race, and that is only possible if you drive the optimal lap. So, whether in the race or qualifying, maximizing performance over the course of your 5-kilometre lap is key.

Aside from using a series of stopwatches to monitor individual driver and car performance, together with that of team mates and the competition, early performance management included examining a range of variables that would provide valuable information. Key among these would be temperature of the tyres, and the range of temperatures across the surface of the tyre that provide an insight into how the tyre's contact patch with the track is behaving. Tyre pressure is also a critical performance factor, and taking tyre pressures along with the temperatures as soon as the car returned to the pit lane was a basic task.

So too was reviewing information from the car's instrumentation: water and oil temperatures, oil and fuel pressure, or any indication of an engine over-rev. Any one of these measurements could point an engineer in the direction of a problem, whether it be overheating caused by a water leak or a deterioration in engine performance reflected in falling oil pressure.

These early systems also relied heavily on the final, most important factor: the feedback from drivers and the way in which they could articulate this to their engineers and achieve consensus regarding the car's performance and where improvements could be made. Having a driver who not only can drive the car at maximum speed but also has the ability to recall key performance points around the race track has always been extremely valuable.

Drivers who can return to the pits and then describe each lap in detail, giving the engineers critical insight into vehicle performance, become a huge asset to their team. Drivers need to drive quickly, but their intellectual ability and technical understanding of the car and what is happening on each straight and each phase of a corner are enormously important. Under braking, drivers may realize that there is a slight bump in the track a few centimetres to one side or the other, and as a result adjust their racing line to achieve a smoother, more stable entry or exit.

Drivers who are 'sympathetic' to their cars possess an important skill, because listening to and feeling the car's performance through the hands on the steering wheel, feet on the pedals and, sometimes, seat of the pants can give important clues to performance. By feeling a vibration under braking or a changing level of resistance in the steering, or perhaps by using their hearing or sense of smell, drivers can sense something that the engineer will find useful.

There is a famous story about Ayrton Senna providing feedback to his Honda engine technicians during a test session in the 1980s that there was something wrong with the engine in the back of his McLaren: a slight change in tone, something 'different'. The Honda technicians checked everything, using some of the early data systems that allowed information to be loaded on to a laptop in the garage, and they came to the conclusion that everything was fine. Shortly afterwards the engine suffered a catastrophic failure, proving that a sensitive and alert driver could spot problems even the experts missed. This added further to the mystique surrounding Senna.

At the opposite end of the spectrum was a driver like Jean Alesi, who early in his career could produce a prodigious amount of speed without fully understanding the reasons behind it, apart from his own innate talent of course. Dropped by Marlboro from its Marlboro World Championship Team programme in Formula 3000 he was snapped up by Eddie Jordan for the 1989 season and would go on to win it in triumphant style, graduating to Formula One the next year.

But it was evident to the engineers at Eddie Jordan Racing that Jean could have good days and bad days, certainly times when if the mood wasn't right his performances would wane. In this case his feedback was invariably that there was something wrong with the car's set-up, and he would recommend changes. This was often to the bemusement of engineers who knew exactly how the Reynard 89D F3000 car should best work, thanks to the input of Alesi's team mate, my old friend Martin Donnelly.

As a result, on one occasion, the team decided that Jean's feedback was such that they opted to tell him his recommended changes had been made to the car – except they had left it exactly the same. Armed with a new frame of mind and belief that his car had been technically improved, the newly motivated Alesi promptly went out and set a much improved lap time.

Although Jean later developed into a very complete Formula One driver, albeit only winning a single Grand Prix during his career, the differences in feedback and analysis between himself and someone of Senna's ability are significant. When the human aspect of performance is introduced to something as technically complex as Formula One race car operation, consistency of performance becomes critical.

Faced with the multiple performance variables involving tyres, suspension, chassis, aerodynamics, engine and transmission, never mind the external variables such as weather and track condition, the engineers have a lot to think about in extracting maximum performance. As a result, the human being behind the wheel of the car should ideally be able to provide a consistent, highly stable degree of performance, which allows the engineers the benefit of knowing that the driver input is entirely reliable.

Imagine one scenario where a driver is producing lap times that are ±0.5 second each lap. That gives you a 1-second variation just because the driver is inconsistent and unable to repeat inputs at the same time and place in successive laps. This makes it extremely difficult for the engineering community to determine the result of any set-up changes they may have made, or to drill into any issues. You are working against an unstable and entirely variable baseline.

Then take a driver who is able to replicate performance lap after lap, to within ±0.1 second, giving a spread of 0.2 seconds against a backdrop of the car's performance at the point in time, including fuel load, tyre wear and so on. This is hugely beneficial to the team, as they can effectively forget about the driver as a variable, and know that whatever changes they make to the car will be reflected in lap time, such is the consistency of driver inputs.

At the 2013 Italian Grand Prix, for example, a quick analysis of the performance of four times World Champion Sebastian Vettel shows the extent of his ability in consistency as much as speed. On laps 7 and 8 of the race he achieved a lap time of 1 minute, 29.119 seconds and 1 minute, 29.101 seconds respectively, a variation of 0.018 second, while on laps 10 and 11 he drove the 5.783-kilometre track in 1 minute, 28.985 seconds and 1 minute, 28.980 seconds, a difference of 0.005 second. Five-thousandths of a second over one lap equates to extra distance of 32.5 centimetres, which might be accounted for by a marginally different racing line at one or two corners, but in reality that performance delta will come from a range of minuscule differences in the performance of driver and machine. From an engineering perspective, it is an entirely consistent performance, the variation being 0.0056 per cent.

This is the kind of performance that sets the great drivers apart from the good ones, and an analysis of the lap times delivered by the Vettels, Schumachers and Alonsos of this world will bear that out. It isn't uncommon to see drivers achieve an identical lap time, down to a thousandth of a second, such is their unerring ability to achieve a high level of driving performance and maintain that level for lap after lap throughout a race.

Obviously other variables will change, affecting lap time as the race progresses: fuel load for one, as the car starts to lighten as the 100-kilogram weight of fuel is gradually reduced. Again, if you look at the 2013 Italian Grand Prix Vettel did his fastest lap on the penultimate lap of the race, as did Ferrari's Fernando Alonso, while Vettel's team mate Mark Webber achieved his personal best on the very last lap when his fuel load would have been at its lightest – a perfect performance trajectory.

Performance management in 2014, however, is on an entirely new level compared with those early stopwatch-based systems combined with vehicle instrumentation and engineer–driver discussions.

As the information technology age started to develop in the late 1980s we began to see laptops appear in the garages, notably used by engine manufacturers like Honda to monitor the performance of their units, adjust the mapping of those early electronic control units and run basic diagnostic systems.

Today that has developed into the entire car being fully instrumented in such a way that the team can performance-manage it through each practice and qualifying session, plus the race itself, optimizing performance and minimizing risk. The instrumentation of the vehicle and development of these sophisticated, real-time telemetry systems mean that we can see precisely how our product is performing as well as the driver operating it.

In some ways telemetry is the ultimate Big Brother system, for we can see in real time how drivers are operating their cars: the precise moment when they brake, steer, accelerate and change gear, the amount of pressure they apply to the brakes, the percentage of throttle being used and, best of all, their ability to deliver sustained performance.

Typically each driver will benefit from a minimum of three data analysis technicians track-side: men and women who sit in front of computer racks looking at the real-time data streams, each focusing on a specific range of parameters to evaluate performance. The systems are designed to highlight anomalies, so that the technicians are immediately alerted to a problem that has started to develop; most of the information is run-of-the-mill, confirming that everything is working fine. The information that is interesting allows you either to tackle a problem, thus mitigating risk, or perhaps to see where some additional performance can be gained.

An example of risk mitigation might come from seeing the front or rear brakes overheating, which enables the data engineer to speak to the race engineer, who can then radio the driver and explain that the driver should change the brake bias front to rear or vice versa, brake less harshly or perhaps use more of the available engine braking. In the closing stages of some races such as in Montreal, a circuit notoriously hard on brakes, this kind of information can make the difference between finishing and retiring, winning and losing.

Aside from real-time analysis and diagnostics track-side, contemporary teams feed the data, audio and TV images back to their headquarters, allowing teams of engineers, managers and strategists to monitor performance away from the heat and emotion of the race track. Enabling the team to make a cool analysis of overall performance is enormously useful since, armed with the 'big picture' rather than the small slice of information available to individual drivers, engineers and technicians track-side, the teams back at mission control have a vast array of information available.

One of the first examples of this approach paying dividends came for the McLaren team at the 2005 Monaco Grand Prix when a serious accident on lap 23 effectively blocked the track. While their competitors took the more obvious decision to use the track blockage and safety car period to carry out a pit stop, McLaren's chief strategist Neil Martin, following proceedings from the team's headquarters in Surrey, made a split-second call for Kimi Raikkonen not to make a pit stop and remain on track. It turned out to be a winning decision based on having the overall picture of what was happening and an understanding of how the optimal result could be achieved.

Aside from the benefit of being able to monitor the car and driver in real time, the significant point about telemetry is the ability to sit down and review every aspect of performance in practice, in qualifying and after the race.

This means that the team's management, engineers, key suppliers and drivers can sit down together and debrief after each occasion on which the cars have been run and examine the precise detail of what happened. The data is available, together with audio and video recordings, combined with the notes taken by race engineers, the information provided by the engine and tyre technicians, and the feedback from the drivers.

There is no room to hide. This is not a performance review being carried out once a quarter or once a year. This is every day, after every session, and everyone's performance is open to scrutiny. It is not for the faint-hearted.

I remember one of my Cosworth engine technicians going into his first engineering debrief with the Williams team in 2010 and emerging, ashen-faced, after facing the reality of having a legendary driver like Rubens Barrichello criticizing the dip in the torque curve of the engine. You need to know your facts, stand your ground, and be prepared if necessary to tell anyone – even a highly paid and famous driver – if you agree or disagree and have the data-based evidence to support your statements.

Everyone in these debriefs can face detailed analysis of their performance; it could be a driver who made mistakes out on the track, a chassis engineer whose set-up changes failed to have the desired effect, or an engine supplier whose specific circuit mapping did not provide the right combination of performance, power delivery and fuel economy.

For the drivers in particular it can be an uncomfortable moment, especially if you are being consistently beaten by your team mate. The data from both cars is made available for all to see in the meeting, with theoretical optimal lap times compared to the reality of what the drivers achieved and, of course, the differences between drivers examined.

Given that the race track is divided into three sectors, an examination of sector times will be made during qualifying, for example, with each driver's best sector times being added together to show what the best lap time could have been. Often the drivers will themselves have managed to achieve three best sector times to put together the optimal lap, and ultimately that's what drivers should be trying to achieve. In reality they often will have a best lap time, which sees a great performance over one or two sectors and a slight underperformance in the third. This is why so much emphasis is put on a driver 'putting a lap together', which is racing jargon for achieving a personal best performance in each sector over the course of a single qualifying lap.

By examining the data the team can show drivers exactly where each gain or loss in performance is achieved as they drive, right down to individual braking points, where they changed gear, which gear they were in and how much steering input they were making. Drivers can be shown how they performed not only over a given lap, but over a series of laps, concentrating on any inconsistencies.

It is also very useful to overlay the data from one driver with that of the driver's team mate. Taking their two best laps, we can then see where the delta in performance arose, and this is closely scrutinized.

When Sebastian Vettel qualified on pole position for the 2013 United States Grand Prix in Austin, Texas, with a lap time of 1 minute, 36.338 seconds and his team mate Mark Webber was second with a time of 1 minute, 36.441 seconds, the team was able to go into the debrief and see exactly where that 0.103-second delta in performance came from. As the data traces were overlaid there will have been tiny differences in performance visible in terms of vehicle speed, braking and acceleration that together added up to a tenth of a second over the course of 5.513 kilometres – an incredibly small margin, but sufficient to be the difference between first and second.

At the Williams team in the same event, however, the margin of difference between its drivers Valtteri Bottas and Pastor Maldonado was significant: a full 0.53 second, which was the difference between Bottas making it through to the second period of qualifying – or Q2 – and ultimately starting the race in ninth, and Maldonado being eliminated after Q1 and starting 18th. Considering they were driving the same-specification car, focus in the debrief will have been on why there was such a significant difference in performance. The team and drivers will have been able to see where that half a second was gained by Bottas, in this instance around the entire lap, and ultimately the data led the team to deduce that the Finn had been better able to get his tyres up to working temperature than Maldonado.

This relentless performance monitoring is an accepted part of the Formula One culture. David Coulthard told me that when he retired from racing and became a commentator for the BBC he expected that after each broadcast everyone involved in the production would have a meeting and discuss what went right, what went wrong, and where they could improve next time out. It didn't happen and, when David asked why, he was told that such an approach might risk upsetting some people if their mistakes or gaffes were discussed in an open forum.

Applied to business, it is interesting that many businesses do indeed review performance constantly, but more often the performance review is taken on the basis of historical financial data, or sales figures, often on a quarterly basis. Reviews of human performance are usually much less rigorous or frequent. We all dislike being scrutinized.

But F1's lesson is that constant performance review is required to drive a culture of relentless improvement. It requires certain things to be in place: honesty, openness and transparency for all parties. It also requires that criticism is seen as constructive, that we are all in this together and everyone has to deliver, every time. And it cannot succeed where there is a lack of trust or, worse, a blame culture. The purpose of continuous performance management in F1 is to learn how we can do better, not to find someone to blame. And most people, most of the time, will welcome the opportunity to see how they can improve and learn from it. If the process unveils a weak link, a system or person who continuously underperforms, then you can do something about it.

One of the things that often happens in managing performance is that so much time is spent looking at the historical data, seeing what went right and what went wrong, that too little time is spent on applying the lessons learned to make sure that the future is better. This was one of David Coulthard's comments to me when he joined Red Bull Racing and witnessed some of the old systems still in place from the team's time under Jaguar ownership; people were obsessed with producing long reports on what had happened in the past. Part of the culture shift under Red Bull, and in part using David's knowledge from driving for McLaren and Williams, was to learn quickly where the improvements could be made and then apply solutions as rapidly as possible. You don't win any race by looking in the mirrors.

LESSONS IN PERFORMANCE MANAGEMENT

Every aspect of Formula One is dedicated to achieving high performance, whether in the sophistication and quality of the engineering, the unerring focus on delivery, or ensuring that the car and driver can outperform the competition.

Owing to the competitive nature of the sport, and the sheer complexity of the activity, we need to apply clear targets and constantly measure our performance against them. The key performance indicators (KPIs) are essential in order for us to know where we stand in relation to our overall objectives.

A KPI might be an individual car's lap time given as a percentage of the optimal time achieved by any Formula One car on that circuit, or it might be a measure of one driver's performance set against that of the driver's team mate. But our KPIs are also going to include measurements of quality, safety and human performance, including absence from work and time keeping – any one of dozens of KPIs that, when put together, can show us how well we are performing externally against our competitors and internally as a team striving to achieve ambitious goals.

Performance management is therefore a key discipline, requiring rigorous and systematic processes of setting targets, agreeing strategies to achieve them and reviewing our progress.

Human nature being what it is, many people struggle with the notion of continuous review and performance appraisal, but it need only be feared whenever the culture of the business is negative and destructive. In a competitive Formula One team the leadership knows that the targets can only be achieved if all involved, suppliers included, work together as a team, win and lose as a team, and continuously learn from collective mistakes and inefficiencies.

When Formula One teams perform pit stop practice, for example, the team manager times each practice stop, reviews the overall performance with the pit crew, and discusses reasons for mistakes or hold-ups, and together they apply the lessons learned. The outcome of many dozens of practice pit stops is that not only does the team come to regard them as second nature, but incremental improvements in performance are turned into time saved.

KEY FACTORS TO BEAR IN MIND:

⫸ *Be very clear about your goals and objectives.* Only by doing so can you measure actual performance and put in place the steps needed to achieve your goals and objectives.

⫸ *Make sure that everyone is aligned behind the goals, and understands why they are there and what the KPIs mean.* Getting buy-in is essential.

⫸ *Create a culture where constant review is welcomed, not feared.* This means honesty, transparency, trust and eagerness to improve.

⫸ *A high-performance culture learns from its mistakes.* Everyone makes mistakes, and we learn most from them. A blame culture is a lame culture.

⫸ *Do not compromise on your goals; otherwise that may become the norm.* If you want to be number one in your field then make that your target even if there are intermediate milestones.

⫸ *Visualize what achieving your goal will look and feel like.* Project yourself into that position; consider what it will take to capture that kind of performance.

⇒ ***Break your performance into its constituent parts.*** Think about F1 drivers and their performance engineers, scrutinizing each centimetre of a lap in order to build towards achieving the optimal performance.

⇒ ***Examine where the gains are coming from, and the losses.*** F1 drivers will want to see where they might be losing time. They can then focus on making precise improvements.

⇒ ***Remember the human factor.*** Whatever the activity, human performance will affect the outcome, so look at the KPIs affecting your people and their ability to deliver.

⇒ ***Be consistent in how you measure.*** Top teams want consistent drivers, because they realize that having a consistent baseline performance provides a solid foundation.

⇒ ***The truth is in the data.*** Invest in IT systems that give you speedy access to relevant data, enabling you to see the anomalies in performance and pinpoint weaknesses.

CHAPTER TEN
COMMUNICATION

I have a Ferrari Formula One steering wheel, which sits in a case in the corner of my office. It's a replica of the steering wheel from the Ferrari F10 that Fernando Alonso and Felipe Massa raced during the 2010 Formula One World Championship, and I often use it to illustrate a number of points about contemporary Formula One. One point is the degree of functionality provided to the driver by means of toggles, switches, levers and dials on the steering wheel; on the F10 wheel there are 29 in total, including dials for the fuel and air mixture going into the engine, one for 'strategy multifunction', another for the engine torque map and even a button to operate the pump on the drinks bottle.

When you examine the wheel carefully, and hold it in your hands, it becomes clear that the engineers have carefully thought through the ergonomics of the unit and agreed with the drivers the best location for each switch or dial. With both hands on the wheel, for example, only the thumbs remain available to operate functions; four buttons are within immediate reach of the thumb, and two sit naturally in range of the thumbs when at rest: the radio and the oil pump.

This tells us quite a lot about the key priorities for the driver to be considering, for the auxiliary oil pump is essentially to ensure effective operation of the engine – in reality the very heart of the car – while the radio button enables the driver to do the one thing that can help more than anything else: communicate with the team. Taking all the other complex systems into account, and assuming for one moment that the car is operating precisely as it should do, any driver knows that, when it comes to implementing race strategy, developing tactics, mitigating risks and seeking optimal performance, communication is all important.

I would go as far as to say that, above all other skills, the ability or inability to communicate has been central to some of the greatest successes and failures I have witnessed during my career. Craig Pollock, former manager of World Champion Jacques Villeneuve and later team principal of British American Racing, has said that more races have been lost as a result of communications problems than for any other reason. I would agree, since the teams and drivers who communicate most successfully and consistently invariably achieve a competitive edge over their rivals simply by having a more complete picture of what's going on and being able to respond accordingly.

I often say that the ability of drivers is proportionate to their communications skills, for, when you examine how the great World Champions like Ayrton Senna and Michael Schumacher worked, their ability to process information, communicate with the team during the race and provide excellent feedback were core skills. And when I say 'communicate', I mean listen as well as talk.

I remember early in the 1998 season the team manager at Jordan Grand Prix commenting to me that one of the revelations of working with former World Champion Damon Hill was the fact that, when he entered the pit lane during a race, preparing for a pit stop, he had the presence of mind to press the radio button and simply say the words 'In the pit lane'. This simple communication meant that the pit crew, prepared for the pit stop but perhaps uncertain about the car's exact track position, knew that they had perhaps 10 to 15 seconds to ready themselves for the rapid-fire pit stop that is such a key aspect of the race.

The previous year we had worked with Giancarlo Fisichella and Ralf Schumacher, two relative rookies, and good communication was not their strong point. In Hill we had a driver who had seven years and 21 Grand Prix victories behind him, and whose experience of working with the Williams F1 team had taught him much, particularly in respect of good communication.

It's these little moments of discovery that are so important in racing, and something as simple as a driver recognizing that it's a good idea to inform the team when he is in the pit lane may seem incredibly obvious, yet is so easily overlooked.

Television viewers watching Formula One racing have become used to hearing short radio messages from the drivers as part of the broadcast.

These messages are delayed, partly to avoid any unfortunate language that may have been used in the heat of battle, but they are also a tiny fraction of the radio communications that actually take place.

For drivers sitting in their race car, perhaps leading the race without the benefit of a reference point in front of them to gauge performance, having the right information at the right time is critical. The drivers' view of the world is confined to the tight cockpit in which they sit, with the steering wheel in front of them providing some information via the read-outs embedded in its face. Dashboards have long since disappeared.

The drivers can see the track in front of them, perhaps for 300–500 metres, and they are primarily focused on steering the car through the best trajectory on the race track. They will glance down at the steering wheel read-outs, of course, but only on the longer straights, and aside from that the only other obvious information can be gleaned from a quick look at the rear-view mirrors delicately situated on either side of the cockpit. They are not very large, 150 millimetres wide and 50 millimetres high, so at best drivers can use them to confirm that there is a car behind and, from its colour, which team it belongs to.

The information available to drivers is quite limited, therefore, providing only a small slice of the information necessary for them to get the most out of the race, adjust their strategy and respond to what is happening around them. Quite often the most critical factors affecting the drivers' race are happening somewhere else on the circuit, far beyond their vision or understanding; a competitor may have pitted unexpectedly, an accident may have occurred or rain might be falling on just one part of the track.

It's interesting in the modern era that F1 drivers' desire for information is so great that it is quite common for them to log the position of the giant spectator screens situated around the track and glance up at them. Watching TV at 320 kph may not seem the best idea, but even a quick look at a screen may divulge some piece of vital information, particularly given that the TV broadcasters will necessarily be focusing on the most interesting developments in the race. Awareness of an accident, or seeing a rival in the pit lane, might just provide a winning edge.

One of Ferrari's senior engineers confided in me at the height of Michael Schumacher's five consecutive World Championship wins that one of the most impressive aspects of his ability was the constant dialogue he maintained with the team throughout each race. He wanted to know how the strategy was developing, what their rivals were doing, which McLaren was parked at the side of the race track and so on. Driving the car flat out came naturally to him, so he was using his intellectual bandwidth to the fullest extent by communicating as much as possible. Schumacher knew the importance of sending and receiving the right information in a timely manner.

Jordan Grand Prix won the 1999 French Grand Prix in Magny-Cours because we had a secret weapon standing in a field down the road from the track and radioing in pinpoint information about the weather and particularly the arrival of heavy rain during the first half-hour of the race. That secret weapon came in the form of Dave, the driver of our hospitality unit, who had seconded himself into the role of rain-spotter and as a result was able to tell us that the rain that was on its way was not a shower, but a prolonged deluge.

Based on that critical information our engineers were able to switch Heinz-Harald Frentzen from a two-stop strategy to a single stop. Initially maintaining his fifth place he later was elevated one place at a time when Rubens Barrichello, Michael Schumacher, David Coulthard and Mika Hakkinen had peeled off into the pit lane for more fuel. Against the odds, but thanks to fantastic team work and vital communication from Dave, Heinz-Harald moved into the lead and won the race.

Standing in our hospitality unit with 450 guests from all our major customers, I was delighted to be able to share with them the fact that while Heinz had driven superbly, and the Jordan 199 was a great car, the deciding factor was our 'bus driver' and his ability to communicate the right piece of information to the team at the critical moment.

'How on earth did you guys manage to do that?' television commentator Murray Walker asked me afterwards. I was able to introduce him to our secret weapon.

If great communication is vital in the heat of battle, the day-to-day life of any business requires no less attention in this respect.

In terms of maintaining good relationships with two key audiences, communication with customers and suppliers is sometimes overlooked. Customers are the lifeblood of any business and, while winning new customers is essential in driving growth, maintaining existing relationships and benefiting from customer loyalty are no less important in Formula One than any other activities.

One of my major criticisms of motor racing teams was the huge effort they could put into securing a sponsor only to forget about the importance of servicing them. Why put yourself in the position of having to find a replacement for a disgruntled customer in two or three years' time when a better course would be to create a long-lasting relationship where the customer keeps coming back because you deliver value for them year in, year out?

At Jordan Grand Prix I looked outside the business towards McLaren and wondered how they could maintain relationships with their customers for so long. McLaren had decades-long customer relationships with companies like Marlboro, Hugo Boss, Exxon Mobil and TAG Heuer. At Jordan we had struggled to maintain relationships longer than two to three years.

As a result I implemented a series of initiatives aimed at delivering more value to our customers, and providing means of interacting with them day to day. This included appointing dedicated account managers to maintain communications with the customers on a day-to-day basis, hosting an annual customer conference where we could outline our plans for the season and enable them to network, and launching an intranet that would enable customers to place orders for assets such as hospitality, show cars and driver appearances. Looking back, I met a lot of resistance to the intranet, but as time would show it was an online customer relationship management system – and ahead of its time.

Similarly we initiated a range of tools that enabled us to communicate better with our suppliers. This included an annual supplier conference, and access to day-to-day communication tools including *J Magazine*, our in-house publication. We were the first F1 team to produce a commercially viable, quarterly publication enjoyed by all the team's core audiences and stakeholders.

Supplier communications is important for a number of reasons. First of all the culture of delivery within Formula One teams has to be cascaded within our suppliers; otherwise we'd have everything ready to go only to find that a key supplier is working to an entirely different deadline.

A business consultant criticized Jordan's management for enjoying relationships with key suppliers that were regarded as being 'too close', and potentially a threat to the business because of overfamiliarity and a lack of corporate governance. Frankly this was entirely wrong and missed the point about F1 teams; the very reason we are able to deliver is that we keep our suppliers close and make them feel part of our team. It is not an arm's length relationship.

It is very important that suppliers tender for business in the normal manner, face regular reviews and understand that they have to remain competitive. But once that process has been put in place my experience has been that you need both formal and informal systems in place to communicate with and manage that relationship.

The formal systems, such as the ordering of goods and services facilitated by enterprise resource systems (ERPs) such as SAP and Microsoft Dynamics, are essential. The benefits of having a correctly integrated ERP system featuring the functionality required to manage the business more efficiently outweigh the inevitable issues that are created during its implementation.

Suppliers are well used to responding to demand created on such systems, but it is equally important to have informal systems that can support that. Chris Jilbert, a talented engineer who ran factory operations for me at Cosworth, once said that the most important part of an F1 engine was the part you don't have. F1 engines are assembled by hand, the engine builders working from a kit provided for each unit, and not having one small component, seal or grommet can stop the entire operation. With an F1 customer like Frank Williams expecting his engines to be delivered precisely to schedule, a weak message saying that it's been delayed because a supplier didn't deliver on time isn't going to hold water.

The culture within the sport requires that it should be possible to call a supplier 24/7. A Friday night telephone call at 8 pm asking for an overnight machining job to be loaded should not be unexpected. It may not be ideal, but if that is what is required to get the job done then there should not be an obstacle to it. Equally, the team will require that the supplier can accommodate such a request, because that is the very nature of our business. It's all about delivery and doing what is necessary to make that happen.

Our colleagues in finance invariably wave their hands in horror at that moment and point out the cost of unplanned production, outside of normal hours, with a correspondingly high charge rate or penalty price. But of course, considering that such an eventuality is highly likely in a fast-paced R&D-centric industry such as Formula One, factoring those emergency jobs into pricing at the contract stage should help avoid financial shocks.

Being the last member of staff to fly to a Grand Prix can be a challenging experience, since the team's supply chain managers will know that you could potentially bring out any last-minute components or supplies required by the team on the other side of the world. As a result I have been variously asked to carry items such as a wiring loom, suspension components, carbon fibre bodywork and even a spare steering wheel in my luggage. It can make for an interesting check-in conversation.

I recall standing behind Jackie Oliver, boss of the Arrows team, when he was checking in for a flight. In answer to the question about luggage he had to admit he would need a little excess allowance as he had a Formula One engine weighing 110 kilograms in a freight container. It wasn't a cheap flight.

So maintaining close relationships with suppliers can be vital in our delivery-focused environment, and the combination of formal and informal communications systems ensures that surprises are removed from the system for both parties.

Staff engagement is another area where I have seen great communication make a difference in significant ways. Considering that 85 per cent of the staff in a Formula One team never travel to races, with all the glamour, prestige and life experiences that travelling around the world can bring, keeping them motivated and fully focused on the job in hand is just as important as for the mechanics geared up for a 3-second pit stop.

If you put yourself in the position of a factory-based member of a Formula One team, perhaps working in marketing, administration, sub-assembly or the design office, imagine the feeling when, on a Monday morning, your race team colleagues arrive in the office. Perhaps they are sporting a suntan, complaining about being tired after a week in Monte Carlo or Melbourne, and then telling stories about some restaurant in Montreal or a hilarious episode in their hotel in Milan. It's not necessarily what the factory staff want to hear.

Maintaining morale is important. We want to make the all-important factory-based staff feel that they are every bit as valuable to the team as any mechanic, engineer or manager gracing the pit lane. Good communication becomes an important tool in the recognition process.

In the early stages of Jordan Grand Prix's history Eddie Jordan, team manager Trevor Foster and technical director Gary Anderson literally knew every single member of staff. There were around 35 of us in January 1991. This close-knit team had great morale and excellent communications; Eddie could stop while walking through the workshop and ask a mechanic how his girlfriend was, or debate a football result. The relationship was personal.

Later, as the team grew, Eddie stated that he didn't like not knowing all the staff any more. He didn't even know the names of some of the people he was meeting in the corridors or canteen. He even said that if the team ever employed more than 100 people he would sell up and do something else.

Years later, with staff levels approaching 300, we dealt with the issue of staff engagement by communicating on a number of fronts and providing activities that could bind the workforce together at least twice a year, typically with the family events at the British Grand Prix and then the end-of-year Christmas party.

In respect of communications, debriefs were held, to which every member of staff was invited, on the Tuesday or Wednesday following each Grand Prix. These were held in the race shop, which had the largest available floor area, and attendance was usually good, though never 100 per cent. We did have a second facility, the wind tunnel centre in Brackley, and often the debrief would have to repeated for them, since their workload meant that a trip up to headquarters at Silverstone was regarded as lost time. This in itself was interesting because, as sure as we would hold the debriefs, the very people who failed to attend were invariably those who then complained about a lack of communication from the management.

The debriefs were very regular, therefore, and hosted by Eddie as CEO, a managing director or a technical director. There would be a review of the past race weekend, an update on developments from both a technical and a commercial viewpoint, and then a Q&A. Individual members of staff might be recognized for their particular achievement, or some issue affecting the company discussed. The whole point was that the communications channel was open and it was two-way.

The walk-about by senior management remained an important aspect of engagement and communication with the staff. It might take only 30 minutes, but it meant that personnel could discuss topics, share a joke and most importantly feel that their work was being appreciated.

Eddie Jordan also initiated an ideas box, which personnel could use to post ideas to be considered by the management board, principally split into the categories of 'making the car go faster', 'improving efficiency' and 'saving money'. These ideas could be sifted through each month and considered at senior management level.

The importance of having great communications from the top down was shown in Dietrich Mateschitz's inaugural address to the workforce at Red Bull Racing shortly after his purchase of the team from Ford Motor Company. In spite of being head of a multibillion-euro business he came to Milton Keynes to address the staff personally, laying out his vision of what he wanted to achieve with the team and the foundation for its development. It was personal, heartfelt and credible. There may have been sceptics in the audience that day, but no one who was present can look back today and say he wasn't a man of his word. Everything he envisioned came true, and more besides.

The other audiences that were always important to me were our fans and the media. If sponsor–customers pay the bills, suppliers provide the thing we need to do the job, and our staff make it all happen, the world's view of how we are regarded as a business is provided by the public and media.

Owing to the popularity of Formula One we enjoy an enormous, multinational fan base, and at Jordan Grand Prix we built a formidable following that undoubtedly placed us among the top five most popular teams in the sport. This was partly due to the 'brand' we represented in being an Irish-registered team owned by a larger-than-life team principal with a love for rock'n'roll and celebrity. Our image was slightly anti-establishment, avoiding the corporate tones of McLaren or the elitism of Ferrari.

We also liked to have fun; Jordan became known for being a team that knew how to enjoy itself whether it won or lost, and since we did more of the latter than the former it came in quite handy. Eddie's decision to host an after-race barbecue at the British Grand Prix, to wait for the traffic queues to subside, developed into the Jordan rock concert, which became a great favourite for fans, media and even our rivals at Silverstone each year.

The point was that we communicated our sense of enjoyment, and our passion for what we were doing. These were appealing brand attributes.

This interest in linking with the fans manifested itself in the creation of Club Jordan, a fan club I initiated in 1997 and had managed by the father–son combination of Paul and Russell Banks. Although we charged a subscription, the monies were ploughed straight back into creating a range of added-value benefits that fans could enjoy, from regular newsletters and bulletins, to team guides, autograph cards, discounts on merchandise and the opportunity to attend tests.

We even arranged an official trip to one Grand Prix per year, the race in Belgium, starting with a tour of our factory at Silverstone followed by a coach trip to Spa-Francorchamps for the weekend. On the Saturday evening we would host our annual Club Jordan dinner, which Eddie Jordan and the drivers usually attended, and to see the look on the faces of the fans when they walked into the room spoke volumes.

At its peak, starting from the time we had Damon Hill and Ralf Schumacher driving for our team in 1998, we had over 10,000 fans on our database, of whom around 50 per cent were fully paid-up members of the club.

These are small numbers, but you have to consider the disproportionate effect these fans had on the impression of Jordan worldwide. We only needed 20 or 30 in a grandstand opposite the pits to create a noise such that other teams were left wondering why Jordan was attracting such attention. The activities we arranged at Silverstone and Spa were so successful that the international media often picked up on the great support we had and began to rate Jordan as among the most popular teams in F1.

Our core of die-hard fans had an enthusiasm that was infectious, and when our sponsors came to races they often were left beaming by the huge attention being levelled on the team by its devoted followers. All of this stemmed from our maintaining a consistent, credible and active dialogue with our fans.

Club Jordan, interacting with the public and our fans, was one of my most pleasurable roles, and it always helped to bring me down to earth about the reality of our business. It could only live thanks to the members of the public who followed Formula One in general, and us in particular.

One afternoon I received a telephone call from a sponsor, German consumer electronic company Grundig, asking if we could arrange a factory visit for a young fan of our team who was suffering from terminal cancer. We duly obliged, and the boy, aged about 12, had a sufficiently 'good' day to step from his wheelchair and tour our facility with his family. At the end of his visit he had his photograph taken with our car, and we presented him with a full Club Jordan pack and a set of team merchandise.

A few weeks letter I received a letter from his mother saying that it had been the best day of his life, and that sadly he had passed away not long afterwards. His dying wish was that he should be buried in the Jordan team clothing we had presented him with. I don't suppose there is a month that goes by that I don't think about him and the fervour he had for our team because of the fact we liked to communicate with our fans.

Reaching out to the media was until recently the primary means of communication with the world, but the advent of social media and proliferation of digital platforms have radically altered the communications landscape.

Within Formula One there is a travelling media corps of several hundred journalists, broadcasters, film crews and photographers servicing the demands of the world's media across a multitude of traditional and digital platforms. The matrix structure of contemporary media means that we have a fusion, and sometimes a confusion, of journalists who might be writing for trade media, national press and international websites and doing a spot of broadcasting and blogging on the side. Very few of the media can afford to work in mono; most have a wide spectrum of outlets and platforms to service.

Having said there are hundreds of them, as with any industry there are the key opinion formers: the media who have covered our sector for many years and/or report for the most prestigious outlets, know the key industry figures on a personal basis and are regarded as having the gravitas and credibility to influence world media opinion. That doesn't necessarily mean that the key opinion formers are the elder statesmen and women of the press office, or that they report on the sport for a multitude of outlets. It might just as easily include a young journalist who reports for a particularly important trade or business magazine that has a disproportionate influence.

Media communications should always be consistent, honest, credible and informative. When people talk about 'spin' it refers to taking the truth and spinning it into something quite different. Spinning the truth invariably moves into the realms of bending it to breaking point, and as soon as you start lying to the media you will quickly be found out, especially now that social media mean that professional media have potentially hundreds of informal touch-points within your organization.

At Jordan we maintained a strong relationship with the media in a number of ways. We were always responsive to requests; my view was that we should always try to accommodate media requests for interviews, access to the team and the creative stunts they might suggest. Inevitably the tendency among our major rivals who had less media-savvy team bosses than Eddie Jordan was to reject outlandish media requests. We were the team that liked to say yes.

We also liked to share our sense of fun with the media, and the regular media receptions, lunches and dinners that we hosted with our sponsors ensured that we had good personal relationships – important when we wanted to communicate the positive things we were doing, but even more vital when times were more difficult and we had issues to address.

I recall Ron Dennis, team principal of McLaren, complaining that the Jordan team was getting too much media coverage relative to its results. It was a compliment indeed, for it was precisely because we couldn't be sure of winning the race on Sunday that we put so much effort into working with the media Monday to Friday.

One of the basic ways in which we cultivated a strong relationship with the key opinion formers was to host a breakfast on a Friday morning in the Jordan motor home. This was a very informal affair, and it achieved a number of things.

First of all it helped us to set the media agenda for the weekend, because invariably the journalists who turned up would ask us for our thoughts on whatever the current big topic was within the sport.

Secondly it gave us the opportunity to deliver key messages about our own team direct to the key media in an informal way. Eddie Jordan would join one table of media, head of business affairs Ian Phillips would sit at another, I'd host several more, and our operations and technical directors would similarly come and join the conversation. This informal session for an hour or so also helped to underline a core brand value of Jordan – that of being a welcoming team. Being 'Irish', we took the cultural attribute of being hospitable and made it a core value. We also made sure we had plenty of storytelling, chat and banter – what is known in Ireland as 'craic' – and a sense of fun. It was also popular with the media because, wherever we were in the world, we served a full cooked breakfast, which went down very well with the UK-centric media corps. When a travel-weary journalist staying at an inexpensive hotel in Japan or Brazil turned up on a Friday morning, you could see the delight at being presented with some home comfort food.

The communications landscape has changed dramatically in recent years, the development of digital media creating a whole new set of challenges and opportunities for communicating with stakeholder audiences. Television companies now broadcast on TV and online, with services such as BBC's iPlayer, Sky Plus and Sky Go giving viewers the opportunity to watch our sport at the time and place of their choosing and also the ability to self-edit the coverage they watch. All media have moved towards an online offering, with industry publications such as *Autosport* augmenting their weekly magazine publication with rolling news 24/7 and subscription-based services offering a deep-dive view of the business. Such developments are being repeated across our industry, and across the world of business around the globe.

In many cases teams and sponsors have struggled to keep up with the pace of development. I built the Jordan website in 1996. Jordan was the second company in F1 to do so after Ferrari. It was a text-based site and we had to email or fax (!) the website agency to have copy updated, because there was no content management system. In 1999 I then developed the intranet to service customers. In each case these initiatives met with resistance internally, and externally, but as history shows being an early adopter of new communications platforms is important.

The most recent communications revolution in our industry has been social networking, with providers such as Twitter, Facebook, Pinterest and LinkedIn giving unprecedented opportunities to communicate consistently and directly with all our audiences: the public, the media, suppliers, customers, staff, investors – the whole world.

I recently met the marketing director of a major business who told me she couldn't convince their CEO of the benefits of social networking because he couldn't see how the opportunity could be monetized. This is to miss the point. If you don't use the channels that are now the most favoured way for customers to interact, you will most surely fail to take advantage of the opportunities it offers, and fail to protect your brand and its reputation. Worse, you will leave a gap in your communications that will be filled by others.

In Formula One we have seen that, while it may indeed be difficult to monetize the opportunities presented by social networking, there are many examples of why it is vitally important. This is particularly the case if you wish to manage the messages reaching audiences about your business, protect yourself against misunderstandings, handle crises quickly, and direct the way in which your business is viewed by the online community – which is, essentially, everyone.

In the spring of 2012 I watched as Fernando Alonso joined Twitter for the first time. He personally managed his account and, since then, has added 100,000 followers per month. At the time of writing he has 2 million fans with whom he can personally interact. Sometimes he tweets a photograph of his bicycle's computer to show his training performance; at other times it might be some rather odd-looking food he has to eat because of his weight management, or maybe a photograph taken on a beach on holiday. His fans love that interaction.

He has also been able to tweet about the Ferrari team's performance, good and bad, which has sometimes put him at odds with the official line. In 2012 Lewis Hamilton shocked his McLaren team by tweeting a photograph of some data from qualifying at the Belgian Grand Prix – company information being shared on social networks, which their rivals will have found it interesting to examine!

There are enormous opportunities that come from being able to communicate directly with audiences in this way, and challenges that need to be met. But as an overall point social networking represents the 21st-century communications revolution that business must embrace.

Today every Formula One team has its digital media strategy. Among the drivers, 20 of the 22 competing in the World Championship in 2014 were managing their own Twitter accounts, with a cumulative total of 9.7 million followers, while sponsors, promoters and the FIA were beginning to harness the power of social media at long last.

I often reflect on the fact that the great communications culture we enjoyed at Jordan would have been ideal for the social media age. The opportunity is formidable.

For winning teams excellent communication is the cement that holds the whole enterprise together and enables delivery. Time and again great communication has unleashed the potential within a team; bad communication has been blamed for failure. 'No one told me' is probably the worst thing you can hear from an employee, supplier or customer, which is why it is given such significant priority within competitive Formula One teams.

LESSONS IN COMMUNICATION

As with any business, Formula One teams can get the best out of their technologies, systems and processes only by harnessing the capabilities of their people, so having excellent communications across internal functions is of critical importance.

We can see this from the way in which F1 drivers use their two-way radios throughout a race to communicate constantly with their engineers and strategists, and how the teams themselves are receiving a steady stream of data from the cars, which are communicating every facet of their behaviour to enable teams to manage risks and optimize performance.

Understanding whom we need to communicate with, how we plan to communicate and what we are going to say – and listen to – has never been more important. In an era when the informational technology revolution has created a global social media phenomenon, we now see our stakeholder audiences connected as never before. Customers can contact suppliers, staff can communicate with the world's media, and for Formula One's businesses the need to define strategies around this has become critical.

TAKING THE KEY ASPECTS IN TURN:

➤ *Good communication operates in both directions.* Good business leaders should therefore be prepared to listen as much as speak. Indeed the old adage that we have one mouth and two ears, so that we can listen twice as much as we speak, is worth remembering.

➤ *Communication should be consistent, honest, credible and informative.* In Formula One the communications flows during a race are a constant. We want to know exactly what is happening and when it happens, and we stick to the fundamental points. There is no time to waste, and communications need to be precise.

➤ *Cross-functional communications fuel operational excellence.* A silo mentality can quickly develop in a busy organization whose functions are focused on their own urgent tasks and targets.

➤ *The winners in Formula One are hungry for information so that they can process it, communicate and make the right decisions.* As a result they are gathering information from several channels at once – the formal systems provided by the team combined with their own observations. Winners like Michael Schumacher understood the importance of great communication.

➤ *Getting hold of that vital piece of information at precisely the right time, and using it to good effect, can make the difference between winning and losing.* Jordan's experience with Dave, their hospitality bus driver, showed what can happen when just one member of staff feeds a key piece of information up the hierarchy – and is listened to. Empowering our staff to communicate, eliminating the obstacles to doing so, is hugely advantageous.

⟫ ***Work out with whom we are going to communicate.*** At Jordan we saw how customers, suppliers and employees were only part of the communications matrix. The general public, in the form of F1 fans, was extremely important in order to understand and influence public opinion, while the world's media were engaged very closely. You can add investors, regulators and professional advisers to the list. The point is that the range of those with whom we should be communicating is often much broader than first imagined.

⟫ ***Strong communication is a key aspect of customer relationship management.*** In any customer-centric business the ability to sustain customers is driven by effective delivery of products and services backed up by consistent communication that enables us to listen to their needs and add value.

⟫ ***Given the importance of supply chain management, communicating with this group is essential, particularly where we need the culture of our suppliers to be in step with that of our business.*** Formula One teams need their suppliers to have the same 'can do' attitude and to be focused on delivery, quality and service.

⟫ ***Engaging staff, securing their buy-in to the company strategy, gaining alignment: these are only made possible by effective internal communications.*** As Dietrich Mateschitz showed when he addressed the staff when he created Red Bull Racing, good leaders should have the confidence to articulate their vision for the business and communicate that directly to the people expected to implement the plan. The regular team updates at Jordan illustrated the importance of continuous dialogue, and the 'ideas box' was a simple but clear example of how important two-way communications are to a performance-oriented business.

▥➤ ***Ultimately the benefit of having great communications with stakeholder audiences is that this enables us to build strong relationships with people.*** And, whether those relationships are with staff, suppliers, media, investors or regulators, having excellent communications not only can help us deliver the right messages when business is good, but is hugely advantageous when things go wrong. Any crisis can be significantly mitigated in its effects through excellent communications.

▥➤ ***The 21st century's digital media revolution is having a significant impact on Formula One businesses, and everyone is learning how to engage with stakeholder audiences through multiple channels, particularly in social media.*** This is opening up huge opportunities to communicate very personally and directly with people. With everyone more connected than ever before, having those consistent, honest, credible and informative communications strategies in place has never been more important. Entire business and brand reputations are being built, or burned, on the altar of social media.

CHAPTER ELEVEN
LEARNING FROM
F1'S TOP DRIVERS

Who is the best Formula One driver? Which F1 driver did you most enjoy working with? Who is the greatest Formula One driver of all time? If you had to choose one F1 driver, who would it be?

These questions, and similar variants, are among those I am most often asked, and it underlines an important truth about the business of Formula One. For all the technology, business and organizational requirements, the world is fascinated by the men and women who can sit inside the tight confines of the cockpit of a racing car, drive it to the limits of its capability and tame the forces that threaten disaster at every turn.

Courage, skill, lightning reflexes: these are the qualities people often ask about. And of course these are indeed some of the requirements inherent to being a Formula One driver. It definitely takes courage to commit yourself to overtaking a rival in a wheel-to-wheel battle at the entrance to a high-speed corner, or to dig deeper in finding that extra tenth or two of a second that might make the difference between qualifying first and qualifying third. Especially when you think you have already driven the car as fast as it will go around a particular track.

But what about intellectual bandwidth, spatial awareness and timing, or the ability to visualize a lap before it has been driven? What of the ability to recall a qualifying lap so perfectly that when the driver articulates it to the engineers they are then able to match that feedback to the data gathered from the telemetry system? Now we are getting into the detail, and of course this is much closer to the reality of what drivers need to do, day in, day out, in their quest to get the most out of the car.

Then there are the additional elements, unseen and seldom discussed: drivers as leaders who inspire their team, motivate, and help deliver a tone and direction that weld the team together. Or drivers as salespeople and brand ambassadors, customer-focused kingpins who can hold court with assembled sponsor guests in hospitality units from Silverstone to Shanghai, Singapore to Suzuka.

So maybe the question should really be: what can we learn from the most successful Formula One drivers, and is there anything to be gleaned that we can apply in business?

I have selected the following drivers, not only for their brilliance behind the wheel of a racing car, but because they possessed the traits of successful people in any walk of life. In some cases they went on to create successful businesses beyond Formula One, but in each example they demonstrated strong leadership skills, built winning teams around them and did everything in their power to be the very best they could be. They are each inspirational in their own right.

When I first attended a Formula One race in a professional capacity, at the 1983 Dutch Grand Prix in Zandvoort, I already had my favourite drivers, notably three times World Champion Niki Lauda and a man who was in many ways his successor, Alain Prost.

I admired Niki for many reasons: he possessed a formidable intellect, matched only by a fierce determination to succeed. He made his own way into Formula One by borrowing money from a bank in Austria and carving a career straight to the top, winning two World Championships for Ferrari in 1975 and 1977. In the intervening year there was the small matter of a near-fatal accident at the German Grand Prix in Nurburgring, when he came within a whisker of being burned to death. As has been recorded many times, he returned to the cockpit only six weeks later, overcoming fear and a range of life-threatening injuries, and was only beaten to the title by Britain's James Hunt when Niki elected to retire from a rain-washed Japanese Grand Prix.

As if that wasn't enough, he would retire from Formula One in 1979 – making an instant decision during the Canadian Grand Prix – only to make a comeback in 1982 and win the 1984 World Championship for McLaren, beating team mate Alain Prost by half a point. Again he had not been quiet in the intervening period, this time setting up an airline –

Lauda Air – which he would later sell to Austrian Airlines before starting a second successful airline, Air Niki, in 2003.

Niki is a straight-talking individual, a shrewd negotiator who understood the 'value' he brought to a team, and in my opinion the first of the modern generation of Formula One drivers. I say that because he was one of the first to understand fully the importance of physical preparation, diet, and ensuring that your lifestyle outside of the cockpit did not detract from your performance in it. Much has been made of his competition and friendship with Hunt, an old-school playboy, and it's certainly the case that James showed Niki how to have a little more fun in his life. But Niki remained very focused on being the best, and doing whatever was necessary to give himself the slightest advantage.

Nicknamed by some 'the computer' because he was dispassionate, calculating and focused on every detail, Niki Lauda showed that his approach guaranteed success not only in Formula One but in the cut-throat world of civil aviation. In some ways his achievements in that field have been all too easily overlooked.

It came as no surprise when Niki teamed up with Ron Dennis's McLaren team that the two would produce success with their combined focus on detail, continuous improvement and leaving no stone unturned in the quest for performance.

When 'the computer' gave way to 'the professor' it was a seamless transition, for as Lauda's career ended so his McLaren team mate Alain Prost would take up the mantle of being the driver whose approach to Formula One took performance management and delivery on to new levels. With an ultra-smooth driving style reminiscent of Jackie Stewart, Prost had a measured, intellectual approach to driving a Formula One car, conserving brakes and tyres, pushing only when needed. Five times World Champion Juan Manuel Fangio famously said that the objective is to win the race at the slowest possible speed, but the words could have come from Prost. This mechanical sympathy illustrated his knowledge and understanding of the car. His speed was more cerebral. He would win four World Championship titles, three for McLaren in 1985, 1986 and 1989, followed by one for Williams in 1993.

Prost's career is often benchmarked against the careers of three contemporaries: Nigel Mansell, Nelson Piquet Sr and Ayrton Senna. In the 13 seasons between 1981 and 1993 inclusive, these four won 11 of the Drivers World Championship titles. It was his rivalry with Senna when they were team mates at McLaren in 1988 and 1989 that is most often talked about, however. As team mates in identical McLaren-Honda cars they dominated both seasons, yet fell victim to the most bitter internecine rivalry. Between them they won 15 of the 16 Grands Prix in 1988, and 10 in 1989, and there was no love lost between them. The fascination came from observing how two very different characters fought for prominence within a team whose management had the unenviable task of trying to control them.

On the occasions I met Prost during this time I found him to be measured in his replies during interviews, with a quiet sense of humour, a very clear focus on what was needed from the team and its key suppliers in order for him to be able to win, and an unerring conviction in his ability. This never came across as arrogance, simply the natural outcome of the commitment he gave to his craft, the skills he had honed through endless hours of testing, and – as with Lauda – a recognition of the importance of fitness and preparation for the task of racing a Formula One car for two hours on a Sunday afternoon.

As something of a Prost fan I spent the 1988 and 1989 seasons watching very closely as Senna appeared to gain the upper hand in terms of outright speed while his team mate deployed mechanical sympathy, guile and consistency. In reality the speed differential was often insignificant, although there were times when the Brazilian moved on to a different plane, such as during qualifying for the Monaco Grand Prix in 1988 when Senna lapped the shortest track on the Formula One calendar a full 1.4 seconds faster than Prost and a massive 2.7 seconds quicker than third-placed Gerhard Berger. Come the race, Senna dominated until making an unforced error on lap 67, which resulted in his car being damaged and retiring from the race. It was Prost who inherited victory, and in some ways that race summarized the fortunes and talents of this formidable pairing.

It emerged that Prost, after being held up behind Berger, had finally overtaken the Ferrari driver only to find himself almost a minute behind race leader Senna. Prost knew there was no way he could catch up, but instead he deployed the tactic of setting fastest lap after fastest lap. When this was communicated to Senna the Brazilian changed his race pace, making that fateful error that caused him to crash.

This was typical of Prost; he was fast and clever and knew how to deploy tactics that would unsettle the competition, making them rethink their own strategy even when it seemed they were beyond threat – not a bad strategy for competitive businesses, or determined Formula One drivers.

Senna's crash in Monaco in 1988 was a low point for him, but 24 hours earlier his pole position margin over Prost had been a quite extra-ordinary achievement.

I remember that qualifying session well because I opted to walk down to the Armco barrier at the entrance to the Swimming Pool section of the Monte Carlo track, a fast left–right sequence that follows a daunting left-hander, Tabac Corner. In those days, pre-internet with no mobile apps to give us live timing, I used a humble stopwatch to gauge who was quick and who wasn't. I put the watch away that day because I could *hear* that Senna was faster, never mind see it. With each lap he simply arrived, braked, turned in and was gone faster than anyone.

Two years later Senna told eminent Canadian Formula One journalist Gerald Donaldson of that qualifying session:

> I was going faster and faster. One lap after the other, quicker and quicker and quicker. I was at one stage just on pole, then by half a second and then one second and I just kept going. Suddenly I was nearly two seconds faster than anybody else, including my team mate with the same car. And suddenly I realized that I was no longer driving the car consciously. I was driving it by a kind of instinct, only I was in a different dimension. It was like I was in a tunnel, not only in the tunnel under the hotel but the whole circuit was a tunnel. I was going and going, more and more and more and more. I was way over the limit but still able to find even more.[1]

At the end of the 1988 season I had the opportunity to interview Senna and made the mistake of implying that it had been relatively easy for him and his team mate Prost to win 15 Grands Prix and both the World Championship for Drivers and the World Championship for Constructors because the McLaren-Honda MP4/4 was such a good car. He wasn't very happy with that proposition.

'Look, there is only one reason why we are the successful,' replied Senna:

> and that is the commitment that we have put into the car and the team in
> every race, every practice and every qualifying. Of course the car is good
> but that was only because we have made it that way, and the reason Honda
> has done a good job is because me and Ron [Dennis, McLaren's team boss]
> have pushed and pushed all the way. Winning is difficult and you only can
> achieve this level of success by putting in more effort than anyone else.

In many ways it is a great shame that the pinnacle of success for both
Senna and Prost came at the expense of their professional relationship
and prevented friendship. It is fortunate indeed that when they raced
together for the final time at the Australian Grand Prix in 1993 Senna
chose their meeting on the podium to embrace Prost, who would be
retiring from the sport after clinching his fourth title with the Williams
team.

Six months later, with the Prost era over, Senna would lose his life in the
fateful San Marino Grand Prix on 1 May 1994. This enormous tragedy
not only went on to frame contemporary Formula One in ways that few
of us could imagine, but ensured that the career of Ayrton Senna became
legend. That he died doing what he loved most, leading a Formula One
race with new rival Michael Schumacher hot on his heels, meant that
when his crash was witnessed by tens of millions of television viewers
around the world neither his legacy nor the sport of F1 would ever be
the same again.

There have been dozens of books written about his life and career, but
in my opinion you need only watch the documentary *Senna* by Asif
Kapadia to understand the appeal, fascination and legacy of the man
from São Paulo. Two personality traits stand out: his complete and utter
commitment when behind the wheel of a racing car, and his compassion
for people around him. He gave his all, and demanded the same in
return from those he worked with.

Of course he had enormous talent, but it was his ability to work hard
at his profession and strive to understand where the smallest gains could
be achieved that enabled him to transcend normal levels of competition.
Put simply, he knew that talent alone was not enough and applied himself
to improving whenever and however possible, and to working with the
best people he could find.

Approaching the 20th anniversary of his death in 2014 his sister Viviane gave Andrew Downie of the press agency Reuters an insight that sums up Ayrton Senna's commitment to the task of being the most complete racing driver in the world.

'Ayrton was considered the king of the rain, but to be king of the rain he had to fail first,' she recalled:

> He was leading a kart race in Interlagos when he was 12 and he lost control of the kart in the race and he spun off. And so, every time it rained, he got in the kart and he drove, wherever he could, he drove till it was dark and he'd come home completely soaked. And that was how he learned to drive in the rain. He had talent, and that talent wasn't enough, he had to have the discipline and the persistence to develop his talent. Those attitudes are as important as opportunities.[2]

Taking opportunities, and then applying himself to making the most of them, was a Senna trademark. Memorably he almost won the 1984 Monaco Grand Prix in his debut season for the unfancied Toleman team, dancing his car around the soaking wet streets of the famous principality while drivers with vastly more experience, driving far better cars, fell by the wayside. I say he 'almost' won the race because victory was within his grasp when the organizers opted to shorten the race owing to the weather conditions, handing a premature win to Prost.

Jo Ramirez, long-time team manager at McLaren, a close friend of Senna and someone who witnessed the Senna–Prost battles at close quarters, told me in the early 2000s that, while Senna was unquestionably an astonishing talent, it was not for nothing that he could become upset with Prost. There were, he said, occasions when Alain could produce a lap time that Ayrton simply couldn't understand. He knew he had a battle on his hands.

Watching the competition closely is something we all do in Formula One, but drivers have a particular version of this, and it starts with their team mate. The reason is very simple: there are 11 teams, 22 drivers, but there is only one driver who has exactly the same equipment as you do – your team mate.

You cannot argue that he has a superior car to you, because in modern, professional Formula One it is a fundamental requirement for the teams to provide their drivers with the same opportunity. Of course there are some occasions when this is tested, such as when a new specification of component is fitted to one car before another, but overall the engineering policy is to ensure that both drivers have the benefit of the same equipment, and therefore that the team has two chances to achieve success in the race.

For a driver like Senna, therefore, it was standard procedure to benchmark himself against his team mate and set out to take the prominent position within the team. The quote from his interview with Donaldson is notable for that reference to 'my team mate with the same car', because that was his ultimate measure of performance. He wasn't just 1.4 seconds faster than the next car. He was 1.4 seconds faster than Alain Prost.

The progression from Lauda to Prost and then Senna leads us inexorably to Michael Schumacher, the German ace who would win seven World Championship titles and rewrite the record books.

When I first met Michael Schumacher at Silverstone on the occasion of him testing the Jordan 191 Formula One car for the first time in August 1991, little did we realize the career that lay ahead of him. What we did realize, even at that early stage, was that he sported a prodigious talent, keen attention to detail, determination to learn quickly and an unerring belief in his abilities. The first time he drove our car, which was the first time he had ever driven a Formula One car, he disobeyed the instructions of our team manager to complete an installation run. Instead he kept circulating until we sent a mechanic to stand on the track and wave him into the pits.

He clearly knew what he was doing, because his objective was to get to know the car as quickly as possible and find its limits. The first time he came past us at speed he missed the apex of the corner into the chicane, which was part of the short Silverstone South circuit. Unperturbed, he simply applied a little opposite lock, kept his foot on the accelerator and disappeared on to yet another lap.

'I have a younger brother called Ralf who is even quicker than me,' Michael told me when I interviewed him in order to compile his biography for our press pack. 'He is only a young teenager but winning in kart racing. I like to practise by racing him in karts even still.'

These were not the words of an egotist, and as time would tell Michael had nothing to fear from his younger brother. On top of his formidable talent Michael combined many of the elements we had already witnessed with Lauda, Prost and Senna: a calculating approach, dispassionate bordering on brutal in execution, and a deep interest in understanding everything about the car, its systems and how the engineers were working in order to make it faster. He knew the importance of data, continuous improvement, relentless performance management and benchmarking against himself and the opposition.

He was also supremely fit, and recognized the importance of putting time and effort into all of the team members, including the 85 per cent of staff who work only at the factory and are chiefly responsible for the car and its developments. In this role as team leader Michael developed very close relationships with his teams at Benetton and Ferrari during the heyday of a 19-season career that witnessed 91 Grand Prix victories, 68 pole positions and 155 podium finishes. When he won a race the enthusiasm with which he greeted his mechanics and engineers was notable, and you could see that the respect and appreciation were mutual. Michael Schumacher believed strongly in the power of giving recognition.

He never failed to thank the team members back at the factories for their hard work and dedication in providing him with a car that featured the safety, reliability and performance he needed to achieve their combined objectives. Simply put, if the team gave him the car with which to do the job, he could be sure of delivering in the race.

In this respect Schumacher showed compassion within his teams that few people witnessed outside. He knew the importance and power of engagement with the factory workers and recognition of their achievement. As a result, team members would do anything for him, and no job was too great or too small if it meant giving Michael the edge he was looking for.

His five consecutive World Championship titles for Ferrari between 2000 and 2004 demonstrated what happens when great leadership and talent come together to create a high-performing team. Ferrari had not won a Driver's World Championship for 20 years, but a reorganized and rejuvenated team under the leadership of Frenchman Jean Todt, British technical director Ross Brawn and South African chief designer Rory Byrne unleashed the potential in this quintessentially Italian team, producing world-beating cars with which Schumacher was able to dominate.

Such was his focus on the job in hand that Schumacher had little time for distractions, and this included cultivating close relationships with the British-dominated Formula One media corps. On top of that he was guilty of pushing his quest for dominance too far on occasion, notably causing collisions with Damon Hill at the Australian Grand Prix in 1994 and Jacques Villeneuve in Spain in 1997. He also appeared to block the track in Monte Carlo intentionally during qualifying in 2006, in an effort to prevent Fernando Alonso from beating his pole position time. Not only was he roundly criticized, but the race stewards decided to penalize him by making him start from the back of the grid.

The lack of close relationships with some key media allied to pushing the performance envelope beyond acceptable limits at times tarnished Schumacher's reputation. However, I think it is more of a commentary of his critics that they have often preferred to focus on these few indiscretions during a career that lasted almost two decades and achieved such profound success.

As with Lauda, Schumacher opted to retire for a period of time only to return to the sport that he clearly missed. His last race for Ferrari was in Brazil in 2006, but he returned to Formula One in 2010 driving for the Mercedes-Benz Grand Prix team under the leadership of Ross Brawn. In the three seasons that followed he failed to add to his winning record. There were many mistakes, particularly in his first season back in the cockpit, but it became quite evident that he regarded this comeback as a challenge to be enjoyed rather than endured. He applied himself rigorously and, although he was in his 40s, a lifelong commitment to achieving peak physical condition paid dividends and he acquitted himself extremely well against team mate Nico Rosberg. It was apparent to most observers that his talent had diminished slightly, but it was even more obvious that his Mercedes-Benz car did not possess race-winning capability. With the passage of time since his second retirement at the end of 2012 we can see that he was part of a development phase for a team that only realized its full potential in 2014.

I have been privileged to meet and to work with a large number of racing drivers, though few have possessed the very complete range of skills needed to reach the very top of Formula One and achieve World Championship-winning success. It is commonplace within our industry for drivers who have not achieved their goals to bemoan the inequity of a sport where talent alone is insufficient. This is particularly true when the subject of money is raised. It is certainly the case that, in order to reach Formula One, sustain a career and secure a drive in a championship-winning car, it requires many millions of dollars in sponsorship and career investment.

However, as with anyone who wishes to reach the top in their chosen profession, industry or sector, it is never enough simply to have talent and ambition. You must also surround yourself with the best people to support your quest and be prepared to work relentlessly to improve yourself every step of the way. Generating the resources to support your ambition and putting the right plan in place to achieve your goal are often more important at certain moments than possessing raw talent.

Damon Hill deserves a special mention because he not only brought our team at Jordan Grand Prix its first Formula One victory, in Belgium in 1998, but showed me how sheer guts and determination can win out. He took his natural talents, worked hard to improve them and took every opportunity he could find to advance his career, even when his ultimate goal of reaching Formula One must have seemed hopeless at times.

He had started his motor racing career very late, in his early 20s, and was already 31 when he made his Formula One debut for the Brabham team in 1992. Many people thought that since his father Graham had been a double Formula One World Champion in the 1960s Damon would find it easy to generate sponsorship and go motor racing. But the opposite was true, and I recall meeting his management in the mid-1980s and them explaining to me the pitfalls. Erroneously many people thought Damon's family were rich, but the truth was that when Graham was tragically killed in a plane crash in 1975 he left his family relatively penniless.

Damon fought for many years to reach Formula One and when he did, with Brabham, it was with a team that was dying on its feet. His talent, commitment and dedication to the task were very clear, however, and now that he was actually in Formula One his name became pretty useful too. He won an opportunity to test for the Williams team, and then graduated to racing for them in 1993 alongside Prost before being joined by Senna in 1994. Prost's retirement and then Senna's fatal accident played their part in promoting Damon to the position of team leader at Williams, and when he won the Formula One World Championship in 1996 it acted as a example of the benefits of willpower and bloody-minded determination to succeed.

When he joined us at Jordan in 1998 I found a man much more at ease with himself as a result of having scored that world title two years earlier, but irked to some extent by the critics who said he had only achieved his success because the Williams-Renault car had been the class of the field. In Spa, Belgium, he qualified our Jordan car with its customer Mugen-Honda engine in third position on the grid, behind the two McLarens but ahead of Michael Schumacher's Ferrari. We knew we had something special on our hands that weekend. The resolute focus that Damon Hill possessed would bring him a remarkable win the following day, showing the world that he didn't need a Williams alone to win, and giving Jordan an insight into the benefit of having a proven winner in your team.

His team mate at Williams in the post-Senna period was David Coulthard, whom I had worked with in Formula 3000 in 1993 at Pacific Racing. 'DC' shared much in common with Damon in terms of a life devoted to racing and a relentless quest to get to the top. In a 15-year career that lay ahead, DC would go on to drive for three of the great teams in Formula One: Williams, McLaren and Red Bull Racing. A tally of 13 Grand Prix victories, 62 podium finishes and 535 career points made him Britain's highest-points-scoring driver of all time, but he also brought something else to his teams: he was ultra-professional with the media and hugely popular with the customers (sponsors) and fans, and he had the dedication to training, engineering and focus on continuous improvement that marked him out as one of the foremost talents of the modern era.

Our paths crossed a second time in 2005 when I was working at Red Bull Racing and DC moved to join the team from McLaren. He talked to me at length one day about the opportunity, quizzing me about Red Bull, its owner Dietrich Mateschitz, the structure that was in place, who was influential and who was not. He was building up a picture of the opportunity, assessing how best to approach the team, and indeed whether this was a team worth considering.

Not only did he join, and help turn what had been the struggling Jaguar Racing team into the giant of the sport that Red Bull Racing has become, but he played a pivotal role in attracting top talent such as Adrian Newey, designer of multiple title-winning cars. They had worked together at

Williams and then McLaren, and in reigniting their partnership at Red Bull Racing paved the way for the team's consecutive titles between 2010 and 2013.

A tall driver, DC had a rigid discipline not only in keeping super-fit, but also keeping his weight down, and even since his retirement he has maintained a high level of preparedness given that he frequently drives a Red Bull F1 car at promotional events. He has admitted that his determination to keep his weight down led him to develop an eating disorder in his teenage years, when every additional 0.1 kilogram of weight could place him at a disadvantage when karting, and it is a measure of his commitment to his career that he has spent 30 years of his life maintaining a regime most would find difficult.

Perhaps not as shatteringly quick as a Senna or Schumacher, a fact that DC can be disarmingly honest about, he compensated for that final percentage point of talent by applying himself fully, working hard at his profession. DC has calculated that he spent 400 hours actually racing a Formula One car and 1,500 hours looking at data, and he believes very strongly in the need to review performance speedily, learn where improvements can be made, make the necessary changes and move on. His focus on continuous improvement has clearly stood him in good stead during 15 years at the top of his profession.

So what can we learn from these drivers that we can apply in business?

1 *If you don't believe in yourself, you cannot expect others to.* Niki Lauda and Damon Hill had to borrow money to kick-start their careers, with no guarantee of future success apart from conviction in their own ability. Ayrton Senna fought pressure from his father to go into the family business, and worked hard to find the sponsorship that enabled him to leave Brazil and come to England to pursue his dream.

2 ***Talent alone is never enough.*** Be honest about your weak-nesses, and work hard to fill in the gaps. All World Champion drivers have added immeasurably to their raw talent by applying themselves to every aspect of the job.

3 ***Don't fear failure; use it to learn.*** Senna's reaction to a karting accident in the rain in Interlagos was to drive a kart as often as possible in the rain until he became a master at it. His first F1 win came in Portugal, in the pouring rain. He finished over one minute in front of the second-placed car and lapped everyone up to and including third place.

4 ***Focus on continuous improvement.*** Top drivers are never satisfied; there is always room for improvement, which is why they engage so closely with their engineers, examine performance data, and benchmark themselves against past performance and that of their competitors.

5 ***Surround yourself with the best people.*** One of the key attributes of top drivers has been their ability to work with the very best teams and managers at every stage of their careers. Michael Schumacher's manager Willi Weber not only oversaw his victory in the 1990 German Formula 3 Championship and prestigious Macau Grand Prix, but also helped secure a contract for him to drive for Mercedes in sports cars in 1991, which ultimately led to them paying for him to start his F1 career with Jordan Grand Prix in that year's Belgian Grand Prix.

6 ***Develop the complete set of skills to be the best in your business.*** This is the David Coulthard approach: Fitness, media training, the ability to work with sponsors, personal presentation, dietary discipline. Complete focus on the job with no time for distractions, the ability to work in a large multinational team with people much cleverer than you in many technical disciplines: the list goes on. By applying themselves to each of these areas and more the top drivers gain advantages when racing, and career opportunities.

7 **Benchmark yourself against your own previous performance and that of your competitors.** Top F1 drivers are focused on beating their own lap times, those of their team mates and all the other competitors. As David Coulthard explains, it is all about reviewing your performance, seeing where the improvements can be made, making the changes necessary and moving on to the next goal.

8 **Accept that there is no easy route to success, even when you appear to have advantages.** Damon Hill did not become a Formula One champion because he was Graham Hill's son – the only father–son champions in the history of the sport. In some ways he achieved it in spite of his start in life, since sponsors and teams felt sure he had access to money and family connections. He applied himself with utter determination and took every opportunity that came his way, even driving uncompetitive cars at times, to gain experience that would stand him in good stead whenever fate came knocking.

9 **Be more focused than the next person.** Lauda, Prost, Senna and Schumacher all possessed an intellectual focus on their career that set them apart from the majority. Their single-mindedness did not win them hosts of friends, but their interest was in working with the best people to secure the best drives in the best cars. When Schumacher retired, his former Ferrari team mate Eddie Irvine commented that he hoped he would enjoy a more relaxed retirement, since the only things that had been important to him during his career were his racing and his family. Therein lies another clue to the statistically most successful career of any Formula One driver.

10 **Set ambitious targets and push hard to reach them.** The top drivers want to win every single time they sit in a car, and they are ruthless in their quest for dominance. Although Schumacher was singled out for overstepping the

boundaries of what was acceptable on a handful of occasions, the same could be said of Prost, Senna and others.

11 *Be compassionate and remember the importance of engagement and recognition.* Senna and Schumacher were ruthless competitors, but they invested in the people around them, built strong relationships, communicated constantly and were quick to recognize the accomplishments of the teams of people at the race track and in the factories.

12 *Be fit for purpose.* Most people do not realize just how fit a Formula One driver has to be to drive an F1 car, but there is also the question of being fit enough to cope with the rigours of constant international travel, 18- or 20-hour days, changes of time zone and inconsistency of diet. Being fit in body, with the right nutrition and physical regime, enables drivers to have the stamina and mental agility to perform at the highest levels. That can also apply to those seeking to get the most out of themselves for the benefit of their business.

And, finally, back to those questions at the beginning of this chapter:

1 *Who is the best Formula One driver?* Today, in 2014, it is Fernando Alonso and, although that view has been somewhat dampened thanks to him being given a series of below-par Ferraris to drive, there is little doubt in my mind that, in the same equipment as a Lewis Hamilton or Sebastian Vettel, Fernando would win over the course of a season.

2 *Which driver did you most enjoy working with?* Germany's Heinz-Harald Frenzten. He had huge reserves of raw speed and enormous focus and yet understood and accepted the other aspects of the job, including working with the media and our customers. He finished third in the 1999 Formula One World Championship for Drivers in our Jordan car powered by customer Mugen-Honda engines, enabling the team to secure third in the Constructors Championship. It was a giant-killing act, and he was a pleasure to work with.

3 *Who is the greatest Formula One driver of all time?* This is a question that cannot be answered, simply because you cannot compare drivers from different generations given the changes in technology and safety within Formula One. How can you compare a Michael Schumacher, who enjoyed 19 years in Formula One, with a Jochen Rindt, who competed for seven years only to lose his life in Italy in 1970 and become the sport's only posthumous World Champion? Safety has prolonged driver careers to the point where racing in F1 for a decade or more is not uncommon, and naturally the results accumulate in ways their predecessors could not enjoy. The reliability of cars is also on a different level, thanks to quality systems and processes in the engineering facilities that produce modern cars.

4 *If you had to choose one driver, who would it be?* Of the current generation, Fernando Alonso; of previous eras, Scotland's Jim Clark. Clark scored 25 wins, 32 podium finishes and 33 pole positions from 72 race starts between 1960 and 1968, and was revered by team mates and competitors alike. His career ended in a fatal accident that occurred during a Formula 2 race in Germany in April 1968, but one only has to spend a little time talking to those who knew him to realize he was in a different league. The late Jabby Crombac, a Swiss journalist who became a close friend of Jim Clark's and shared his Paris apartment with him for a time, talked about him with me when we were caught in the same airport lounge in the late 1990s. 'There was Jim, and then there was everyone else,' he recalled. 'And sometimes I still think that's the case. There has never been anyone quite like him, as a racing driver, as a man and a friend.'

Notes

1 Gerald Donaldson (1990) *Grand Prix People: Revelations from Inside the Formula 1 Circus*, Motor Racing Publications, Croydon.

2 Interview on **www.uk.reuters.com**, 25 April 2014.

CHAPTER TWELVE
COULTHARD IN CONVERSATION

MG   David, as winner of 13 Grands Prix, driving for three of the top teams in the world, what are the characteristics of building a winning mentality?

DC   A lot comes from the target you set. Sometimes that target is winning the race, or at least taking a step on the road towards being able to win a championship; we should all have a specific goal in mind.

When I started racing as a young boy, initially in karting and then progressing into the different categories of racing that lead up to Formula One, I always had targets, and right from the very beginning I knew that I needed the best team of people around me to help achieve my goals. At the beginning it was my family helping me, and later when I started racing with professional racing teams I realized that it was my engineers, mechanics and the team management who would give me the tools and support necessary to go out and win.

MG   So you always knew you need to have the right people around you?

DC   Right from the start I realized that if I wanted to win it would require a joined-up approach from everyone involved in my teams, irrespective of the level of racing, from karting to F1. Motor racing is a highly complex sport, and so, although I would love to sit here and tell you that all my achievements were down to me, I recognize and embrace that I have always worked in a team environment throughout my career and understand that we win as a team and we lose as a team.

MG Presumably it wasn't just about finding the right people, but getting them to gel, to really act like a *team*.

DC Having that great team culture is vital. Let me give you some detail, because as a driver I always had to rely on certain key people; otherwise I wasn't going to win anything.

When I was driving a Formula One car in a race for teams like Williams, McLaren and Red Bull Racing, as you know I had a two-way radio link with my race engineer; he is the guy who works directly with me on a day-to-day basis to help correlate all the information available to us and help me to optimize the performance of the car in the race. I am not an engineer, so while I don't understand all of the details of the car's aerodynamics, its vehicle dynamics, control systems, engine, gearbox and tyres, I do know what I want from the car to enable me to give a race-winning performance against the competition. I know what I need in order to succeed.

The race engineer has to take my feedback and set about translating that into helping the engineering team understand where we have weaknesses and have to improve.

My race engineer will be supported by a small group of engineers and technicians at the track who are specialists in all of the systems within the car, and of course in each two-car Formula One team I will have a team mate who also has a race engineer along with his own support team. So we already are looking at a couple of dozen engineers and technicians responsible for helping me and my team mate extract the best performance possible. All the information is shared between us, so that even my team mate, who I am also racing against, is working alongside me in the meetings where we are trying to get the most out of the car each weekend.

To carry out the instructions of the engineers in terms of any adjustments to the cars, we have a chief mechanic who oversees all the physical, mechanical changes to the cars and their specifications, to ensure that the correct adjustments are made, the right upgrades fitted and the overall set-up of the car is precisely as we want it. The chief mechanic will then have mechanics on each car who have overall responsibility for different areas of the car, for example the front suspension, the rear suspension, brakes and so on. So we have a clear hierarchy and responsibilities within the team, with everyone fully accountable for their area. If the wheel falls off, we know exactly who is responsible...

MG   And you had something of a baptism of fire in terms of relying on your team to give you a safe car, as well as a fast one.

DC   Indeed, in 1994 I was a test driver for the Williams Formula One team, driving the car to test new developments so that our race drivers, Ayrton Senna and Damon Hill, could have the latest upgrades from one race to the next. At the San Marino Grand Prix in Italy that year, Ayrton, one of the finest racing drivers we have seen, was killed in that tragic accident, and as a result of his loss I was promoted to becoming a race driver.

This meant that a couple of weeks after Senna's fatal accident, I was having to drive the same specification of car at 320 kph – and none of us knew exactly at that time what the cause of Senna's accident was, although it was suspected that it was a combination of factors leading to a driver error. So my job was to take that car and race as hard as I could, totally trusting in my engineers and mechanics to have prepared it to be completely safe, reliable and high-performing. My life, quite literally, was in their hands.

Sometime after that I did suffer a serious accident, and it was caused by the steering failing at very high speed. It turned out that one of the mechanics had not bolted everything together correctly, and a bolt had actually fallen out of the steering column and caused my car to crash. The team owner, Frank Williams, called me in to see him and he brought the mechanic concerned into the meeting. Naturally the guy was upset – although maybe I should have been the one who was upset! – but we didn't blame him and fire him; we just discussed what had happened and agreed to learn, and to make sure we had processes in place to ensure it wouldn't happen again.

MG   So blame culture is avoided and in your experience it's all about learning from mistakes and moving on?

DC   Absolutely, it's just about finding the way to make the steps, whether small or large, to improving performance next time out. And we want everyone in the team to feel part of that process, focusing on relentless improvement. If someone makes a mistake then in most cases you can be sure that is the safest person to do that job again because they'll never want to screw up a second time!

We'll have over 20 mechanics in the team to service the two cars, and these guys also act as the pit stop crew during the all-important stops which we have during the race to change the four wheels and tyres, adjust the aerodynamics and also carry out any repairs such as when we damage a front wing or nose section. So the mechanics do a lot more than build the car to the right specification; they also have to deliver service – call it customer service in business terms – to me during the race. And I tend to be a demanding customer, because I want the pit stop to take only a few seconds.

Aside from the mechanics who prepare the cars and carry out the pit stops, the engineers take personnel numbers to over 40, and then we have logistics and operational staff to manage our freight and supply chain, as each team will bring two cars and around 30 metric tonnes of equipment to each race. Sometimes people want to know what the most important part of a Formula One car is; the answer is the part you don't have. So we need to have all the right parts, of the right specification, at the right time and place on one of the 20 Formula One race tracks around the world. No excuses.

MG   What about the rest of the team track-side?

DC   The team management also attends the races, looking after the business side of the sport, and then every team has its commercial and marketing department which is handling the customer relations with the sponsors, the hospitality, event management, public relations and so on. We are now talking about a small army of perhaps 60 to 70 people at every race, working flat out for five or six days to ensure that everything is in place to give us the best chance of success. Even our catering staff are vital because, as the saying goes, an army fights on its stomach and, when we are racing in countries as diverse as Korea, Brazil, Singapore or Canada, having the correct diet, eating at the right times and keeping your energy level up is as vital for the mechanics as it is for me as a driver.

So, I have just described for you how at each Formula One race we have over 60 team members present to help us get the most out of the car, and give me the support necessary to go out and win the race. But, again, this is only the tip of the iceberg, because that represents only 15 per cent of our workforce, since 85 per cent of people who work for a Formula One team are based in a factory in the UK, or Italy or Switzerland, designing, manufacturing, building and developing our product, the Formula One car, bringing it to the marketplace to sell to our customers – the sponsors – and providing all the back-office support from marketing to finance, HR to IT, that would be familiar to any business.

MG But the race team is only the tip of the iceberg. What about the factory staff?

DC A complete team of 600 full-time staff is pretty standard among the top teams in Formula One, and they will then be supported by a supplier base of perhaps 200 companies providing everything from nuts and bolts to raw carbon composite materials, brake components and even the engine. At Red Bull Racing, for example, our engines are provided by Renault, who themselves employ several hundred people on the Formula One engine business in Viry, near Paris.

The sheer number of people involved in this means that we absolutely have to get everyone aligned, working together and making sure they deliver in their respective areas. That means we cannot have anyone who is not delivering. We also don't want people who don't trust their team mates and start overreaching themselves into areas which aren't their responsibility, or area of expertise.

We want team players at every level, from the most basic job at the factory right up to the technical director and me as a driver; we all have to deliver.

And, rather like many businesses with an international context, Formula One has some added problems such as the fact that we have our headquarters in Europe but are racing all over the world. So we need everyone in the team to work across time zones, especially when the heat is on. If we have a problem at the track in Suzuka, Japan, we want to be able to get information or perhaps even components from the factory with an eight-hour time difference and a 12-hour flight for anyone who has to bring an upgrade out. And we don't expect everyone to have gone home at 5.30 in that case.

The culture is therefore to work to deadlines together, even if this means accepting that on some occasions it will require a very early start or a late night to give the team the chance of doing the best job. It's the least that can be expected if we are genuine in our passion to win.

The other resource that I have when driving the car, trying to race to win, is information, and it's that combination of people working together as a team, and then accessing and sharing the right information, that really gives us the edge.

MG Talking about information leads smoothly into the topic of the IT age and in particular big data. How has that affected your career?

DC I started testing F1 cars in 1992 and racing them in 1994, so my career has almost perfectly coincided with the information age, and the IT revolution which has swept the world in the last two decades.

Sitting in my Formula One car, racing 23 other guys who are equally determined – and sometimes a little bit crazy – I have to spend around 1 hour, 40 minutes pushing myself and the equipment to its limit. I can only see the track directly in front of me, and maybe a little bit of colour of the car behind in my wing mirrors. Other than that, it's the steering wheel in my hands.

So, the big picture of what is happening is actually not clear to me, because I am on my own, out on the race track, pedalling the car as fast as it will go, and my team mate will be doing the same things.

The car, however, is on a wireless network, relaying about 50 gigabytes of data back to the race team during a typical race weekend, and monitoring every system imaginable, including me.

A lot of people don't like annual performance reviews; just imagine what I have had to put up with during my 15-year career. With every single aspect of the car's performance being monitored real-time through 120–150 sensors, it means that every single thing I do as a driver is immediately visible to the team.

It is the ultimate Big Brother system; in the old days the drivers could tell little white lies about the car and make out that the car was rubbish but that they were driving perfectly. In my era that was impossible, because if I braked half a metre too early or too late for a corner, shifted gear at the wrong time, put in too much or too little steering, or went off the track by a few centimetres, the team knew immediately. So if you have made a mistake, you know that by the time you get back to the pit lane the whole team will know. There is no room to hide.

But that's a good thing because, just as a mechanic is expected to do his job properly, be fully accountable and recognize when they could do things better, the same applies to me as a racing driver.

So data is our friend, even if we sometimes think it isn't!

MG But data acquisition systems are only part of the story; what about back at base?

DC One reason we are so reliant on IT is that a Formula One car is designed and developed on the basis of information, and its entire configuration defined back in a factory using a combination of technologies including computer-aided design, computational fluid dynamics, finite element analysis and so on. It is tested using both sophisticated computer modelling and physical testing of its aerodynamics in a wind tunnel.

And we are also able to use the availability of data systems to simulate races for the driver. The simulator technology that we have, such as Red Bull's sim, is incredibly accurate; it's mounted on a multi-axis rig rather like an aircraft simulator, and we can load every circuit on to it, drive the track using different inputs and configurations, giving both the driver and the team highly valuable information before we ever go to a race track.

When we finally build the car and take it to a race track we want to ensure that the car is behaving as we expected it to, reviewing the performance of all the systems and trying to make sure that there is a correlation between what we developed at the factory and what is happening on the race track. If we aren't getting the outcome we expected, if there's an issue which we need to understand, looking at the data and combining it with the knowledge within the team and my feedback as a driver will usually help us understand what the problem is.

The data analysis engineers in a Formula One team are therefore crucial to helping translate what is happening to all the systems and give us a clear understanding of where the opportunities and challenges lie. They sit at the back of the garage, watching the data streaming from my car real-time as it goes around the track, with all the different parameters being shown on the screen.

It's been estimated that 750 million numbers are transmitted from the car to the data systems during a Grand Prix – that's around twice the number of words each of us will speak in an average lifetime – and those numbers are turned into colour-coded data traces which come up on the screens track-side, and are also relayed back to our mission control centres at our headquarters in the UK.

Most of the data is run-of-the-mill information which tells us that everything is fine, so what we spend a lot of time and energy doing is looking for the data which tells us there is a problem, or better still helps us to anticipate a problem before it becomes serious and allows us to react accordingly. Again, this is about the team working together, sharing information, reacting swiftly and being completely focused on the target.

Sometimes it is not possible to stop a problem developing, or find an immediate cure, such as when we suffer the failure of one of the gears in the gearbox, or a fault in a system such as if the brakes start to overheat and you could suffer a catastrophic failure if you didn't react. But if the team can spot the problem, tell me on the radio and we agree a new strategy, for example not using that gear again or being easier on the brakes during the final laps of a race, it can make all the difference between winning and losing, or finishing the race or retiring with mechanical failure.

They say there isn't an 'I' in 'team' but, if there was, I suspect it would be the 'I' from IT, because everyone in Formula One these days knows the importance of information, of data, and of harnessing it and using it to give us a competitive advantage.

MG You've talked about the team and the technology. But an F1 team is a business and as a driver you are the very public face of that organization. How much do you get involved with the customers, the sponsors, who ultimately make the business pay?

DC One thing people soon learn is that the sponsors are no longer merely looking for some publicity at 20 Formula One races around the world, but a 365-day marketing programme which covers a wide range of activities and goals they have set for us to achieve. It used to be that big sponsors came into Formula One hoping that they would benefit from the television coverage generated by winning races and seeing their brands on TV.

But even the top teams in Formula One cannot guarantee that they can win every race. A team like McLaren, where I won 12 Grands Prix, has a fantastic record, but ultimately their achievement of winning 25 per cent of all the Formula One races in which they have competed since the 1960s means that 75 per cent of the time their sponsors are going to be disappointed if the only thing that matters is winning.

So, for teams like McLaren, Red Bull and Williams, my experience as a driver is that we are working to add value to our customers all year round, seven days a week, and the racing becomes only one part of what we do for them.

As an example, even though I retired as a Formula One driver over five years ago, I am still working hard for companies like Red Bull and AMG Mercedes doing promotional and marketing events all over the world.

So, in the last couple of years I have been driving a Red Bull F1 in Texas to make a promotional film ahead of the inaugural United States Grand Prix in Austin, and giving Formula One street-racing demonstrations in key markets around the world. I even had to perform doughnuts in an F1 car on the helipad of the Burj Al Arab in Dubai; so the stunts can be pretty spectacular!

For me as a driver, I am an ambassador of the company and obliged to do a lot more than just think about my job driving the car; I am also heavily involved in helping the company to provide a comprehensive solution to the customers.

MG So even for you as a driver there is an understanding of the big picture for the team commercially?

DC Of course, and you soon realize that in a team of several hundred people we are trying to do everything as well as possible, whether racing or running hospitality events or putting together some major customer event. It's all about coming up with a comprehensive solution.

The best analogy of our approach to focusing on complete solutions, rather than just one or two areas of excellence, is in the Formula One car itself. An F1 car is made up of more than 5,000 individual components, and within these we have significant systems or structures that have to perform very highly and also work together in harmony.

You have the chassis, which is made from carbon fibre and has a number of jobs to do; it has to first of all provide somewhere for me to sit, which is quite useful, be physically large enough for me to operate all the systems, yet small enough to make the car aerodynamically efficient. It also has to have the strength to protect me in the event of a 300 kph accident, perhaps with multiple impacts, and be stiff and strong enough to carry all of the other components of the car which are bolted to it.

Then you have the power unit, which not only produces almost 800 bhp and powers me around the track, but is itself part of the chassis, so it has to be rigid, as well as reliable and fuel-efficient. These days the power unit is a hybrid petrol–electric unit, and extremely complex. The gearbox comes next, transferring the power to the wheels, the suspension on all four corners, and finally the bodywork including the front and rear wings, the floor section and all the other efficiently designed pieces of carbon fibre which enable the car to produce over 2 tonnes of downforce at top speed. The car could quite literally drive on the ceiling, as the downforce generated is more than double the weight of the car and driver combined.

We call this assembly of all these elements, all these independently designed systems which go into making a car, the 'package'. The 'package' is what we are looking for, and a good package is a car which has all of these systems working in harmony, complementing each other and enabling me as a driver to take performance on to a new level.

At our factories, therefore, we have hundreds of skilled people responsible for the design and manufacture of the different systems – experts in structural design, vehicle dynamics, aerodynamics, powertrain design, electronics, software and control systems – but, although each of these people might like to come up with simply the best in their respective area, the fact is we have to develop a complete solution that works together for the benefit of me, the driver, as the end user.

You can't win races by producing only the best engine, or the best gearbox; we have to be focused on packaging the best overall solution, and ultimately that's what the championship-winning teams are able to do. At McLaren we won the team's championship in 1999 and 2001 because we produced the best overall car solution over the course of the season.

And it's the best overall solution that not only enables us to be successful, but also to attract the best customers or sponsors because they realize that depth of capability is extremely important. Being a one-hit wonder is never enough; we have to deliver sustained performance week in, week out, and across each championship season.

MG Talking about sustained performance, how do you go about reaching a sometimes seemingly impossible target?

DC The starting point is this; unless we set a clear target we will never start down the road towards achieving it. So it's important to know what the goal is and never take your eye off it.

I have been very lucky to work with some very talented and inspirational people during my career, and one of those has been Dietrich Mateschitz, who co-owns Red Bull and is responsible for turning it into one of the most successful drinks businesses in the world.

But he has done a lot more than start a drinks business from scratch; he in fact created the energy drinks industry – and has gone on to dominate it globally. And he has also had the vision to create the team which has dominated the Formula One World Championship between 2010 and 2013 with Sebastian Vettel, a team which I played a part in developing from relatively difficult beginnings.

When Red Bull bought the Jaguar Racing Formula One team at the end of 2004, it acquired a team which had achieved relatively little, mainly through poor leadership and a lack of vision. But Red Bull could see the potential; this was a team which had a lot going for it, but it needed to be structured in a much more efficient way and for the team to be given the power to deliver the results.

I was brought in by Red Bull in 2005, mainly because of my experience of working with championship-winning teams such as McLaren and Williams, and therefore part of my job was to identify some of the strengths and weaknesses and help them to move forward, step by step, towards their goal of turning the team into winners. They had a core of very good people, but we also had to make some changes and bring in fresh talent to make the team more effective, including recruiting Adrian Newey from McLaren as technical director.

That Jaguar Racing team had huge potential, but it was not until Red Bull took it over, brought its winning culture into play, invested in the right areas with the right people, and set out a very clear target did that group of individuals truly realize their potential as a team – this enabled them to become World Champions.

The best team produced the best package, and the result was that together they achieved the goal they had set themselves.

DAVID COULTHARD'S 10 KEY BUSINESS MESSAGES

▪➡ ***Have a clear goal and stay completely focused on it.*** Whether it is a small 'next step' or the ultimate objective, develop a laser-like focus on that target.

▪➡ ***Work to precise targets and deadlines.*** This is common in F1 and helps to create a goal-oriented culture. Everyone has to know what we want to do, and by when.

▪➡ ***Surround yourself with people who are the very best at what they do.*** None of us can do everything, and part of my success has been to work with incredibly talented people.

▪➡ ***Team work requires everyone to be clear about their responsibility, and accountable for it.*** No one can be a 'spare part'; everyone has to deliver.

▪➡ ***Continuous improvement comes from learning quickly from our mistakes as much as developing new ways of doing things.***

▪➡ ***Avoid creating a blame culture.*** Everyone makes mistakes, and often the people who make mistakes are those who can be most trusted never to repeat them.

▪➡ ***The factory staff are just as important as those out in the field.*** Both have to be aligned, for without the 'back office' the 'front office' cannot function.

▪➡ ***Technology is giving us lots of new opportunities to develop successful strategies, with our ability to mine information making data a vital currency within business.***

▪➡ ***Even as an F1 driver I understand the importance of being customer-focused, a brand ambassador for the company.*** The same should apply to all employees.

▪➡ ***Success in F1 comes from developing the best overall package in terms of the technologies, systems, process and people, with the ultimate goal of winning for ourselves and our customers.***

CHAPTER THIRTEEN
STORIES FROM
MY TIME IN F1

The owner of the house I rented in Long Hanborough, Oxfordshire, did not explicitly allow me to sublet a room. But life sometimes requires the odd risk be taken, and in 1988 I rented a couple of rooms out, one to a photographer, Peter Fox, who would go on to become a highly regarded professional in Formula One, the other to a fellow Northern Irishman, Eddie Irvine. He would become slightly more famous than Peter, finishing second in the Formula One World Championship in 1999 as Ferrari team mate to Michael Schumacher.

Life with Eddie was never boring, even though our personalities and regimes could not have been more different. I was usually up and away to work long before he stirred, while at night I would be in bed and fast asleep before he ever crept in, usually with a young woman in tow. I came to resent the wicker chair in his bedroom, propped up against our adjoining wall. The rhythmic squeaking and banging against the wall of my bedroom, a few inches from my own headboard, left nothing to the imagination as to how he was entertaining his guests.

The phone rang one morning at around 10 minutes to nine. Breakfast in hand, I wondered who could be calling. It was Trevor Foster, team manager of Eddie Jordan Racing, asking me if I'd seen Eddie. As one of the team's three drivers in Formula 3000 alongside Heinz-Harald Frentzen and Emanuele Naspetti, Eddie had been complaining about the lack of testing. Trevor was calling from Donington Park racing circuit to say that all three Reynard F3000 cars were ready to roll but there was no sign of Eddie, and he was scheduled to drive each of them. It was what is known in the business as a 'shake-down test' to check various systems on the rebuilt cars.

I put Trevor on hold and went upstairs, knocking on Eddie's door. Sure enough there was a muffled answer and he opened the door, revealing that he not only had just woken but also had a guest. When I told him Trevor was wondering where he was, two things became apparent. One was that he had completely forgotten the fact that he was due to be testing; the other was that he had no intention of admitting as much. I was instructed to tell Trevor that there was no sign of Eddie, and that it looked as though he had left some time ago.

Being a good landlord I decided to lie for my tenant and protect his reputation, such as it was, while he fired up his car and headed off to Donington Park at breakneck speed. He made it in time for the test, telling Trevor some story about his car having broken down en route, while I was left to make tea for the tearful girl who woke up to find that her beau had departed. Life in the fast lane.

* * *

As mentioned in Chapter 2 on leadership, the first time I met Eddie Jordan he told me to 'f*** off'. I was 16, and he was a nationally famous racing driver. He didn't actually tell me to 'f*** off', to be fair; he actually said 'I'm a bit busy; would you ever f*** off.' I'd summoned up the courage to ask for his autograph at Kirkistown racing circuit, my local race track situated on Northern Ireland's Ards Peninsula. What I didn't appreciate was that he was having a difficult weekend, and when I asked for an autograph it came at the wrong moment.

Fast-forward 10 years and our relationship had improved since Eddie realized in 1987 that I was working for Marlboro and came under the heading of 'someone who might be quite useful'. The following year I found him giving Formula 3000 driver Jean Alesi, later to become a top Formula One driver, a stern ticking-off for ignoring fans on the way into the track that morning and refusing to sign autographs.

'You have to understand the importance of getting these people on board,' said Eddie, Jean looking chastened. 'I mean, it's the least you can do when these people come to see you race and ask for an autograph.' Funny how a decade of working very hard to raise sponsorship and become PR-aware had changed EJ's view of the importance of signing autographs. I didn't tell him about the irony of that for some years, and when I did he was disbelieving. It served to show the importance of never forgetting yourself whether on the way up in your career or the way down. It takes nothing to be polite.

Half a career later, at the Japanese Grand Prix in 2001, I found myself invited to dinner with Jean Alesi, the president of Honda Racing Shoichi Tanaka and Honda's executive Robert Watherston. Alesi, famed for his extraordinary debut season for Tyrrell in 1991, had gone on to enjoy a career that constantly promised much but never quite delivered. Highly rated, he drove for both Ferrari and Benetton, though arguably at the wrong time for both, and a single victory in the Canadian Grand Prix in 1995 was poor reward for the popular and striking-looking Frenchman of Sicilian parentage. He gave much to Formula One fans along the way, however, and that evening he reminisced lyrically about the highs and lows of a career triggered by the faith shown in him by Eddie Jordan 14 years earlier. He even signed a few autographs for the restaurant staff.

* * *

Barry Sheene remains a legend to motorcycle racing fans the world over, and for a generation of Formula One fans he was famous for being the two-wheeled version of Britain's ultimate playboy driver, James Hunt. Together they blazed a trail of dramatic success juxtaposed with high drama on and off the track. They both made headlines on the front page as well as the back page with their blond locks, impish grins and magnetic attraction to the opposite sex.

Sitting in our hospitality unit at the Australian Grand Prix, Sheene asked if he could join me for a coffee and started talking about our prospects for qualifying. By now living in Queensland and working for Australian television, he was a calmer person than in his hell-raising days, but the appeal remained and he was ever popular.

A few minutes later Australian three times motorcycle World Champion Mick Doohan came into the room and joined us, the two starting into some typical banter, two of the great legends of motor sport who commanded the attention of a worldwide fan base in the heyday of their careers.

I had long since become used to sitting in the midst of celebrity, having hosted the great and good from the music industry and Hollywood thanks to our open-house policy at Jordan Grand Prix. Sylvester Stallone, Pierce Brosnan, Michael Douglas, Catherine Zeta-Jones and Bono were all in a day's work. But sitting there with Doohan and Sheene I felt it was a moment to relish, for here were two real superstars of sport.

The fourth person to join our group, balancing the numbers at our table and adding another dimension entirely, was George Harrison. He had become friendly with EJ, each bringing the other access to a shared passion: George for Formula One, Eddie for music. Having a Beatle in our midst was also not unusual, therefore, but it rather added to the moment. As they talked I remember thinking about the achievements of each, their experiences, the people they had met, and their legacy. Mick and Barry both carried the scars of their careers, having confronted mortality at 190 mph on two wheels, while George – well, you could only begin to imagine the life George had enjoyed and endured as a member of the most famous rock group of the 20th century.

I often look back on that day, not least because within five years two of them would be dead, Barry at 52 and George at 58, both victims of cancer. It succeeded where tempting fate on the race track or the lifestyle of rock stars had failed. I don't know if Mick Doohan ever thinks back to that day in Melbourne, but it is for me a constant reminder that while our achievements in life are fleeting we have it within ourselves to leave a legacy, for none of us know what is around the next corner.

* * *

If there was one question that the representatives from Disney and its film distribution business Buena Vista International were not expecting, it was for Bernie Ecclestone to ask them 'What is Disney?'

Before introducing them to Bernie, I had helped them plan the meeting by imagining what topics he would want to raise, which points might be contentious, and how we would play it. I should have known better, for if there is one trait Bernie is famous for it is his ability to say the unsayable, knock you off your guard, and use contrariness as a weapon to destabilize you in negotiations.

Sitting in one of the meeting rooms of his offices in Knightsbridge the two Disney and Buena Vista International executives had already commented on the artwork around its walls and on the shelves: the sculptured pile of dollar bills, the framed *Playboy* front covers, the intricate timepiece clicking and ticking on its way – a countdown to Bernie entering the room.

We were there to present the case for Disney Pixar to launch its animated movie, *Cars*, at the Spanish Grand Prix in Barcelona. The idea was to bring the European movie media to the race, where they would enjoy the racing and meet some of the voice talent, specifically Owen Wilson, who voiced the lead character Lightning McQueen. There was also the prospect of bringing Paul Newman, Hollywood legend and racing driver, who voiced the character Doc Hudson.

Instead of launching into our pitch, however, I found myself telling Bernie about the history of Disney, its film business, theme parks and licensing activities, while the executives from BVI and Disney sat in silence. It was uncomfortable.

'Are you going to use the Formula One name or logo?' asked Bernie finally. No, we said.

'OK, well if you do then you'll hear from my lawyers. Otherwise let's see what we can do to help you.'

Twenty-five minutes later we had an agreement. Dozens of European movie and film media would descend on the Circuit de Catalunya to tell the world about *Cars*, with the noise and spectacle of Formula One in the background. Meantime Owen Wilson would join me on the grid before the race to be interviewed live on TV in front of millions of fans in Disney Pixar's key markets: the UK, Germany, France, Italy and Japan. We did 11 interviews in less than 30 minutes. Disney Pixar got its publicity for *Cars*; Bernie had an A-list star on the grid saying how fantastic Formula One is.

Bernie had cut to the chase and agreed the outline of the deal in less time than many businesspeople take to indulge in small talk. Everyone was happy.

* * *

The group of corporate hospitality guests from Ireland were having a great weekend at the San Marino Grand Prix – so good, in fact, that many of them had failed to make it to qualifying on Saturday such was the fun they had enjoyed in the nightspots and fleshpots of Ravenna. At several thousand dollars per ticket, their non-appearance was not only embarrassing for the sponsor and annoying for the team's account manager tasked with looking after them, but a colossal waste of money.

Sunday morning, race day, and things were looking better. They had managed to rouse themselves after a few hours' sleep or, in a few cases, poured themselves on to the coach to the circuit directly as dawn broke outside their hotel.

In the hospitality unit everything was in order; our guests had arrived in numbers, and this particular group was in situ. I did my usual rounds of the tables, thanking people for attending, answering questions about the team's performance that season and hopes for the race, exchanging hellos with some of the familiar faces we had come to know.

Sometime later my two-way radio burst into life with a message to return to the hospitality suite. There was a problem, I was told.

My first thought was that someone had been ill, or perhaps topped up their hangover a little too quickly, but neither of those turned out to be the case. The problem, I was told, was the man standing in the corner of the unit and refusing to take his place at the table. He had been standing there for some time and was making the other guests uneasy because of his demeanour and complexion. He looked decidedly odd.

I went and spoke with him.

'Hi, how's it going?' was my opening line.

He nodded and said he was fine. Good, I thought.

'Everything OK? It's just that we'd like you to take your place at the table because you can't just stand here in the corner all day, and the other guests are worried about you.'

He looked at me and then, most apologetically, began to explain.

'You see, I have a problem,' he said.

'Go on. What is it?' I replied.

'Well, I have been stabbed. I am bleeding quite badly and I don't want to upset anyone, because I think my shirt has quite a lot of blood on the back of it.'

As explanations went, this was not one I had been anticipating.

It turned out that he had made the mistake of making a play for a woman in a nightclub unaware that her Italian boyfriend would take offence at his advances. When they left the nightclub at 5.30 or 6 o'clock that morning there had been a confrontation outside and the boyfriend had produced a Stanley knife, slashing our guest and causing a deep wound to his back. He had been bleeding for around five hours by this time and, sure enough, the back of his shirt was soaking.

I got a chair, sat him down and we called a medical crew, who attended to him and ensured that he was going to be all right. Fortunately he was and lived to tell the tale.

In customer relations you get to deal with all kinds of people, all kinds of situations and the pendulum swing of human behaviour. You should be prepared for anything. Sometimes the processes can never allow for reality, so you just have to learn to adapt and remember that this person deserves patience, understanding and, in extreme cases, an ambulance.

* * *

If I made a list of frequently asked questions I think number one would undoubtedly be 'What is your favourite Grand Prix?' It's not a question I find easy to answer, rather like someone asking which is your favourite child. My usual response is to say that there isn't one, but that you cannot go wrong with the 'four Ms': Melbourne, Montreal, Monza and Monaco. Each has a unique ambience and place in the heart of Formula One.

Melbourne has been the opening round of the World Championship since 1996, and after a hectic three-month winter back in Europe, building cars, finalizing sponsorships, signing drivers, organizing team launches and dashing around pre-season testing in Spain, the trip to Australia is always welcome.

After the short, cold days back in England the warmth and freshness of Melbourne's Albert Park are a delight. So too is the fact that here's a long-haul destination without any language problems for F1's English-speaking teams: a modern, cosmopolitan city with excellent hotels, beachside restaurants and knowledgeable fans.

Montreal arrives in June, a short diversion to North America after the start of the European leg of the season. As with Albert Park the race is held on a track that is not used for the remaining 51 weeks of the year, in this case the Circuit Gilles Villeneuve on the Île Notre-Dame, an artificial island in the middle of the St Lawrence seaway. The French-speaking locals with their culture clash of European heritage and North

American confidence put on one of the best races of the year. The grandstands are always full, the races produce excitement because of a track layout that promotes overtaking and incident, and the fact that team personnel have to negotiate their way across the Olympic rowing lake by means of a rickety footbridge made from scaffolding only adds to its charm.

Monza, home of the Italian Grand Prix, is a cathedral of speed, a forested parkland where you can go for a walk and, sensing the ghosts of racing from decades long gone, find the moss-covered near-vertical banking from days of old. The fans, Ferrari's Tifosi, flock in their tens of thousands, a sea of red. The traffic outside has never really improved and you can walk to the spot where actor James Garner stood on the pit straight in the final shot of John Frankenheimer's 1966 movie *Grand Prix*.

And then there's Monaco. It really is the jewel in the crown. Graham Hill won there five times because, he said, it was worth it in order to have the chance to kiss Princess Grace. The principality has held its street race since 1929, and it is madly wonderful. If someone tried to invent it today, a race on streets too narrow to promote overtaking, with a lap only 2.075 miles long featuring a tunnel under a hotel and a chicane created by a swimming pool on the sea front, they would be told to forget it. But that is what is so wonderful about Monaco; the racing almost – *almost* – becomes secondary to the beautiful people, their boats and their bling. Being tagged on to the end of the Cannes Film Festival it also helps to ensure a Hollywood A-lister or two along the way.

In 2004 Jaguar's PR guru Nav Sidhu, later to found his own agency Sidhu & Simon, helped mastermind a tie-up between Jaguar Racing, the heist movie *Ocean's Twelve* and the diamond company Steinmetz. Nav put out the word that the Jaguar F1 car had a large diamond inset into its nose section and, when Christian Klien crashed outside the Fairmont Hotel, said that the diamond had fallen off. Cue several dozen people crawling around on their hands and knees looking for the diamond. This generated acres of press coverage. The other coup that weekend was to get the stars of *Ocean's Twelve* to turn up, whereupon we had George Clooney, Brad Pitt and Matt Damon visit us in the pit lane. Not exactly your average PR shoot, that one, but when Brad came by, shook my hand and said thank you it was best to remain cool. 'Any time,' I said.

* * *

Networking is a key business tool, and something I have worked hard to master during my career. I have seen some of the best in the world manage it effectively, and as you become more successful it tends to be the case that your achievements open more and more doors.

EJ was always a master at it. He was determined to network like crazy, and it would annoy me when colleagues at Jordan Grand Prix criticized him for partying too hard. Yes, he often left work early to go to a concert in London, or headed off to a late-night dinner with celebrity guests at the race track, but there was a lot more than partying on Eddie's mind. Eddie knew the value of networking, the publicity it would attract for him and the team, and of course the fact that all successful businesspeople quite enjoy letting their hair down. More than a few serious business leaders have been wooed into a deal by being taken away from the boredom of corporate life and shown life in the fast lane.

At the Australian Grand Prix in 2002 I became aware that Irish prime minister Bertie Ahern was on a state visit and that we would be sharing a table with him at a dinner for the regional Chamber of Commerce in Melbourne. With an Irish theme, EJ was invited with me as his right-hand man for the occasion, and it nicely positioned the Jordan team.

EJ had met Bertie before, and indeed other Irish prime ministers, so he certainly wasn't fazed by the event. Quite the contrary, EJ and Bertie basically held court while everyone else listened, and the evening's formalities went smoothly. Afterwards, to everyone's disappointment, the prime minister's hotel manager told us that his bar was shut, so we retired some distance away to a pub, the Cricketers Arms, that was attempting to close. They were soon convinced to remain open.

Sitting there, chatting to a military attaché and listening to Eddie and Bertie talking about business, politics, sport and music, I reflected on the path the Jordan team had taken over the previous dozen years.

The barman then leant forward and, nodding in the direction of the two men deep in conversation, said 'So, are you with them?'

'Yes,' I replied, 'We've been at a formal dinner and they were desperate for a pint.'

'Ah,' he said, 'I just can't believe it's him, sitting here, drinking in our pub.'

'I know,' I agreed, looking at the Irish PM.

'I mean it's not every day you get Eddie Jordan walking into your bar.'

Funny old world.

Sometime later, at the 2002 Monaco Grand Prix, I was chatting to Bono from U2 when he handed me his mobile phone and asked me to look after it while he went on to the starting grid to have his photograph taken with EJ. I wasn't sure why he was handing it to me.

'Tony might call,' he said. 'Tony Blair. He's at Chequers for the weekend. He wants to have a chat about our aid programmes. If he calls just tell him I'm with EJ and we'll be back in 15 or 20.'

As I said, a funny old world.

* * *

The French Grand Prix in Magny-Cours in 1999 was an important event for my customers. We had around 400 guests in the hospitality units from companies as diverse as Benson & Hedges, MasterCard International, EMC and Brother Industries. It was a busy weekend; the guests had to be entertained, shown around and looked after by a team of accounts managers, events managers and logistics staff.

Matters, however, were made more difficult by bad weather blowing across central France from the Atlantic coast. If it was making for a cloudy and sometimes wet weekend for the guests, it was doing nothing for the race team's strategy as the race approached.

Qualifying had gone well for one of our drivers, Heinz-Harald Frentzen, badly for our other driver, Damon Hill. Heinz would line up fifth, Damon an unhappy 18th. In front of us on the grid were the Stewart of Rubens Barrichello, Sauber of Jean Alesi, Prost driven by Olivier Panis and McLaren of David Coulthard.

But it was the weather that posed the biggest problem as the team sought to find a race strategy that could accommodate the variables brought about by rain showers. Ferrari, we knew, had a sophisticated weather monitoring system, as had McLaren, while at Jordan a fax from the Met Office in London was about as high-tech as it got.

Sunday morning and the pre-race strategy meeting brought forward an idea; a spotter, specifically Dave, who drove our motor home hospitality unit, would be sent off on his scooter with a two-way radio and instructions to head in the direction of the weather and call in details of rain showers. Not the average job for a team bus driver, but Dave duly headed off and made the necessary call during the first stages of the race; rain was on its way, and not just the rain showers we had endured all morning. This was a weather front, and the rain would stay.

That call rather changed our strategy; armed with this key piece of information from Dave, the team opted for a one-stop strategy, filling the car to the brim with fuel and sending Heinz back out on track to maintain the fifth position he had held from the start.

As the laps rolled by the rain continued to fall, and indeed it became heavier, and we saw our lead car promoted to fourth and then third. On lap 66 both Mika Hakkinen's McLaren and Rubens Barrichello's Stewart were forced to stop for more fuel, enabling Heinz-Harald to move into a lead he would never lose. Whatever the capabilities of the Stewart Ford and McLaren Mercedes teams, they were no match for Jordan armed with Dave.

We won the French Grand Prix and, while our world rejoiced, our competitors wondered how on earth Jordan had made the right strategy call. My guests, our sponsors, were ecstatic; I took the winner's trophy across for them to photograph.

'Amazing. How the hell did you guys manage to pull that off?' asked one.

'Simple,' I replied. 'We had a secret weapon. He's called Dave.'

* * *

Working in Formula One may seem glamorous, and indeed there are some occasions when you have to pinch yourself and reflect on the good fortune you've had to enjoy a particular time or place. But like any business it is 99 per cent hard graft, and the moments of euphoria and celebration are few and far between. Winning doesn't happen often, even for the top teams. McLaren is fond of pointing out that it has won 25 per cent of all the races in which it has competed – a terrific statistic and one of which they are rightly proud. But the flip side of that is that they lose 75 per cent of the time.

At Jordan our quest for success lasted seven and a half years. We started in Formula One in March 1991, but it wasn't until August 1998 that we secured our maiden win – and what a win it was.

It wasn't seven and a half years of misery before then. We achieved lots of milestones and made sure we celebrated them: our first finish, first points, first podium, first pole position, first double podium, even a fastest lap or two. But by 1998 we had done everything we could achieve, apart from win a Formula One race, and with major sponsors, top drivers and the expectation of success weighing heavy on our shoulders it was time to deliver.

Spa-Francorchamps in Belgium had always been a favourite track; indeed in 1991, our first season, we had come within an ace of winning the Grand Prix with Andrea de Cesaris before the car's Ford Cosworth engine had failed through lack of oil. Situated in the Ardennes mountains, it was also a track that carried with it some great heritage, a circuit originally built on public roads, following the topography of the forested hillsides. This is a circuit of the old school – it has survived in spite of its remote location, and moved with the times without losing its road-racing character. It has come to represent the antidote to some of the characterless, featureless, cement and tarmac monoliths at which we race today.

Arriving at Spa in 1998 we knew that our team had made good progress. We had produced a competitive car the previous season, making a good foundation for the Jordan 198 car. We had witnessed Peugeot depart as our engine supplier, replaced by 'customer' engines from Mugen-Honda: engines we had to pay for, albeit at a discounted rate. And we had replaced Italian Giancarlo Fisichello with former World Champion Damon Hill, teaming him with Ralf Schumacher.

Damon brought a number of things with him: fame and notoriety, which our sponsors rather liked, but perhaps more importantly the knowledge of how to win. Having driven for Williams, which was at that time one of Formula One's top teams, he had an insight into how they worked, how a quick car behaved and felt, and what it took to win. Knowing what it takes to win is pretty important whether in business or sport, and we hoped to tap into Damon's knowledge.

That fact that he was teamed with the brother of his arch-nemesis, Michael Schumacher, added quite a lot to the story. Michael had controversially robbed Damon of a world title in 1994 when he appeared to drive into him at the final round of the championship in Adelaide. There was bad blood then, and for many British fans Michael's reputation would remain forever sullied.

Damon's demeanour in Spa was positive from the word go. He was fourth fastest in second practice, third fastest in final practice, and in qualifying he produced a stunning performance to place his car third on the grid behind the McLarens of David Coulthard and Mika Hakkinen. When I say it was a stunning performance, I vividly recall standing in our garage and watching the timing monitor as Damon completed his final qualifying lap, separated by only a few hundred metres on the track from Michael Schumacher's Ferrari. After the first two sectors, of a three-sector lap, it looked as though Michael would be quicker, but then Damon's final-sector time came up on screen and he was placed 'P3'. We'd just beaten Schumi's Ferrari in a straight fight, and there was a real sense of achievement.

Ralf had qualified eighth, so we were really hoping to have both cars in the top six points-scoring positions in the race, and to secure a podium if the weather conditions came our way. Spa's infamous microclimate often creates interesting races, with multiple pit stops and tricky decisions as regards tyre choice thanks to the track's length. It can often be raining in one section, dry in another and damp in between.

We had already seen a massive accident that weekend when former World Champion Jacques Villeneuve crashed his Williams at the ultra-demanding Eau Rouge corner. Professor Sid Watkins, Formula One's senior medical adviser, was on the scene soon after, concerned for Villeneuve's well-being. As Watkins recalls in his book *Beyond the Limit*, he said to Villeneuve it had looked like a 'pretty big bang' and got the unexpected reply 'Yes, I really enjoyed that.'

Enjoying accidents wasn't something we were particularly keen on doing, but the race start on Sunday afternoon produced one of the most spectacular multi-car pile-ups in recent times, triggered when pole sitter David Coulthard spun his McLaren across the track at the exit of La Source hairpin. Carnage ensued, cars ricocheting off one another, bouncing into the barriers, carbon fibre and wheels flying in all directions. Mercifully no one was seriously injured, but when the race was halted and a restart declared we noticed that neither Ralf nor Damon had been caught up in the melee. Watching replays, they had both miraculously dodged the chaos all around.

At the second start, Damon sliced between the McLarens to take the lead and, although by lap 8 he had been reeled in by Michael Schumacher who then moved ahead, it was one of those occasions on which Michael drove faster than the conditions suggested was wise. Opening a 40-second lead, he crashed into the back of Coulthard's McLaren; it was an astonishing error, and highly controversial. Michael's view was that David had slowed on purpose and thus caused the incident, while the McLaren driver asserted that he was simply trying to make it easy for the German to pass him. Either way, both were out of the race, and a fracas developed when Michael decided to visit the McLaren garage to vent his fury.

All this left Damon once again in the lead, with Ralf now in second place. We were first and second, 1–2, and in control, or at least as in control as we could be in the miserable conditions, with the added complication that Jean Alesi's Sauber was just behind us in third. Jean was pushing, and Sauber was also keen for a maiden win.

As things turned out, we needn't have worried. Those last laps took forever, not helped by the fact that Ralf's car was faster than Damon's and the young German was keen to overtake! Cue Eddie Jordan, on the radio, asking Ralf to confirm that he would remain in second place and not threaten Damon. It took Ralf a while to reply, but eventually he did as he was asked. We couldn't afford for them to have an accident and, to be fair, Ralf's car was simply quicker because of a better set-up at that phase of the race, and Damon had done the hard work all weekend.

Winning the Belgian Grand Prix, becoming the first team in the history of Formula One to score its maiden victory with a 1–2, was a significant achievement. To do it at Spa, one of the legendary tracks, added to the flavour. We also had all our key sponsors present, including their most senior executives, and I well remember the delight on the faces of MasterCard's Richard Child, Pearl Assurance's Richard Surface and Benson & Hedges' Nigel Northridge. Happy customers, but happy staff too, for this was the only race in our history to which we had arranged a staff outing from the factory. They danced in the traffic jams leaving the circuit afterwards. And we had our fan club there too, Club Jordan, avid fans, passionate about Jordan and about Formula One, many of them having joined since Damon Hill became our driver.

What can be better than to achieve your goal with your staff, your customers and your fans, never mind in front of the world's media and hundreds of millions of television viewers around the world? For those of us at Jordan who had never experienced winning an F1 race before, we knew it was a moment to savour. Damon Hill looked slightly bemused as EJ celebrated as only he could, madly dancing his way to the podium, hardly believing what had happened.

But Damon had achieved his mission. He had shown us how to win, sprinkled some of his World Champion's magic into our team and made it look, well, effortless in the end. Ralf's performance only underlined our strengths at the time, and that the Jordan Mugen-Honda 198 was the car to have on that day. I often wonder what Peugeot's executives thought as they watched us win our first race, eight months after they quit with one of them forecasting that Jordan would never win anything.

In winning, you are often reminded of your original motivations: to bring success and pleasure to your shareholders, staff and customers – and, sometimes, as an answer to those who kept telling you it wasn't possible.

* * *

When I started work as a journalist and broadcaster in the 1980s one of my jobs was to commentate on the FIA Formula 3000 Championship for Eurosport, a new satellite sports channel. As the feeder formula to F1, the F3000 series was at that time very well supported with a good number of F1-calibre sponsors, particularly from the tobacco industry. One of these was Marlboro, and as a media relations consultant to them I often found my duties as a journalist overlapping with my commitments to Big Tobacco.

At Donington Park for the opening round of the 1990 series, a Marlboro-supported driver by the name of Andrea Montermini surprised everyone by claiming an emphatic pole position for the Madgwick International team. As a result I had the task of interviewing the 25-year-old Italian for Eurosport, and getting a quote from him for the Marlboro press release.

I nodded towards him, my camera crew standing just behind me, and he duly arrived, did up his overalls in order for the sponsor logos to be in full view, and we started.

'So, Andrea, congratulations on a maiden pole position for Madgwick,' I said. 'You must be delighted.'

'Fantastic,' came the reply, with a large smile on his face. Here was a man of few words. OK, I thought, he is Italian. English is not his strongest point, and he just needs a little encouragement.

'How would you describe the performance of the Reynard 90D around here?' I offered.

'Eh, fantastic.' This wasn't going to vie with the Frost–Nixon interviews any time soon.

'And for the team, this sets you up for a terrific race tomorrow, doesn't it?'

'Fantastic.'

At this point we decided to halt the interview.

'You don't actually speak English, do you?' I said.

'Fantastic,' he said, and then, 'Non, no inglese.'

In spite of that rather basic communications faux pas, which I have often retold as an example of how to get the basics wrong, Andrea would later become not only a fluent English-speaker but a lifelong friend. Even now, when we meet, he says only one word to start with: 'Fantastic.'

* * *

As a teenager I recall reading a feature in the *Observer* newspaper's colour supplement about Niki Lauda, his fiery accident at the Nurburgring and subsequent comeback just a few weeks later at the Italian Grand Prix in Monza. It was the stuff of legend, particularly as his arch-rival at the time was Britain's James Hunt. As fans will know, the 1976 title fight went down to the wire in the final round in Japan: a dramatic, rain-affected race that saw Lauda quit and Hunt do just what he needed to win the World Championship.

Not surprisingly the Hunt-versus-Lauda duel has remained iconic, becoming the subject of *Rush*, Ron Howard's superb, if slightly 'Hollywood', telling of the story.

My first acquaintance with Hunt came at the Sicilian round of the Formula 3000 Championship in the summer of 1986. I was given a lift to the Enna-Pergusa circuit by Marlboro's Graham Bogle and top freelance racing journalist Ian Phillips, and I later noticed that Hunt was there, employed by Marlboro as an adviser.

The following year Ian Phillips was appointed team boss of the fledgling Leyton House March F1 team, and he passed on to me his contract with Marlboro. I was now working for Bogle and, from time to time, found myself alongside Hunt as he advised, cajoled and sometimes ripped into the young drivers who were part of the Marlboro World Championship Team programme.

As many found, James wasn't easy to get to know. He had charisma, but he could be boorish, argumentative and sometimes just a little bit frightening to be around. A decade after his Formula One success he remained passionate about the sport, co-commentating for the BBC alongside Murray Walker, and quite often cutting in to correct the doyen of British motor sport broadcasting, usually with a barbed comment about some driver's capabilities or mental competence.

On one occasion I was dispatched to James's house in Wimbledon to interview him for a Marlboro-sponsored programme being made by Brunswick Films. Arriving at his house, the first order of the day was to join him in playing a game of snooker. He had a large glass of something alcoholic in his hand, but that didn't stop him carving his way around the table, competitive as ever. It's often been said that if he hadn't been a Formula One champion James would have been a world-class competitive in something else – probably tennis, which he enjoyed, but I can certainly vouch for his snooker. I found out later that he played snooker against champion player Jimmy White.

During our little match I had to go to the bathroom, whereupon I was introduced to Humbert, James's African grey parrot, who sat outside the toilet door and wolf-whistled as you answered the call of nature. He was also an expert at mimicking the ring-tone of a 1980s-style phone, and if you held the phone in your hand the parrot would say 'Yes, uh-huh, yes, uh-huh.' James told me Humbert had picked this up while listening to his mother on the phone.

Eventually we made it into the garden to record the interview. It was a sunny day, and the cameraman thought the light was great. The only problem was the budgerigars, dozens of them, which James collected and bred. The more we tried to do the interview, the louder the budgies became, until finally we moved away far enough to be able to complete the questions and answers as best we could.

Hunt's passing at the age of 45, in June 1993, was a tragedy in so many ways – not least because he would surely have played an increasingly successful role in broadcasting and acting as an ambassador in F1. With the increased commercialism within the sport, James Hunt would have thrived.

When his co-commentator Murray Walker retired from full-time F1 commentary I was fortunate to spend a quiet hour with him over break-fast one morning. I remember two funny moments. The first was when I asked him how his autobiography was going.

'Not very well, lots still to do. I have written about 60,000 words,' he said.

'That's not bad,' I replied, thinking he must be almost finished.

'Well, the problem is, I have only reached the age of 16...,' he smiled.

The second moment came when I asked him about the book's content, and whether there were any juicy stories. He said there weren't, as it wasn't his style and he felt he had to protect his well-earned reputation for giving everyone a little credit for what they did.

He then went on to tell me a very amusing story of how, at one Grand Prix, no one from the BBC could find James Hunt in the run-up to the race. Despite their best efforts, Murray was left to start the race com-mentary on his own, until 20 minutes later the door suddenly burst open and James rushed in, grabbed the microphone and started chatting away.

It later turned out that James had successfully seduced an F1 driver's wife the night before and they realized the only time they could get together was when her husband was in the cockpit of his car, on the grid and at the start of the race. James described how, in spite of being as attentive as possible to his new friend, he kept one eye on the TV screen in the motor home just to make sure the husband was fully occupied elsewhere.

* * *

At the time of the 2000 British Grand Prix I accompanied Heinz-Harald Frentzen to a PR event for one of Jordan's sponsors and brought my son Frank along. He was six years old and as a result of our team's previous sponsorship from PlayStation he had been using a PlayStation 1 games console since the age of three and was something of an expert at playing the official Formula One game.

On meeting Frank and hearing that he liked to drive the PlayStation F1 game, Heinz asked him what his favourite track was. Hockenheim, he answered, going on to explain that he liked it because it was easy to qualify on pole position there and win the race.

Given that Hockenheim was Heinz's home race, he was clearly fascinated by this revelation from a six-year-old. Why was it so easy, he asked? Frank then explained that all you have to do is to switch off 'damage' on the steering wheel and jump the three chicanes flat out in top gear!

Heinz thought this was very funny, but pointed out that unfortunately his Jordan didn't have a 'damage off' mode.

Fast-forward two weeks and we were at Hockenheim for the German Grand Prix. Our season wasn't going well. As my colleague Trevor Foster would later point out, one of the drawbacks for our small team of maintaining a race-winning assault on the World Championship in 1999 had resulted in exhaustion for our relatively small team, and a lack of focus on 2000.

During practice, therefore, we were very surprised, indeed astonished, to see Heinz 'P1' with a lap time much quicker than any of his rivals. What a performance!

It was only a few minutes, however, until the time was deleted. It turned out that he had jumped one of the chicanes and, as a result, taken a short cut. When he saw me later he said he was just trying to do what Frank had suggested, even without the 'damage off' button. It hadn't quite worked out.

'Not as easy as one PlayStation,' he smiled. One of F1's quality people.

* * *

The first time I met Bernie Ecclestone was in 1990 when I walked into the media centre at the Brazilian Grand Prix and found an envelope on my desk containing an invitation to dinner. I assumed it was a general media invitation, so that evening I borrowed a sports jacket from a colleague and headed off to a swanky restaurant.

I was surprised to see that the restaurant was being run as normal, with small groups of guests at tables for twos, fours and sixes. There was no sign of a private function. Maybe, I thought, there's a function room? The maitre d' said no, there was no private function, but instead he showed me to a table for four booked in the name 'Ecclestone'.

There I met two other journalists – Anne Giuntini from *l'Equipe* and Gerhard Kuntschik from the *Salzburger Nachrichten* – and before we had too much time to wonder what was going on Bernie Ecclestone walked in and was shown to the table.

The reason for the dinner, he said, was that the three of us had written stories about him in the recent past and, since he didn't actually know us personally, he thought it would be a good idea to have a chat so that the next time we felt like writing a piece about him we could actually base it on having met him. Point taken.

What followed was two and a half hours of entertaining discussion, chat, argument and debate over every facet of Formula One, Bernie's vision for the future – a vision he achieved, incidentally – and some very candid comments about the drivers, team owners and broader politics of the day.

What did he tell us? Well, that's tricky – because the condition of us having dinner is that if we ever revealed the details of the conversations we ought to think about working in another sport.

I have a hastily typed transcript of the evening on an old floppy disk on a shelf in my office. I typed it out as soon as I got back to my hotel that night, and one day I'll print it out and think about revealing it. But it won't be in the lifetime of the man who built F1 as we know it.

* * *

Sitting in my stocking feet, wearing dirty trousers and an open-necked shirt with grey smudges all over it was not my best look, I admit, especially when I was sitting in a meeting room at 6 Princes Gate waiting for the chief executive officer of Formula One, Bernard Charles Ecclestone, to join me for a meeting to discuss some topics relating to Cosworth.

Arriving in Knightsbridge that morning I had been relaxed, early and able to enjoy a gentle stroll from Scotch Corner up towards the headquarters of the company responsible for the commercial rights to Formula One. Naturally I was thinking about the meeting agenda, and wondering what questions Bernie might field: always best to be prepared when going to see him.

The first I knew about what was happening was when I thought it was raining, but looked up to see blue skies. As I looked down again I realized I was not being rained on but spattered from head to foot by a jet of water coming from a cement mixer parked in a building site that I was walking past. One of the workmen had decided to use a high-powered jet of water to clean the inside of the cement mixer's giant bucket. Unfortunately the jet of water decided to ricochet at right angles, taking with it the residue of cement – and covering me.

For a while I just stood there, slightly disbelieving as I realized my suit, shirt, tie, shoes, briefcase, hair and face were now pebble-dashed in cement. When I finally reacted, the workmen were already converging on me, and the look on their faces confirmed my fears; I looked a mess.

Fifteen minutes later, with some cash from the foreman's office to pay for dry cleaning and the address of the company in case I required compensation, I was on my way. But this meant arriving slightly late for a meeting with Bernie, and looking as though I had walked straight out of a zombie movie.

Fortunately his receptionist did not call security as soon as she saw me and, when Bernie heard, he had one member of staff take my shoes and jacket away to be cleaned up, and so I found myself sitting, half-dressed, in his meeting room.

'You OK?' he said on entering. I said I was, he sat down and the meeting progressed smoothly. As we talked I thought about how often people had prepared to meet Bernie, worrying about how to deal with him, usually fearing the outcome. But today, with me covered in cement dust, it was just another meeting, all very normal, businesslike, concise and satisfactory, in fact exactly like all the meetings I'd ever had with him, suited or otherwise.

INDEX

Note: The index is arranged in alphabetical, word-by-word order. The prefix 'Mc' and numbers in headings are filed as spelt out in full. Organization names spelt as acronyms (eg BMW) are filed as written. Roman numeral locators refer to material within the Preface.

Battles for Wales

Myrddin ap Dafydd

Owain
Glyndŵr

Gwasg Carreg Gwalch

First published in 2017
© Myrddin ap Dafydd / Gwasg Carreg Gwalch
Translated from the Welsh by Susan Walton

Published by Gwasg Carreg Gwalch,
12 Iard yr Orsaf, Llanrwst, Conwy, LL26 0EH.
tel: 01492 642031 Ffacs: 01492 641502
email: llyfrau@carreg-gwalch.com
website: www.carreg-gwalch.com

ISBN: 978-1-84524-257-2

Cover design:Eleri Owen

Acknowledgements

The author is grateful to Visit Wales for
photographs on pages 73, 90, 94, and 110, crown
copyright 2017; to Des Marshall for the
photograph of Glyndŵr's Covenant Stone,
page 97; and to the *Western Mail* for the map on
page 125.

*1. Gwenllian's stone, in front of Kidwelly
castle; 2. Arthur's stone, Dinas Mawddwy*